Contemporary Spanish Poetry

Andrew P. Debicki. Courtesy of Kelly Heese, University Relations, the University of Kansas.

Contemporary Spanish Poetry

The Word and the World

Edited by
Cecile West-Settle
and Sylvia Sherno

Madison • Teaneck
Fairleigh Dickinson University Press

©2005 by Rosemont Publishing & Printing Corp.

All rights reserved. Authorization to photocopy items for internal or personal use, or the internal or personal use of specific clients, is granted by the copyright owner, provided that a base fee of $10.00, plus eight cents per page, per copy is paid directly to the Copyright Clearance Center, 222 Rosewood Drive, Danvers, Massachusetts 01923. [0-8386-4040-0/05 $10.00 + 8¢ pp, pc.]

Associated University Presses
2010 Eastpark Boulevard
Cranbury, NJ 08512

The paper used in this publication meets the requirements of the American National Standard for Permanence of Paper for Printed Library Materials Z39.48–1984.

Library of Congress Cataloging-in-Publication Data

Contemporary Spanish poetry : the word and the world / edited by Cecile West-Settle and Sylvia Sherno.
   p. cm.
Includes index.
ISBN 0-8386-4040-0 (alk. paper)
1. Spanish poetry—20th century—History and criticism. I. West-Settle, Cecile, 1944- II. Sherno, Sylvia.
PQ6085.C576 2005
861'.609—dc22
                                2004021001

PRINTED IN THE UNITED STATES OF AMERICA

Contents

Acknowledgments 7

"What Andy Taught Me"
SARA MARTIN 9

Foreword:
Unas Palabras para Andrew P. Debicki
ANGEL GONZÁLEZ 11

Introduction
SYLVIA SHERNO AND
CECILE WEST-SETTLE 15

Light in the Eyes:
Visionary Poetry in Vicente Aleixandre
SANTIAGO DAYDÍ-TOLSON 25

José Moreno Villa:
Exile and Community
SALVADOR J. FAJARDO 39

Affirmative Action:
Francisco Brines's *La última costa*
JUDITH NANTELL 59

Gloria Fuertes's Last Words:
Mujer de verso en pecho
DOUGLAS K. BENSON 78

Radical Musicality and Otherness
in the Poetry of José Angel Valente
LINDA D. METZLER 98

Old Photographs, New Views:
Interpretation and Creation in
Atencia's *A orillas del Ems*
ANITA M. HART 123

Writing the Book of Life:
Ana Rossetti's *Punto umbrío*
MARTHA LaFOLLETTE   143

Staging Immanence: Of Space,
Time, and Luminous Reality in
Dionisia García's *Lugares de paso*
MICHAEL MUDROVIC   166

Giving the Vampire Voice:
Monstrous Metaphors in Recent
Spanish Poetry by Women
MARGARET PERSIN   180

The Queer Poetics
of Ana María Moix
JILL ROBBINS   204

Three Apologies for Poetry:
Discourses of Literary Value
in Contemporary Spain
JONATHAN MAYHEW   224

Contributors   247
Index   251

Acknowledgments

THIS BOOK NEVER WOULD HAVE COME TO FRUITION WITHOUT THE support of various persons and institutions. To give every one of these fine people and places the merit they deserve would require more space than we have here, so we will reluctantly limit ourselves to naming just a few.

We are of course immeasurably indebted to Andrew P. Debicki, whose mentoring and scholarship inspired this work. We are also grateful to the National Endowment for the Humanities for sponsoring the 1989 Summer Seminar where we first met Professor Debicki. That summer and our participation in the seminar marked the beginnings of rich personal and professional experiences.

Washington and Lee, and UCLA, our home institutions, have supported our professional endeavors through sabbaticals and grants, and we wish to thank them. One colleague at Washington and Lee deserves special mention. Lynn Bennett's help with the preparation of this manuscript has made our lives much easier during the last two years, and we, as editors, are deeply indebted to her.

Moreover, we extend heartfelt thanks to all of our authors, whose essays represent a fitting tribute to Andrew Debicki and his many contributions to our profession. Finally, we thank our families, especially Marty and Frank, for their patience, love, and support through the years.

What Andy Taught Me

Take the poem in your two hands and look inside.
Don't be afraid if you see yourself.
Look again. It will be different this time.
Don't wait for someone else to tell you.
Ask why—there is more than one answer.
Beam on your classmates.
Listen closely to them.
Love the poem.
Don't apologize.
Say what you see.
There will be more than one way.

—Sara Martin

Foreword
Unas Palabras para Andrew P. Debicki
(Some Words about Andrew P. Debicki)

ANGEL GONZÁLEZ
TRANSLATED BY DAVID LEE GARRISON

CONOCÍ AL PROFESOR DEBICKI HACE MUCHOS AÑOS, TANTOS QUE no puedo precisar con certeza la fecha y las circunstancias de nuestro primer encuentro. Creo que nos vimos por primera vez hacia 1970 en mi casa de Madrid, donde mantuvimos una conversación que versó, naturalmente, sobre poesía y poetas. Bastó ese encuentro inicial para que yo apreciara en él una serie de cualidades no muy comunes que lo convierten en una persona y en un crítico admirables. Su simpatía humana, su cultura, su amor por la poesía, la amplitud de sus gustos, la mesura y la tolerancia de sus juicios me impresionaron desde el principio muy favorablemente. Así surgió una amistad "a primera vista" que el paso del tiempo no hizo más que consolidar, y que acabó deparándome multiples satisfacciones y beneficios. El crítico literario Andrew P. Debicki me sacó del "infierno" de la poesía social —lugar al que todavía vuelvo con gusto algunas veces—para instalarme en el ámbito más prestigioso de la post-modernidad. No sé si me lo merezco. En cualquier caso le estoy sinceramente agradecido, pues supo leer mis poemas de una manera nueva, imaginativa y a la vez rigurosa, que repercutió de modo muy positivo en la valoración de mi trabajo.

El profesor Debicki pertenece a la promoción de hispanistas americanos que rompió la barrera de la Generación del 27—de la que también se ocupó—para adentrarse en el estudio de autores más jóvenes, ignorados en los EE.UU y aún no considerados en el mundo académico de su propio país cuando él comenzó a prestarles atención. Su labor, reveladora y orientadora, ha tenido una doble proyección. En el terreno de la investigación, ha conseguido exponer y valorar con objetividad un panorama lírico todavía confuso, que ahora empieza a verse con mayor claridad gracias en gran medida a sus aportaciones críticas. Pero por su original aproximación al hecho poético, en la que se combina el inteligente uso de la teoría con la primordial y respetuosa atención al texto, a la posición del autor y a la reacción de los lectores, Andrew Debicki merece el título de maestro de maestros. Dicho de otro modo, él logró algo que es patrimonio de muy pocos: "hacer Escuela." Son ya muchos—yo conozco a algunos—los investigadores ya prestigiosos que se presentan con orgullo como discípulos del maestro Debicki. A ellos, y a él como causa primera, se debe que se mantenga muy vivo el interés por la poesía española y latinoamericana contemporáneas en las universidades de este país.

Por muchas razones, los poetas españoles tenemos una deuda de gratitud con el profesor Andrew P. Debicki. Mis palabras de hoy sólo pretendieron apuntar—muy insuficientemente—los motivos de esa deuda, y dejar constancia de ella.

[I met Professor Debicki many years ago, so many that I can't remember for sure the date and circumstances of our first encounter. I believe it was around 1970 at my home in Madrid, where we had a conversation that gravitated, naturally, around poetry and poets. In that first meeting I sensed in him a number of the rare qualities that make him such an admirable person and literary critic. His empathy, his appreciation of culture, his love for poetry, the wide range of his interests, the respect and tolerance in the way he expressed his ideas—all of these things deeply impressed me from the start. Thus emerged a "friendship at first sight" that the passing of time has only served to enhance, and that has brought me great personal and professional satisfaction. The literary critic Andrew P. Debicki rescued me from the "inferno" of social poetry—a place that I still occasionally revisit with pleasure—and installed me in the more prestigious environment of postmodernity. I'm not sure that I deserved it. In any case I am sincerely grateful, for he understood how to read my poems in a new way, imaginative yet rigorous, that had a very positive effect on the critical appraisal of my work.

Professor Debicki belongs to that group of American Hispanists who broke through the barrier of the Generation of 1927, which received so much attention, to delve into the study of younger authors, ignored in the United States and still not highly valued in the academic world of their own country when he began to focus on them. His work, pioneering and illuminating, has had a dual impact. As a scholar, he has managed to map out and evaluate objectively a lyric panorama that remains complex, that only now is coming to be seen with greater clarity, thanks in large part to his critical insights. But it is because of his original approach to the poetic act, an approach that combines the enlightened use of theory with primary and careful attention to the text, an approach that considers both the position of the author and the reaction of the reader, that Andrew Debicki deserves the title Teacher of Teachers. In other words, he achieved something that is the legacy of very few: he created a school. There are now many (I know some of them) who refer to themselves with pride as disciples of the master, Debicki. They, and he as their initial inspiration, are largely responsible for the lively and continuing interest in contemporary Spanish and Latin American poetry in American universities.

For these reasons, we Spanish poets owe a great debt of gratitude to Professor Andrew P. Debicki. My words today only begin to point out and record the nature and scope of that debt.]

Introduction

Sylvia Sherno and
Cecile West-Settle

A ROCK WAS PLACED CAREFULLY ON THE TABLE. THE EARNEST YOUNG graduate students contemplated its polished surface, its dark inertness, its silent *quiddity*.

But it was not the rock itself that they were meant, finally, to study and prize. A poem is like this rock, they were told. A poem, too, is an object, utterly finished, coldly unmoving. Like a rock, a poem is untouched by circumstance, impervious to history and personal experience. And whatever mysteries and truths it holds close within its core are also timeless and unchanging.

Those of us who were fortunate enough to take part in Andrew Debicki's 1989 National Endowment for the Humanities (NEH) seminar, "Critical Approaches and Hispanic Poetry," listened to this anecdote culled from Andy's Yale graduate school years, during the heyday of what came to be known as the New Criticism. The story was intended to exemplify the formidable rigor and unrelenting practicality of New Critical formalism. It also was meant to underscore the eruptions and fissures in the topography of literary theory and critical practice occurring over a period of some three decades or more.

Andrew Debicki's knowledge of the theoretical and critical terrain is unquestionable. Since the early 1960s he has been one of the foremost Hispanists in this country, and indeed one of our most distinguished scholars in the field of Hispanic poetry. He obtained his doctorate from Yale University during the time of William Wimsatt and other luminaries of the New Criticism. His academic career, from its beginnings at Trinity College, to Grinnell College during most of the sixties, and finally to the

University of Kansas from 1968 to the present, has consistently been recognized for the excellence both of his teaching and of his scholarly research.

As an authority on Latin American and Spanish contemporary poetry, Debicki's critical approach has evolved, as has poetry itself. His first book, *La poesía de José Gorostiza* (1962), was a close reading in the New Critical style of the work of the Mexican poet. In subsequent volumes (for example, his important *Estudios sobre poesía española contemporánea* [1968, 1980], *Dámaso Alonso* [1970, 1974], and *Poetas hispanoamericanos contemporáneos* [1976]), he employed a wide range of analytic concepts and techniques including point-of-view criticism, archetypal criticism, and reader-response criticism. Moreover, his increasing body of scholarship, especially the influential *Poetry of Discovery* (1982, 1988) and his most recent study *Spanish Poetry of the Twentieth Century* (1994), introduced American Hispanists to the important new voices that have reinvigorated and redefined lyric poetry in Spanish: namely, Spain's now-canonical "Fifties Generation," the younger "novísimos" poets with their postmodern aesthetics and vision, and the authors of the past two decades who are even now exploring new poetic directions and modalities.

Andrew Debicki's philosophy, both as a teacher and a critic, has been eclectic, practical, and, above all, generous. Through his publications, as well as his four National Endowment of the Humanities seminars, he has served as mentor to some of the leading critics of Hispanic poetry. Although his scholarship remains vital and influential, and while he has continued to be a vigorous presence in his capacity as the University of Kansas's vice-chancellor for research, graduate studies, and public service, Professor Debicki has essentially retired from the classroom. To honor his innumerable contributions to, and continuing influence on, the field of poetry criticism, we have collected eleven essays, all dedicated to various aspects of Spanish lyric poetry. We have chosen the title "Contemporary Spanish Poetry: The Word and the World." The unifying theme is poetry's twin impulse: first, to create a self-contained reality and, second, to remain vitally connected to the world. For us, this broad theme most cogently captures Andrew Debicki's attitude of respect for the integrity of the poem and for the art of poetry itself, while also suggesting the ways he has opened up this field of study through his innovative and illuminating application of various critical methodologies and theoretical approaches. We believe that each one of the eleven studies, written by colleagues and former students, not only reflects the esteem and affection in which Andrew Debicki is held, but also represents a significant contribution to the study of contemporary Spanish poetry.

Furthermore, we have found within the very diversity and eclecticism of the collection its unifying thread. Santiago Daydí-Tolson, for example, opens the volume by inviting us to read (or to reread) a poet whose contributions to modern Spanish letters correspond to a significant span of years within the last century. In "Light in the Eyes: Visionary Poetry in Vicente Aleixandre," Daydí-Tolson studies one of twentieth-century Spain's most significant poets. Aleixandre's silence in the ten years following the publication of *Poemas de la consumación* (1968) and *Diálogos del conocimiento* (1974) is in part due to his loss of eyesight. Ironically, given the preeminence in his verse of light and of a sensuous reality concretely and purposefully observed, the poet's blindness brought to a close a poetic corpus that painted, in Daydí-Tolson's terms, "a lyrical world aglow in one of the most luminous poetic visions of the period." Better than most of his Spanish contemporaries, Aleixandre, according to Daydí-Tolson, represents the continuity of visionary poetry not only in Spain but also in world letters—and anticipates the younger writers Andrew Debicki has called "poets of discovery."

Unlike the isolation that ensued from Vicente Aleixandre's loss of vision, José Moreno Villa's experience was not the isolation of physical darkness, but that of exile. Salvador J. Fajardo's study, "José Moreno Villa: Exile and Community," depicts the poet living in Mexico during the Spanish Civil War, geographically far removed from his homeland. For Moreno Villa, Fajardo explains, Spain signifies the physical and emotional space that has formed the poet's very sense of self, and it is from this space that he writes his first poem of exile, "Converso con vosotros." Fajardo's essay shows how Moreno Villa employed the creative power of poetry to communicate with the absent "other," that is, the poet's compatriots in Spain.

Judith Nantell's essay, "Affirmative Action: Francisco Brines's *La última costa*," reconsiders that poet in the light of his 1995 collection. The pronounced elegiac quality of Brines's poetry has been acknowledged by his readers and by the poet himself. Yet *La última costa* foregrounds what has not always been recognized in his work as a whole: namely, Brines's affirmation of intense vitality. Although the title evokes the finality of human existence, the intimate voice speaking in *La última costa* arrives at a heightened understanding that the very fragility of life, made even more poignant by the presence of memory and experienced anew through the act of poetic creation, is reason enough to celebrate being, both as a driving force and as an ontological state.

A very different kind of writer, but one Debicki has seen fit to include among the mid-century "poets of discovery," is the subject of Douglas K. Benson's "Gloria Fuertes's Last Words: *Mujer de verso en pecho*." Fuertes's last volume of poetry is consistent with much of her earlier work because of the pronounced indeterminacy of the verses achieved by a complex blending and juxtaposition of conventions, languages, and genres. In many of her poems Fuertes maintains an attitude of solidarity, while in others she conveys a tone of ironic objectivity. As is true in her work as a whole, *Mujer de verso en pecho* continuously subverts readers' expectations and ultimately extends their notions of poetry.

"Radical Musicality and Otherness in the Poetry of José Angel Valente" is the title of Linda D. Metzler's reading of one of Brines's and Fuertes's *congéneres*. In Metzler's judgment, José Angel Valente's poetry is imbued with a profound musicality crucial to the creation of emotion and ontological meaning. Numerous expressive strategies—the counterpoint of recurrent and varying sounds, contrasting rhythms, the conscious use of silences, to name a few—exemplify the lyric subject's search for release in an "other" portrayed variously as a transcendent harmoniousness, a divinity, a beloved, nature, and nothingness. Valente's musical poems engage readers by obliging them to perform in hearing, breathing, and sounds that make language verge on song.

Anita M. Hart considers the complementary play of visual and verbal images in María Victoria Atencia's *A orillas del Ems*. Her essay, "Old Photographs, New Views: Interpretation and Creation in Atencia's *A orillas del Ems*," regards that volume as a poetic contemplation of life and death, the particular and the universal, the ephemeral and the eternal. By interweaving words and photographs, says Hart, Atencia uncovers and (re)creates multiple levels of reality, and at the same time draws the reader into the process of continually deepening consciousness.

Turning to one of the most intriguing poets now writing in Spain, Martha LaFollette examines the collection that transcended the notoriety surrounding Ana Rossetti's earlier lyric production and assured her a position of literary stature. While in Rossetti's first volumes of poetry sexual and writing subjects frequently converge and, just as frequently, are identified as female, in *Punto umbrío* she pointedly employs a register that goes beyond either masculine or feminine gender. According to Martha LaFollette's "Writing the Book of Life: Ana Rossetti's *Punto umbrío*," this highly introspective volume of poetry at once betrays the poet's awareness of the written word's failure to produce either groundedness or transcendence, yet also reveals her essential affirmation of faith in the writing process as an act of creation, significance, and intense experience.

"Staging Immanence: Of Space, Time, and Luminous Reality in Dionisia García's *Lugares de paso*" is the title of Michael Mudrovic's thoughtful study of Dionisia García's most recent verses. Historical monuments, especially arches, provide the backdrop for some of García's lyrics. Mudrovic finds that such physical structures, grounding the verses within a concrete, anecdotal reality, represent at once the inextricable intertwining of space and time, the immutable and the immanent. In keeping with W. J. T. Mitchell's taxonomic analysis of space in literature, the poems of *Lugares de paso* draw poet and reader together in the complex, interdependent processes that culminate in epiphanic illuminations of both text and life.

Margaret Persin's sprightly "Giving the Vampire Voice: Monstrous Metaphors in Recent Spanish Poetry by Women" studies the vampire as a metaphorical expression, from ancient times to the present, of our desire for power and also our fear of the abuse of power. A social construct that makes possible the confrontation with forbidden thoughts and taboo behavior, the vampire, in Persin's view, represents what lies beyond the norms and strictures imposed by conventional society and culture. In the recent poetry of several Spanish women, Persin discovers the vampire figure not only cast in a distinctly female and feminist light, but also as a metonym for the creativity of the poetic text.

National identity, as defined by the official discourse of the Francoist regime, was based on Castillian, male heterosexual, Catholic models derived from the Spanish imperial past. Jill Robbins, in "The Queer Poetics of Ana María Moix," asserts that the work of this Catalan writer, including *Baladas del Dulce Jim*, calls into question such homogeneous notions of nation, class, gender, and sex, and thereby betrays the fissures in the monolithic schema propagated by the old order.

Finally, Jonathan Mayhew's "Three Apologies for Poetry: Discourses of Literary Value in Contemporary Spain" closes the volume with a panoramic view that defines contemporary Spanish poetry's role vis-à-vis a highly diversified audience. Mayhew posits the notion that contemporary Spanish poetry, informed by a wide range of discourses, metaphysical, realist, and neo-avant-garde, responds to distinct readerships and varied cultural expectations. At the same time, the recent preference of poets and critics for a poetry of "experience" reveals the marginalized status of those lofty literary values that have shaped the canon, while providing clues about the present status of literature as a whole.

All in all, each of these critical pieces, with the author's particular intuitions, methodological preferences, and theoretical framework, reflect the guiding concept of our volume: poetry's engagement with the world. Taken together, these essays are a reminder of the breadth of knowledge Andrew Debicki brings to the practice of criticism, his joyfully pragmatic approach to the individual poem, and his understanding that the art of poetry is an expression of the writer's intimate world, but also a vehicle of connection to the world outside the poem.

Bibliography

Andrew P. Debicki

1962. *La poesía de José Gorostiza*. México: Ediciones De Andrea.

1968. *Estudios sobre poesía española contemporánea; la generación de 1924–1925*. Madrid: Gredos.

1970. *Dámaso Alonso*. New York: Twayne Publishers.

1973. *La poesía de Jorge Guillén*. Madrid: Editorial Gredos.

1974. *Estudios de literatura hispanoamericana en honor a José J. Arrom*. Edited by Andrew P. Debicki and Enrique Pupo-Walker. University of North Carolina Chapel Hill, Dept. of Romance Languages. Distributed by International Scholarly Book Service, Portland, OR.

1976. *Antología de la poesía mexicana moderna*. Selección, introducción, comentarios y notas by Andrew P. Debicki. London: Tamesis, D.L.

1976. *Pedro Salinas*. Edited by Andrew P. Debicki. Madrid: Taurus.

1976. *Poetas hispanoamericanos contemporáneos: punto de vista, perspectiva, experiencia*. Madrid: Gredos.

1982. *Poetry of discovery: the Spanish generation of 1956–1971*. Lexington: University Press of Kentucky.

1989. *Angel González*. Gijón: Ediciones Júgar.

1991. *En homenaje a Angel González: ensayos, entrevista y poemas*. Edited by Andrew P. Debicki and Sharon Keefe Ugalde. Boulder, CO: Society of Spanish and Spanish-American Studies.

1994. *Spanish poetry of the twentieth century: modernity and beyond*. Lexington: University Press of Kentucky.

1997. *Historia de la poesía española del siglo XX: desde la modernidad hasta el presente*. Madrid: Gredos.

Contemporary Spanish Poetry

Light in the Eyes: Visionary Poetry in Vicente Aleixandre

Santiago Daydí-Tolson

After almost six decades of continuous creative work Vicente Aleixandre ceased to write. From 1974, when he published his last book of poems, *Diálogos del conocimiento* (The Dialogues of Knowledge), until his death in December 1984, he did not even plan a book. Toward the end of his life Aleixandre, who had received the Nobel Prize for Literature in 1977, was silent. The Spanish poet was at the same time losing his eyesight. The increasing eyesight problems may have contributed to Aleixandre's poetic silence, as did other ailments of old age. Nonetheless, at a less immediate level, the relationship between blindness and silence appears to be a decisive coincidence within Aleixandre's poetics.

Eyesight might very well be seen as essential to Aleixandre's visionary poetics and to his masterful use of visionary imagery, a stylistic preference that, according to Andrew Debicki, served as a model for the younger Spanish "poets of discovery"(3). Vision and visual images are, in effect, central to Aleixandre's poetry. Blindness, on the other hand, is inconceivable within his poetic world made up of both surrealistic visions of an oneiric nature and very concrete images of an intently observed reality. The sensuality of light, of things seen, is a constant presence in his world, and it is difficult to imagine silence and darkness as belonging to his poetic domain. Thus, with blindness came silence and the end of a poetic work that had given to Spanish poetry a lyrical world aglow in one of the most luminous poetic visions of the period.

But blindness, which has not deterred other poets from writing and, on the contrary, has been interpreted since ancient times as a sign of poetic inner vision (the blind eyes of Homer, Milton, and Borges come to mind), does not necessarily justify Aleixandre's loss of interest in writing. In symbolic terms this concrete manifestation of human physical limitation represents in Aleixandre the opposite; namely, a spiritual condition brought on by old age after having attained his ultimate poetic objective: the wisdom of an inner light. Words were no longer needed once this level of certainty was gained.

Aleixandre's last two books, *Poemas de la consumación* (Poems of Consummation) and *Diálogos del conocimiento*, support this interpretation of his silence. They are the work of a poet who, having attained an ultimate level of consciousness and knowledge, decides that his poetic life has come to an end and chooses silence instead of repetition. The poetry of an old man, these last two collections bring closure to a long poetic process that had taken Aleixandre from his beginnings as a poet (somehow influenced by the exercises of pure poetry in *Ambito* [Ambit]) to the mature and almost oracular voice of profound wisdom found in his last two collections. The title *Poemas de la consumación* points unequivocally to an end, a consummation, the attainment of a goal. With old age comes death and the completion of life, but also with age comes knowledge, the subject of *Diálogos del conocimiento*, his final book. The poem "Conocimiento de Rubén Darío" (Knowledge of Rubén Darío) (1978, 1:65–67) from *Poemas de la consumación* combines, albeit implicitly, key terms from the titles of Aleixandre's last two works. The ineffable knowledge gained at the end of life is the lyrical motive that makes of this poem a special example of Aleixandre's last writings. The poet presents this composition as distinctly meaningful as he sets it apart from the rest of the collection in a section labeled "Intermedio," (Intermission). As Gimferrer observed (24), the title "Conocimiento de Rubén Darío" is closely related to the theme of Aleixandre's final book. Using the figure of the Latin American master, so admired by Aleixandre, the poem explains why the latter considered his work as a poet completed.

The poem is a last homage to the Darío who inspired Aleixandre's own poetic career from the moment when Dámaso Alonso lent him an anthology of Darío's works in the summer of 1919 (Cano, 181). "Conocimiento de Rubén Darío" is also a statement on poetry itself, on the nature of poetic inspiration. For Aleixandre, one of the Spanish poets who best represents the essence of modern poetry in the twentieth century, returning at the end of his career to the poetry and figure of Rubén Darío is a clear recognition of the visionary roots of his own poetry and the poetry of his contemporaries. An explicit declaration of his poetic principles, "Conocimiento de Rubén Darío" is the *ars poetica* of one of the best representatives in the Spanish language of Darío's poetic legacy and its dependence on a centuries-long Western tradition of lyrical *poetry as revelation*.

Rubén Darío, a poet who never ceases to exert influence over contemporary Spanish and Latin American writers, appears in Aleixandre's poem as a figure that represents the essential elements of poetry as he conceives it. By recognizing the poet who inspired his first writings, Aleixandre is acknowledging not only the influence of Darío's poetic views on his own conceptions, but also his own accomplishments or shortcomings as a poet.

"Conocimiento de Rubén Darío" points to Aleixandre's allegiance to the romantic tradition of visionary poetry. The poem focuses on the poet's powers of understanding, proclaiming an exalted view of the former as an exceptional individual whose talents are distinctly related to his capacity to see reality in a profoundly meaningful way. At once sensual and spiritual, Darío represents the Aleixandrian poet to perfection. In Aleixandre's poem he appears as a man mysteriously touched by a sense of transcendence in the most material aspects of his human nature.

Because the senses are designed to grasp the material world in all its complexity and beauty, they find in Darío a level of enhancement that Aleixandre claims for himself, as most of his highly sensual poetry attests. Among the senses, the most strikingly effective to understand the world is sight, precisely the sense that Aleixandre lost in his old age. Thus, when he decides to write his poem about the old master, he begins the composition with these telling words: "Los ojos callan" (The eyes are silent). These are the eyes of the poet who in his visionary knowledge has gone beyond language.

From this startling, rather oracular statement the poem develops around the image of the eyes as the organ of physical and poetic sight. To see is to understand. Darío, the poet of sensual materialism, looks around and sees even in darkness, as darkness becomes light in his visionary eyes.

> Rubén que un día con tu brazo extenso
> batiste espumas o colores. Miras.
> Quien mira ve. Quien calla ya ha vivido.
> Pero tus ojos de misericordia,
> tus ojos largos que se abrieron poco
> a poco; tus nunca conocidos ojos bellos,
> miraron más, y vieron en lo oscuro.
> Oscuridad es claridad. Rubén segundo y nuevo.
> —(Darío, ll. 31–38)

[Ruben, who once, with your extended arm, / mixed foams and colors. You watch. / He who watches, sees. He who is silent has already lived. / But your compassionate eyes, / your big eyes that opened slowly, / your unfamiliar beautiful eyes, / looked more, and they saw in the darkness. / Darkness is light. Second and new Ruben.][1]

The simple, sensual visual perception of the young Modernist poet who was initially fascinated by form and external beauty contrasts with the meditative gaze of his older persona, the poet of "Lo fatal" (Fatality) and the anguished realization that matter and the senses will not last forever. The contrast between the youthful embracing of materiality and the mature recognition that life is but a brief illusion comes as a frightful realization. Better yet, this transformation of seeing underscores the interpretation of sight as much more than the simple visual contact with light: it is in darkness where the human eye can really perceive its own internal light. And that kind of seeing is what in traditional visionary terms represents true knowledge: "Rubén callado que al mirar descubres. / Por dentro hay luz. Callada luz, si ardida" (Silent Ruben, who discovers upon looking. / There is light within. Silent light, but burning.) (ll. 40–41).

This internal burning light, the light of poetic vision which Aleixandre tried to reach from the very beginning of his poetic career, is what he saw and admired in Darío's work. From the moment when as a young man he read for the first time the poems of the Latin American master and was inspired to write his own poetry, he set himself in his "camino hacia la luz" (journey towards light) (1978, 2, 528).

Obviously, in the search for light eyesight is fundamental. The eyes become central images in the representation of poetic imagination and its powers of vision. Because of their peculiar relation with light—a term that would require much more than a few pages to discuss in its many functions as a poetic image representative of poetic knowledge—the eyes have attracted the attention of poets, artists, mystics, and scientists. As Arthur Zajonc points out in *Catching the Light*, those endowed with special creative talents in arts and sciences as well as those longing for a spiritual life have always marveled at light and vision, symbols of the most elusive of human objectives: absolute knowledge.

Throughout time and across cultures, eyes have been endowed with special qualities and magical overtones. The eye represents the mysterious side of the human spirit and reality. More than the other organs of sensual perception, the eye seems to grasp the whole of reality, while at the same time reflecting the inner world of the individual. Thus, since antiquity, eyesight has been interpreted as a higher and more spiritual or intellectual sense, superior to the other four, more material and lower, senses (Korsmeyer, 11–37).

Poetry and science, myth, philosophy, and religion find themselves entangled in a similar obsessive search for light, the physical phenomenon invisible to the eye, as science proves, if not reflected on some form of matter. In the emptiness of the void light is invisible. Darkness is not so much the absence of its opposite—light—but the absence of matter that can make light visible in reflection. At the same time, matter is invisible if no light makes it appear to the eye. Matter and "spirit" or light alternate in these simple physical facts, and the vulnerability of the one to the other suggests the elusive nature of reality.

Human feeling for light and its perception is enormously complex and cannot be easily summarized. The mere reference to light and the eyes brings to mind a rush of images that encompass a whole spectrum of sensations, from the most sensuous one of light bringing reality to consciousness through the eye, to the most abstract view of light as divine essence, the blinding presence of God, so magnificently expressed by Dante at the end of the *Commedia*, in Canto 33 of "Paradiso." The poet, who has finally reached the divinity, cannot stop himself from raising his eyes "all'eterno Lume" (to the eternal Light) (l. 43), the eternal light of God, even before St. Bernard signals him to look up:

> ché la mia vista, venendo sincera,
> e più e più entrava per lo raggio
> dell'alta Luce che da sé è vera.
>
> (ll. 52–54)

[Because my sight, becoming truer, / entered slowly into the ray of / that high Light which in itself is true.]

The essentially visual component of reality, and in particular of beauty, is also treated by Dante in exalted terms. Eyesight is the superior sense, the only one capable of recognizing beauty, the material manifestation of the utmost spiritual value. In Canto 31 of "Purgatorio," Dante is taken to the presence of Beatrice. When she unveils her face in front of him the poet loses all sensory capacities with the exception of sight. Canto 32 begins with the expression of such experience:

> Tant'eran li occhi miei fissi e attenti
> a disbramarsi la decenne sete,
> che li altri sensi m'eran tutti spenti;
>
> (ll. 1–3)

[My eyes were fixed / and so intent in satisfying the decennial thirst, / that all my senses were lost.]

San Juan de la Cruz in "Canciones entre el alma y el esposo" (Songs Between the Soul and the Husband) (105-14) also makes use of the eyes and sight to represent the experience of God's presence. The eyes of the poet exist only because of the divine light, the beauty of the beloved:

> y véante mis ojos,
> pues eres lumbre dellos,
> y sólo para ti quiero tenellos.
>
> (ll. 48–50)

[And may my eyes see you, / because you are their light, / and only for you I want them.]

The eyes of God, in turn, are ever present in the poet's mind as he looks for them in the visual forms of nature:

> ¡O christalina fuente,
> si en essos tus semblantes plateados
> formases de repente
> los ojos desseados
> que tengo en mis entrañas dibujados!
>
> (ll. 51–55)

[O crystal fountain, / if only in your silvery faces, / suddenly appeared the beloved eyes / I have in my heart engraved.]

The poet yearns to fix his eyes on those of the loved one. For the mystic, as for Dante, the poet's eyesight is absorbed by the blinding light of God, which is, in turn, the source of all light and beauty, the objects of desire.

A romantic poet changes the mystical value of the divine eyes that materialize in the water of a stream. In Gustavo Adolfo Bécquer's legend "Los ojos verdes" (Green Eyes), the absorbing eyes of God are transformed into a suggestively magical force that uncannily represents the lure of beauty as the material manifestation of true knowledge (133-41). The legend tells of the man who sees in the water of a lake the fascinating green eyes of a woman who leads him into drowning. The tragic end of this legend might very well be understood as a consequence of the disproportionate desire to know, represented by the enchanted quality of the eyes that promise the bliss of full happiness. Again, the utmost manifestation of knowledge is personified in the figure of the beloved, her beauty, that calls for total abandonment in the embrace of love.

In "Rima LXXI" (Bécquer, 480) the same romantic poet talks about two forms of light, two forms of seeing: the physical light, seen by the normal eyes that bring the soul the reality of the world, and the internal light of the poetic imagination, the light seen only by the eyes of the visionary. The "green eyes" of the legend belong to this second kind:

> De la luz que entra al alma por los ojos,
> los párpados velaban el reflejo;
> mas otra luz el mundo de visiones
> alumbraba por dentro
>
> (ll. 9–12)

[The eyelids veiled the reflection of the light that through the eyes reaches the soul; but another light shone in the world of visions.]

The symbolic representation of the eye as the organ of the highest form of perception is supported by a popular conception of the eyes as mirrors or windows of the inner self. In the case of the divine eyes it means omniscience; when referred to the eyes of the loved one it signifies also an absolute possession by virtue of both lover and beloved, looking into each others' eyes. As such, the eyes are mentioned time and again in relation to love, and in many cases represent much more than just love for another. They are the manifestation of a mystery, the physical representation of a desire to see. No image is more expressive of this modern understanding of the eye and eyesight than *Eye-Balloon*, the almost surrealistic drawing of an eye in the form of an aerostatic balloon that Odilon Redon imagined flying in a barren landscape, its pupil ardently fixed in the sky.

Eyes, then, not only receive the rays of light from the outside world, but also emit their own light on the world, expressing or visualizing a nonvisual reality. It seems appropriate to think that because of this double function of the eye as perceiver and illuminator, the traditional image has become extremely persuasive and pervading to the point of affecting everyday language and conceptions.

Knowledge, as represented by vision, is much more than a simple perception or an intellectual act: it involves the whole spirit, with its emotional and deeply rooted feelings, and it engages the forces of imagination. Poetic knowledge, then, is neither scientific, nor philosophical, nor religious—it encompasses a visionary act, a true creation, as suggested by Andrew J. Welburn (1–15).

Few could express more vividly this visionary nature of poetic invention than Arthur Rimbaud in his sonnet "Voyelles" (Vowels) (104). After coloring the vowels, thus giving them a visual value in a completely arbitrary and imaginative way, he makes at the end of the poem a direct reference to the mysterious character of the eyes: "—O l'Oméga, rayon violet de Ses Yeux!" (O the Omega, violet ray of Her eyes) (l. 14). These are the eyes as seen in the beloved face of the other, the eyes whose rays illuminate the inscrutable and suggest true vision. In Rimbaud, the visionary poet of *Illuminations* (189–241), sensual perception and magical poetic gnosis are entangled in the fantastic visual capacities of the eye.

Charles Baudelaire, another French symbolist poet who had profound influence on Rubén Darío's poetic views, also uses eyes to represent inner knowledge and mysterious longings. To the eyes of the beloved he adds those of cats who, lovers of a sort, contain in their secret gaze the hidden light of mystery. Cats, for Baudelaire, are sensuous and at the same time profoundly mysterious beings who possess a knowledge humans desire. The cat that walks in the poet's brain in the poem "Le Chat" (Cat) (55–56) is a symbol of the writer's spirit:

> Quand mes yeux, vers ce chat que j'aime
> Tirés comme par un aimant,
> Se retournent docilement
> Et que je regarde en moi-même,
> Je vois avec étonnement
> Le feu de ses prunelles pâles,
> Clairs fanaux, vivantes opales,
> Qui me contemplent fixement.
> (ll. 33–40)

[When, as if attracted by a lover, my eyes turn obediently to the cat I love and I look into myself, I see with astonishment the fire of its pale pupils, lighted lamps, live opals, that look at me fixedly.]

The real cat that lazily lounges around the room in another poem also titled "Le Chat" becomes a symbol of the lover (39). As he would with her, the poet looks in the cat's eyes for that state of sensual and spiritual abandonment in the lover's embrace:

> Viens, mon beau chat, sur mon coeur amoureux
> Retiens les griffes de ta patte,
> Et laisse-moi plonger dans tes beaux yeux,
> Mèlés de métal et d'agate.
> (ll. 1–4)

[Come to me, my handsome cat, hold the claws of your paw over my loving heart, and let me dive into your beautiful eyes made of mixed metal and agates.]

Its eyes, like those of the woman, are "deep and cold," and pierce like a dart producing that frisson of passion:

> Je vois ma femme en esprit. Son regard,
> Comme le tien, aimable bête,
> Profond et froid, coupe et fend comme un dard,
> Et, des pieds jusque à la tête,
> Un air subtil, un dangereux parfum
> Nagent autour de son corps brun.
>
> (ll. 9–14)

[I see my lover in spirit. Her deep and cold eyes, as yours, friendly beast, hit and hurt like a dart, and from toe to head, a subtle wind, a dangerous perfume swim around her dark body.]

Obviously, fervent lovers and austere wise men love cats because they embody that visionary knowledge poetry tries to attain. Cats are "sphinx allongés" [elongated sphinx] with "prunelles mystiques" [mystical pupils], beings endowed with a rare capacity to see.

Returning to Aleixandre, and keeping in mind these references to the eyes of animals, one cannot but consider another of his poems in which animal eyes again play a fundamental role. "A mi perro" (To My Dog) (1975, 337–38), a composition originally published in 1965 in the book *Retratos con nombre* (Named Portraits), begins with a situation very much related to the one seen in Baudelaire. The poet looks at the "profound" eyes of his dog and reaches the timeless and innocent realm of the animal conscience, which he calls "noon":

> Oh, sí, los sé, buen "Sirio", cuando me miras con tus grandes ojos profundos.
> Yo bajo a donde tú estás, o asciendo a donde tú estás y en tu reino me mezclo contigo, buen "Sirio", buen perro mío, y me salvo contigo.
> Aquí en tu reino de serenidad y silencio, donde la voz humana nunca se oye, converso en el oscurecer y entro profundamente en tu mediodía.
>
> (ll. 1–5)

[O, yes I know them, my good Sirius, when you look at me with your large and deep eyes. I go down to where you are, or I climb to where you are and in your kingdom I become one with you, my good Sirius, my good dog, and I save myself with you. Here in your kingdom of serenity and silence, where no human voice is ever heard, I talk at sunset and walk deeply into your noontime.]

The animal, whose eyes are referred to in the poem as "profundos ojos conocedores" (profound knowing eyes) (l. 8), "hondos ojos apaciguados" (deep peaceful eyes) (l. 13), and "ojos misericordes" (compassionate eyes) (l. 22), receives in Aleixandre a treatment that cannot be interpreted as purely nostalgic or playful. On the contrary, Aleixandre's basic belief in the unity of nature becomes apparent in this poem, just as his views on the fallen nature of humankind are also apparent. The dog is not a symbol, as the cat might be in the case of the French poet: its eyes really look at reality under a different light, a light the poet wants for his own.

Rubén Darío comes to mind again when reading "A mi perro." The miraculous story of an animal and a mystic, Darío's poem "Los motivos del lobo" (The Wolf's Reasons) (946) retells the old story of the wolf of Gubbia and Saint Francis. Here the eyes of the wolf are first described as those of a beast:

> bestia temerosa, de sangre y de robo
> las fauces de furia, los ojos de mal
> (Darío, ll. 5–6)

[fearful beast, bloody and sinful, with furious jaws and evil eyes]

But when Saint Francis, the medieval mystic whose own eyes in the words of Gabriela Mistral "[e]staban como la hondura de la Flor, mojados siempre de ternura" (like the depth of the flower, they were dampened with tenderness) (55), convinces the animal to hurt no one, the wolf's eyes become as loving as those of the saint. Thus, when the transformed beast goes to church and listens to the psalms, its eyes are now "clear" and humid:

> Sus bastas orejas los salmos oían
> y sus claros ojos se le humedecían
> (Darío, ll. 86–87)

[Its rough ears listened to the Psalms and its clear eyes got wet]

These eyes, so different from the eyes of Baudelaire's cats, are the reflection of the animal's "simple" and "pure" soul. "Mas el alma simple de la bestia es pura" (But the simple soul of the beast is pure) (l. 55), writes Darío in the same poem (946). As such, they also point to that knowledge commonly related to light and sight.

Closely related to this view of animals is Pablo Neruda's moving poem "Un perro ha muerto" (A Dog Has Died) (1974, 93–96) written to his dead dog:

> Mi perro ha muerto.
> Lo enterré en el jardín
> junto a una vieja máquina oxidada.
> Allí, no más abajo
> ni más arriba,
> se juntará conmigo alguna vez.
>
> (ll. 1–6)

[My dog has died. I put it in the ground, next to an old rusted engine. There, neither deeper nor higher, it will be next to me again someday.]

The materialist poet hopes, though, for a dog's heaven, expressing with this view one similar to that presented by both St. Francis and Aleixandre:

> Y yo, materialista que no cree
> en el celeste cielo prometido
> para ningún humano,
> para este perro o para todo perro
> creo en el cielo, sí, creo en un cielo
> donde yo no entraré . . .
>
> (ll. 9–14)

[And I, the materialist who does not believe in the celestial heaven promised to a human being, I do believe that for this dog there is a Heaven, a Heaven which I will never reach.]

Again in Neruda's poem, the eyes of the dog are "más puros que los míos" (purer than my eyes) (l. 34), purer than the eyes of men, as they look at the poet with infinite love. Animals, with their profoundly mysterious eyes, are much more than just symbols of the mystery: they are the mystery of life, of nature free from human complexities. Human beings cannot but look at their eyes and wonder.

The gaze of the loved one, human or animal, holds the true knowledge that everyone looks for; a knowledge that cannot really be obtained, even when eyes meet. As Darío feared, such knowledge will be obtained only in death, the ultimate experience, when the eyes open to another, quite different realm. "Per tutti la morte ha uno sguardo. / Verrà la morte e avra i tuoi occhi" (For everyone death has a face. Death will come and it will have your eyes.) (77), wrote Cesare Pavese at the end of his life. The eyes of death are those of the beloved, filled with mysterious revelation.

It is obvious, then, that when Vicente Aleixandre centered his attention on Darío's eyes he was doing it with a full understanding of the many meanings that would be met in that image. His own view of the poet as a seer is based on his acceptance of Darío's poetic beliefs on the visionary character of the poet's art.

A poet whose poetic roots have been traced to romanticism, Vicente Aleixandre represents, better than most of his contemporaries in Spain, the continuity of a poetic tradition that brings him nearer to German and English Romanticism, French Symbolism, Latin American Modernism, and Surrealism than to most of his contemporaries in Spain. Although Aleixandre is not precisely a visual poet, in the sense that one could not pretend to relate his images with mainly visual forms, light and its opposites, shadows and darkness, are common elements in his poems. They serve to represent two basic Aleixandrian concepts: that of human life as a sudden and brief bolt of light amidst a pervading darkness, "Entre dos oscuridades, un relámpago" (Between two worlds of darkness, a sudden lightning) (1975, 262–63) and that of his poetic venture as a "journey towards light."

Notes

1. All translations are my own.

Works Cited

Aleixandre, Vicente. 1975. *Antología total*. Ed. Pere Gimferrer. Barcelona: Seix Barral.
———. 1978. *Obras completas*. 2 vols. Madrid: Aguilar.

Alighieri, Dante. 1949. *La divina commedia*. 3 vols. Milano: Rizzoli.
Baudelaire, Charles. 1961. *Les fleurs du mal*. Paris: Classiques Garnier.
Bécquer, Gustavo Adolfo. 1973. *Obras completas*. Madrid: Aguilar.
Cano, José Luis. 1986. *Los cuadernos de Velintonia: Conversaciones con Vicente Aleixandre*. Barcelona: Seix Barral.
Darío, Rubén. 1961. *Poesías completas*. Ed. Alfonso Méndez Plancarte. Madrid: Aguilar.
Debicki, Andrew P. 1982. *Poetry of discovery. The Spanish generation of 1956–71*. Lexington: University Press of Kentucky.
De la Cruz, San Juan. 1990. Canciones entre el alma y el esposo. In *Poesías*. Ed. De Paola Elia. Madrid: Clásicos Castalia.
Gimferrer, Pere. 1974. La poesía última de Vicente Aleixandre. *Plural* 32: 23–27.
Korsmeyer. Carolyn. 1999. *Making sense of taste: Food and philosophy*. Ithaca: Cornell University Press.
Mistral, Gabriela. 1965. *Motivos de San Francisco*. Santiago de Chile: Editorial del Pacífico.
Neruda, Pablo. 1974. *Jardín de invierno*. Buenos Aires: Losada.
Pavese, Cesare. 1968. *Poesie del disamore*. Torino: Enaudi.
Rimbaud, Arthur. 1962. *Illuminations*. Paris: Hachette.
Welburn, Andrew J. 1989. *The truth of imagination. An introduction to visionary poetry*. New York: St. Martin's Press.
Zajonc, Arthur. 1993. *Catching the light: The entwined history of light and mind*. New York: Bantam Books.

José Moreno Villa: Exile and Community

Salvador J. Fajardo

On November 29, 1936, José Moreno Villa left the Residencia de Estudiantes in Madrid, after having lived there for twenty years.¹ He and other intellectuals, Antonio Machado among them, were moved to Valencia where the Republican government was located at that time.² Moreno Villa would reside in Valencia until February 3, 1937, when he was sent to the United States as a cultural representative of the Republican government. He would remain in the United States for approximately two months before traveling to Mexico to assume the post of cultural attaché. At that time he still believed his stay in Mexico would be relatively short: "¿Pensaba también en la interinidad de todo, como había pensado siempre? La idea de interinidad no podía borrarla porque es consustancial en mí. Yo pensaba que mi estancia en México podía ser de unos meses o de dos años a lo sumo" (Was I also thinking about the transitoriness of everything, as I always had? I could not erase the idea of transitoriness because it is consubstantial with me. I thought that my stay in Mexico might last a few months, or two years at most) (1944, 243–44).³

Entitled "Topografía de la casa paterna" (Topography of father's house), the first chapter of Moreno Villa's autobiography, *Vida en claro* (Life Made Clear), is a meditation on his childhood home and the relationship of its inhabitants to the various spaces they inhabited. Recalling that his own room was located "entre norte y sur, con luz de oriente" (between north and south, with light from the east) (14), he muses, "[p]odría decir que, nacido en oriente, me atraía el occidente. Pero también podría decir que, habiendo nacido en el sur, me atraía el norte, puesto que salí de Málaga a los dieciocho años, España arriba hasta Alemania, y más tarde, al bajar del norte, me quedé en Madrid" (I could say that, born in the east, I was attracted by the west. But I could also say that, having been born in the south, I was attracted by the north, since I left Malaga at eighteen, going up through Spain to Germany, and later, upon coming down from the north, stayed in Madrid) (15). Indeed, Moreno Villa's attention to *place* is one of the most fascinating aspects of his autobiography, and, in my view, a constituent element of its exilic character (of course, the same could be said of Alberti's *La arboleda perdida* [The Lost Grove]). In effect the poet is very explicit on the connection between his sense of self and the space wherein it develops:

> Yo quería hacer de mi cuarto un refugio donde, reinando el orden, pudiese abrir o extender mis planes, mis creaciones juveniles, sin que mis hermanos me devolviesen nada, sin que la vida exterior penetrase en la vida que yo iba forjando dentro de mí. Pero mi cuarto estaba entre norte y sur y decidió sobre mi vida. Mi destino fue abandonarlo y vivir siempre, desde entonces, interinamente. (Villa 1944, 18)

> [I wanted to turn my room into a refuge where, order prevailing, I could start or extend my plans, my youthful creations, without my siblings mixing up anything, without external life penetrating into the life I was framing within me. But my room lay between north and south and was decisive in my life. My destiny was to abandon it and to live always, since then, transitorily.]

Such reflections on the idea of "orientation" led Moreno Villa to the other key signpost along his vital and poetic itinerary; "transitoriness" ("interinidad"). Moreno Villa considers one's stay anywhere as but a passage because life is an essentially unstable, fleeting phenomenon, and it is this sense of "transitoriness" that shaped much of the poet's life and work. Moreno Villa conceived *Jacinta la pelirroja* (Jacinta the Redhead) as a kind of farewell to an impossible love affair, and wrote the poems of the collection in 1927 on a return voyage to Spain from the United States. Likewise, his creative energies were renewed during his exile in Mexico; it was also in Mexico that he had a family and rooted part of himself through his son, as he tells us in "Nos trajeron las ondas" (The waves brought us), his great poem on exile.

Moreno Villa wrote *Vida en claro* in Mexico in the early forties, when he knew he was destined to remain there. Still his sense of *interinidad* had not abated. It was the emblem of his retrospective *Vida en claro* both when he started to write it and at the end:

> Un constante aterrizar y despegar es la acción del poeta en la vida. Le es tan necesaria la tierra como el cielo. Sin el apoyo duro, no puede dar el salto. Pero su tragedia es que ni la tierra ni el cielo le satisfacen. La vida en la tierra es demasiado complicada y violenta; la vida en el cielo demasiado simple o llena de nubes. Por esto su acción es de fuga constante. (263)

> [The poet's action in life is a constant landing and taking flight. The earth is as necessary to him as the sky. Without the first support, he cannot jump. But his tragedy is that neither the land, nor the sky, satisfies him. Life on earth is too complicated and violent; life up above too simple or full of clouds. That is why his action is a constant flight.]

Such considerations of life as transit suggest a being in constant self-transformation, always engaged in reevaluations and learning, consciously actualizing a sort of Bergsonian *devenir*. In 1944, at age 57, Moreno Villa had established a new home in Mexico and yet he still sees himself in transit. When the poet hands over his autobiography to his son as a parting gift, it is handed over as one would a baton in a relay race.

It is perhaps because he recalls his life as a prolonged passage that Moreno Villa shows an exceptional sensitivity to the disposition of the various locales he inhabits. These are not inert but rather highly magnetized spaces that contribute to and energize the poet's inner orientation. For the poet, the magnetizing force of these habitats arises from his reflection on the human bonds they generate. For instance, the liaison with Jacinta developed and gained strength in Madrid and then weakened and disintegrated in New York.[4] New York astonished and ultimately repelled the poet. His inability to orient himself properly in this alien space went hand in hand with the emotional turmoil that Jacinta's as well as her family's behavior provoked in him.[5] He regained orientation on his way back to Spain, his inner compass guiding him again to the context and community that gave fullest play to his sense of continuity, and to his identity as poet, painter, scholar:

> [E]n las crestas de las ondas internas se entrelazan las luces de Nueva York y las madrileñas. Sé que en este preciso momento el pintor Juan Echevarría está pintando su enésimo retrato de Pío Baroja; que Ortega está preparando su clase de filosofía; . . . que García Lorca lee, con ahogos de alegría, su nueva comedia; que los eruditos afinan, que afinan los poetas y los filósofos; . . . ¡Qué maravilla! durante veinte años he sentido este ritmo emulatorio, y he dicho: Así vale la pena de vivir. (1944, 140–41)

> [In the crests of internal waves the lights of New York and those of Madrid interlace. I know that at this precise moment the painter Juan Echevarría is painting his nth. portrait of Pío Baroja; that Ortega is preparing his philosophy class; . . . that García Lorca reads, choking with happiness, his new play; that erudites are polishing their work, as are the poets and philosophers; . . . How marvelous! For twenty years I have felt this competing rhythm and I have said: this is the way to live.]

Moreno Villa, unsettled momentarily by the discord between inner and outer spaces, reorients himself mentally and physically toward his creative community by composing the poetic journal *Jacinta la pelirroja*. That journal will reflect his inner crisis, while contributing to his exploration of innovative poetic forms and renovation of the community's spirit. The poet needs both to depart and to arrive, to create in transit. Moreno Villa's relationship to his environment is at once committed and free. It is, in fact, characteristic of the particular spatial qualities of Moreno Villa's poetry that they represent at every step the fundamentally linguistic interface between man and his environment, replaying the Gadamerian contract with the world:

> To have a "world" means to have an attitude towards it. To have an attitude towards the world, however, means to keep oneself so free from what one encounters of the world that one is able to present it to oneself as it is. This capacity is both the having of a "world" and the having of language. Thus the concept of "world" or "environment" (Welt) is in opposition to the concept of "surrounding world" or "habitat" (Unwelt), as possessed by every living thing. (Gadamer, 402)

As I said earlier, Moreno Villa conceived his "attitude" toward the world according to a sense of transitoriness, a view affected by circumstance as well as predisposition. But the Civil War, as it redistributed the political and social spaces of the Peninsula, forced upon all Spaniards the need to reconstitute or at least clarify their allegiances, to confront their ideological identities and refashion community bonds. Moreno Villa, though not a political man, was strongly committed to the cause of the Republic, as were most Spanish intellectuals of that time. Thus, although surprised and not entirely comfortable with the idea, he accepted the government's request to travel to the United States.[6] What began as an officially sanctioned displacement became for the poet permanent exile.

While in the United States, Moreno Villa was asked by the Spanish ambassador (probably at the suggestion of his Mexican friend Genaro Estrada) to assume the post of cultural attaché in Mexico. A lingering concern for his lecture tour and the cultural amenities available in the United States made the poet less than enthusiastic about his subsequent departure:

"Dejaba Norteamérica con cierto fastidio. Me hubiera gustado vivir allí, entre buenos museos, buenas bibliotecas, gente respetuosa y un nivel de vida material suficientemente elevado. Pero el misterio, valiéndose de Genaro Estrada, me llevó a otro sitio."(241)[7]

[I left the U.S. with a certain irritation. I would have liked to live there, amid good museums, good libraries, respectful people and a sufficiently elevated material existence. But mystery, by means of Genaro Estrada, took me elsewhere].

Moreno Villa's reaction to the United States may have been born of an effort to escape the confusion experienced in Spain, to prolong the apparent calm that the United States offered together with the possibility of retreat into the satisfactions of unthreatened intellectual labors. Nonetheless, only a few pages later he muses:

[p]oca ilusión me hacían ya los libros y el arte después de la tremenda experiencia de España. Me sentía desligado de todo lo anterior, de toda forma y todo contenido. Respiraba el fracaso de Europa, de España y de todos nosotros, pero a pesar de esta crisis

de la fe en los hombres y en sus sistemas, me reconfortaba la idea de ser útil a alguien y a algo. (243)

[books and art no longer held the same excitement for me after the Spanish experience. I felt detached from everything previous, from all form and content. I breathed in Europe's failure, that of Spain and of us all, but in spite of this crisis of faith in men and their systems, the idea of being useful to someone and something comforted me].

Actually such diminished faith in strictly intellectual pursuits was not new. As the war broke out, in an effort to join the "popular" front in craft and spirit, Moreno Villa moved away from his more daring poetic experimentation and toward the ballad, adding his "romances" to all those others that came to integrate the *Romancero de la guerra civil* (Ballads of the Civil War).[8] A similar down-to-earth spirit informs "Converso con vosotros" (I speak with you), Moreno Villa's first "exile"[9] composition, written in Mexico in January 1938, and published in *Hora de España* (Hour of Spain) in March of the same year.

On his way back to Spain in 1927, Moreno Villa anticipated his reentry into the high energy intellectual world of the Residencia and composed formally demanding, detached, ironic poetry. In contrast, straining toward the war-torn Peninsula from Mexico in 1938, he writes in a straightforward, conversational manner a gritty salutation to the defenders of his Spain. Clearly Moreno Villa's responsibilities as cultural attaché for the Republic would intensify his sense of displacement. At this moment his official function and his personal sense of uprootedness led to the evocation of powerful human bonds with the defenders of the Republic and the government they represent.

When a poet provides us with an autobiography,[10] the temptation is strong to read the poetry in light of the biography and, in particular, to read the poetry according to the autobiographer's own interpretations. Certainly in these conditions there can be contextual enrichment of our reading of the poetry that shouldn't be discarded, but we should, of course, guard against the tendency to grant excessive "authority" to the poet's views at the expense of our own independent reading practice. I say this because I want to address the function of self-narration in "Converso con vosotros." By "self-narration" I don't mean autobiography (which the poet gives us in *Vida en claro*). Rather, self-narration is the silent dialog one carries out with oneself, sometimes just below verbalization, often in an almost unconscious manner. Self-narration accompanies our circulation in space or our attention to others. It subtends our anticipations and bears upon our instinctual as well as conscious memory. Self-narration is the foundation of the plot of our life. "Converso . . . " intersects with self-narration through a cluster of interrelated components such as space (place), identity, and personal ethics. While the spatial element in the condition of exile may seem obvious, it would be worthwhile to look at it in some detail in order to gauge with precision what displacement actually entails.

According to William Poteat, "space is primordially a pre-reflective vectorial orientation, and this precisely is my body in its pre-reflective integration into a world . . . It is within an oriented *whence* that primordial spatiality lies and it is from within this *whence* that all orientation derives" (italics in the text [182]). Our ideas of space begin with the location of our body and how we relate it to our environment. Principally we place ourselves in our topography through speech and sight. We generate our relationships from our location in space, and we articulate those relationships through speech *from our places.* Our speech commits our position and commits us to it as well. This notion has been described as "faithfulness to speech":

> The ground of all my discriminations and articulations of space, both reflected and as yet unreflected—visual, olfactory, tactile, audial, kinaesthetic, proprioceptive—is the radical *whence* of my lived, as yet unreflected mindbody in its worldly circumambience. It is in other words a *place: the archaic place* from "within" which all my *acts of placing*—both gestural and spoken—proceed. Spatially as *place* is a *whereon-to-stand* from which you and I and all others jointly make our mindbodily appearance with one another in our mutual world. (Poteat, 271, italics in the text)

As we contextualize our speech and our location, we contextualize as well our relationship to others and form our ethical positions with respect to them. The boundedness of our body, its bonds to the generating space of our communications, is essential to both our sense of identity through time (and space), or sense of self, and to our responsibility to be attentive to the presence and voice of others. We understand, reveal, and commit ourselves from our place of being through conversation/communication. This mutual placing and boundedness of the self reveals our responsibility to one another as equal ethical subjects and our dependence on one another to sustain our identities.

Our placedness is equally an indispensable element of our self-narrative. As we proceed through the spaces of our circumstance, we narrate ourselves to ourselves according to the *telos* of our existence, that is of our self-narrative. Alasdair McIntyre suggests that:

> [w]e live our lives, both individually and in our relationships with each other, in the light of certain conceptions of a shared future, a future in which certain possibilities beckon us forward and others repel us, some seem already foreclosed and others perhaps inevitable. There is no present which is not informed by some image of some future and an image of the future which always presents itself in the form of a *telos*—or a variety of ends and goals—towards which we are either moving or failing to move in the present (200–201, italics in the text).

For Calvin S. Schrag, embodiment is also indissolubly linked to self-narrative: "Bodily presence announces a texture of spatialization that remains existentially coordinated with the temporalization of the subject as a coming from a past and a moving into a future. The embodied presence of the subject integrates spatiality and temporality"(153). Charles Taylor further clarifies the notion of embodiment for us when he says of the "principle of embodiment" that it is:

> the principle that the subject and all his functions, however "spiritual" they may appear, are inescapably embodied. The embodiment is in two related dimensions: first, as a "rational animal," that is as a living being who thinks; and secondly, as an expressive being, that is a being whose thinking is always and necessarily in a medium. (85)

In "Converso . . . " Moreno Villa articulates the principle of embodiment by expressing the need to enter into contact with his fighting compatriots; here he turns language into its most engaged and concrete manifestation, a conversation. Through this conversation the poet generates a mutual space for speakers, orienting himself fully from his place of speech toward the place of his interlocutors. The poem is a turning toward his brothers abroad. It is also an articulation in another sense, the sense in which a musing takes linguistic shape, a conversation with oneself, a moment of self-narration that becomes an actual conversation, albeit with absent others. Thus, this very absence, this truncating of the verbal and bodily gesture or facing across the ocean, seizes the exile condition not only as a need for completion through community, but also as the generation of this very community through the communication itself. In this manner, as he links with his community, the poet wants to alleviate the anguish of exile by making of it a contribution.

"Converso con vosotros" is, then, Moreno Villa's first poem of exile and expresses the poet's hope not only that he will be reintegrated with his struggling brothers in the Peninsula, but also that present divisions will turn into future concord. Although it evokes and successfully persuades the reader of fundamental truths, it is important to see the poem both as a universal, humanly valid statement and a political one. In this sense it becomes important to ascertain what the poem seeks to enact or to do; ultimately we want to know how this "act" connects the personal and the public domains of Moreno Villa, the individual who wants to reach his fighting compatriots in Spain, and the official (cultural attaché) who wants to affirm his allegiance, the exile and the government representative.

As the title "Converso con vosotros" indicates, the poem unfolds a conversation, a dialogue with absent others who are also intimately conceived as being one with the speaker.[11] Indeed the poem follows the pattern of a conversation that begins by establishing the relationship of the interlocutors, develops a topic, arrives at a new point; in this instance the new point is a hopeful forward look. We move from "Converso con vosotros" (I speak with you) (l. 1), through "Conversamos sin odios" (We speak without hatreds) (l. 33), to "Y sé que hemos de hablar hasta que un día / no crucen por el cielo balas, sino canciones" (And I know that we will speak until one day / songs, not bullets cross in the sky) (ll. 36–37).

The poem flows in the pondered pace of a leisurely exchange of views, in thirty-seven lines of preponderantly "verso llano" and varied length (6 to 14 syllables), with occasional assonance. Only four lines, ending in "fusil" (rifle), "cañón" (cannon), "moral" (spirit), and canon, are "versos agudos." These lines stand out prosodically in descriptions of the present difficulties that conversation is asked to palliate. The reading tempo is slow, marked by the strong pauses of short sentences. In the otherwise reposed flow of articulation a phonetic knottedness stands out in lines 5 to 9 to reinforce the materiality of the martial scene (alliteration in *s* in ll. 5–6, until "tocan" (touch); statistically significant occurrence of the phoneme *r* in ll. 8–9):

> 5 Yo voy con vuestras balas silbando
> 6 y recibo en silencio las que nos tocan.
> 7 Pego mis alas con las del buitre,
> 8 me aferro a los paquidermos rampantes,
> 9 brinco en el potro y enfilo el cañón.

[I whistle along with your bullets / and receive in silence those that touch us. / I glue my wings to those of the vulture, / I fasten to the crawling pachyderms, / I jump on the colt and aim the cannon.]

The first four lines of the poem establish the parameters of the situation as well as its figurative architecture; the informing trope is a double integrative synecdoche:

> 1 Converso con vosotros porque estáis en mis venas
> 2 en mi garganta y en mi frente.
> 3 Y porque yo, a mi vez, estoy viviendo
> 4 en el gatillo de vuestro fusil.

[I speak with you because you're in my veins / in my throat and on my brow. / And because I, in turn, am living / in the trigger of your rifle.]

The speaker creates the space of interlocution within himself through the triple synecdochal representation of his body, whose essential components of lifeblood, voice, and thought are substituted for the absent referent, "cuerpo" / "ser" (body/being). The speaker conceives himself as an aggregate of parts that act as containers for "vosotros" (you). The self is reinstituted in the second statement in three corresponding iterations, "yo" (I), "a mi vez" (in turn), "estoy viviendo" (I am living), which are regathered in the tripartite focusing of line 4: "en el gatillo de vuestro fusil" [in the trigger of your rifle]. At the same time the three components of "vosotros," sited in "venas" (veins), "garganta" (throat), and "frente" (brow), are fused in a three-tiered process of concentration to "gatillo." This lexeme, near the center of line 4, where flesh meets metal at the edge of a release/explosion, contracts and contains both "yo" and "vosotros." The notion conveyed here is that of a mutual and shared refocusing on the defensive task.

I have looked in some detail at these opening lines because they present both the figurative and the conceptual thrust of the poem: the pattern "yo"—"vosotros"—"yo," is a part/whole synecdoche that anticipates the integration that the conversation is meant to achieve. Conceptually this integration is seen also as the reconstitution of a self shattered by exile, whose identity is menaced by "incertidumbre" (uncertainty) (l. 14).

The conversation thus begins with an assertion of commonality in thought and action. From the point of view of the speaker the conversation is also meant to reshape his identity, his subjectivity vis-à-vis the fight in which his Republican "brothers" are engaged. Furthermore, the thrust toward concreteness seeks to assuage in the speaker the sense that he has been *abstracted* from the context of responsibility represented by the other "speakers," that is, his compatriots in Spain. For this to be achieved, for the present site of the speaker to acquire legitimacy or meaning for the self, this site needs to be reconnected to the space of the struggle. This can only be achieved through speech, the conversation that will give a personal orientation to both "places." The speaker's displacement has momentarily disrupted the linkage between his self-narrative and the tradition that nurtures it, that is to say his agency and the context of its practice.

In a conversation one may consider antagonisms, discrepancies, frictions, the obstacles that the dialogue might be expected to "dissolve," to transform into mutually acceptable discourse/narrative. (In fact the present stage of the war will not allow this, as is recognized by the resurgence of the instruments of violence near the end of the poem—ll. 31–32). Implicit in this conversation is a reference to the one that is not taking place between the war's contending factions. That conversation will be a future one when "balas" (bullets) have become "canciones" (songs) (l. 37). Before that happens *in the poem* there is a materiality that needs gradually to be resolved, or mitigated at least, into communication. The images (metaphors) deployed in lines 5 to 9 represent the thickest presence of such obstacles, instruments of death. The speaker espouses their action because he would want to participate also, to risk his life as "vosotros" (you) are doing. But in the process of attaching himself imaginatively to the engines of war and animalizing them, he does somewhat reduce their matter and asperities. As prolegomena to the pursuit of this conversation the speaker needs to establish his solidarity with his addressees, claiming a presence in spirit in the field of battle.

Lines 10 to 13 summarize the preceding development. Line 10, "Cuando quiero vivir converso con vosotros" (When I want to live I speak with you), does so most explicitly—on an existential level, equating separateness and death. That is to say that his life, like those of the Republican soldiers, is in the balance, and that he owes it to them as his interlocutors:

> 10 Cuando quiero vivir converso con vosotros.
> 11 No hay mejores amigos,
> 12 mejores hermanos,
> 13 mejores inteligencias.

[When I want to live I speak with you. / There are no better friends, / no better brothers, / no better brains.]

This is the level at which he can converse with them and which the first lines of the poem establish: the place of speech of both conversing parties has been defined as the speaker's inwardness and his interlocutors' field of battle, for in order for the exchange to be effective there has to be a common space. But what comes to be as well with the poem's opening is a communicative action, an *event*, which is what the conversation actually enacts. It also exhibits the coming to be of a language for present use, a language whose fundamental aim is to maintain a threatened community:

> [L]anguage has its true meaning only in conversation, in the exercise of understanding between people . . . [i]n linguistic communication "world" is disclosed. . . . All forms of human

community of life are forms of linguistic community: even more, they constitute language. For language, in its nature, is the language of conversation. (Gadamer, 404)

To be who he is, the speaker needs to converse with his brethren. Lines 11 to 13, "No hay inteligencias" (There aren't . . . brains), conclude the opening development with an echo of lines 1 and 2, as the speaker reiterates the bonds between his addressees and his inner being. Essential components of the speaker's inner self have now been externalized and are components of his addressees' selves (ll. 3–4). In this conversation there is more than an exchange of views, there is an exchange of life.

We may consider this first part of the poem a legitimizing of the conversation as it asserts the commonality of the parties and the level of their voices. The section that follows, "Cuando la incertidumbre . . . conversar" (When uncertainty . . . speak) (ll. 14–28), expands the notion of interdependency. First it attends to the speaker's need to engage the others (ll. 14–22), and follows with considerations on mutuality (ll. 22–28). It is in line 14 that the speaker refers to his condition as exile, which leaves him vulnerable to uncertainty; "—pena del exiliado—" (sorrow of the exile) is set out from the flow of speech, in apposition to "incertidumbre," graphically and syntactically representing that very condition ("pena" should be understood as sorrow and lot together). The exile's isolation produces uncertainty because, deprived of expressive contact with his community—a situation which this "conversation" wants to remedy—the conditions of his speech and of his identity are threatened. That is why he feels that "incertidumbre" wants to sink him, reduce his selfhood, and dry up his voice (ll. 14–15), separating him from his communicative, active context. Murray Jardine comments on such possible conditions:

[T]he critical question in [the] conception of place is whether or not the speaker has become abstracted from the context of responsibility to other speakers—*something the other speakers can probably answer better*. The concept of place articulates . . . the absolutely critical dimension of attentiveness to the voice of the other. ([159–60] italics in the text)

The speaker understands his need for the voice of others in his moments of greatest danger: thoughts of exile and of the imminence of death: "Y a vosotros recurro cuando veo / que el curso de mi vida se ha acortado" (And I resort to you when I see / that the course of my life has been shortened) (ll. 17–18).

The next four lines (ll. 19–21) return to the idea of codependency as necessary mutual support, a notion that is further expanded in lines 23 to 26:

> 19 Sois vosotros, amigos infinitos,
> 20 Los que eleváis mi caduca moral;
> 21 así como soy yo quien os ayuda
> 22 a levantar la vuestra si decae.
> 23 Es el pájaro quien alegra a la rama
> 24 y es la rama quien alegra al pájaro.
> 25 Es el río quien sostiene al cauce
> 26 y es el cauce quien sostiene al río.

[It is you, innumerable friends, / who elevate my failing spirit; / as it is I who help you / to lift yours if it declines. / It is the bird that gladdens the bough / and the bough that gladdens the bird. / It is the river that sustains its banks / and it is the banks that sustain the river.]

These lines suggest a pastoral interlude that anticipates the conclusion where bullets have become songs. But before we arrive at that desired future, the present must be once more addressed. In the conclusion "Converso . . . canciones" (I speak . . . songs) (ll. 29–37), the speaker iterates the constancy of his support and his communication. His conversation has become consubstantial with his self. It is significant that he should describe this temporal constancy in spatial terms "la luna" (the moon), "el sol" (the sun). These commonplace referents are effective, nonetheless, in their universality, for they abrogate the distinction between the two shores of the Atlantic, an idea that is reinforced in the next two lines, "cuando enmudece la ametralladora / y cuando bosteza el cañón" (when the machine gun goes mute / and when the cannon yawns) (ll. 31–32). The same sun and moon shine on the battlefield, the place of his addressees.[12] The last four lines want to recapture a serenity (adumbrated in the pastoral interlude of ll. 23–26) seen as the necessary consequence of this conversation. They anticipate a calm that may include the contending factions when speech overcomes violence:

34   En paz, como el regato y el pájaro que pasa.
35   En paz, como la muerte del que cae de un tiro.
36   Y sé que hemos de hablar hasta que un día
37   no crucen por el cielo balas, sino canciones.

[In peace, like the brook and the bird that pass. / In peace, like the death of he who is shot down. / And I know that we shall speak until one day / not bullets, but songs cross the sky.]

The speaker has learned from this conversation, where "[c]onverso" (ll. 1, 10, 16, 29) and "[c]onversamos" (l. 33) become "Y sé"(l. 36). This conversation is the first of the songs that "cru[zan] por el cielo." In his first experience of exile, Moreno Villa creates a speaker who finds it necessary to reinvent himself in terms of his community by understanding the place of his speech. In *Sources of the Self* Charles Taylor addresses this question in terms which, though of a general nature, are especially pertinent to notions of identity that we have examined in the poem:

> To know who I am is a species of knowing where I stand.... People may see their identity as defined partly by some moral or spiritual commitment, say as a Catholic or an anarchist. Or they may define it in part by the nation or tradition they belong to.... Put counterfactually, they are saying that were they to lose that commitment or identification, they would be at sea, as it were; they wouldn't know any more, for an important range of questions, what the significance of things was for them. (27)

Moreno Villa wants the poem "Converso con vosotros" both to express and to generate, through language, a space on which to stand, from which to speak. The poem is not only an expression of his solidarity with, and his need of, his struggling community in Spain. It is also a communicative act, an event in his self-narrative. As he seeks to answer the question, "who am I?" he finds that the question only makes sense in the interchange of speakers. He defines who he is by defining from where and with whom he speaks, creating in this conversation a space of moral orientation where his most important defining relations are enacted.

"Converso..." explores the need to establish an actual present, that is, a location for the interpersonal exchange from which a possible future may take shape. The future, however, is inscribed in the present conditions of the "verbal" exchange (a text that conceives itself as an interlocution), and has existence only as an intention. That is to say, the future is a disposition of the present, an orientation of the self in its present concrete spatiality. The "conversation" performs a convergence *in its space* of the speaker's self-narrative and the projected narratives of the addressees in a dialectic of intention and expectation. It is meant to generate a common "place" in which to engage the others from a condition of faithfulness-to-speech. Such a commonly defined "place" will produce speakers who realize their assumptions of a context of communication (and practice) from the confluence of their self-narratives and the community/tradition to which they connect. Such a realized "true" place reveals to the participants in the conversation—to the speaker who now generates it—the universal through the particular.[13] The conversation aims at this universality in the sense in which Heidegger, commenting on the "essence" of poetry as he understands it in Hölderlin, sets it forth:

> The being of men is founded in language. But this only becomes actual in *conversation*. Nevertheless the latter is not merely a manner in which language is put into effect, rather it is only as conversation that language is essential. . . . But now what is meant by "a conversation"? Plainly the act of speaking with others about something. Then speaking also brings about the process of coming together. . . . [T]he unity of a conversation consists in the fact that in the essential word there is always manifest that one and the same thing on which we agree, and on the basis of which we are united and so are essentially ourselves. Conversation and its unity support our existence. (277–78 italics in the text)

Although thoroughly committed to the Republican cause and to participating in its defense, it is the bringing about of a community of intent that in this poem interests Moreno Villa. His poem anticipates a communal, national healing: a vaster effort at agglutination amid the dispersals, dislocations, and sundering of war.

Notes

1. He had been invited there in 1917 by the institution's first director, Alberto Jiménez Fraud: "Vente a la Residencia de Estudiantes. Yo necesito en ella unos cuantos hombres jóvenes que, por su rectitud moral, su afición al trabajo y su entusiasmo por las cosas nobles, influyan, sin reglamento ni cargos determinados en el ambiente de la casa. Tú no vas a ser pedagogo, pero vas a ayudarme más de lo que te figuras" (Come to the Residence. I need some young men who by virtue of their moral rectitude, their love of work and their enthusiasm for noble things, will influence, without rules or specific instructions, the atmosphere within the house. You won't be a teacher but you will help me more than you can imagine) (Moreno Villa 1944, 101).

2. The first group of intellectuals was evacuated from Madrid by the "Quinto Regimiento" (Fifth Regiment) in late November 1936. Moreno Villa was joined as well by the painter Gutiérrez Solana, the scholar Navarro Tomás, and others. They were transported to Valencia and housed in an old hotel, turned into the "Casa de la cultura" (House of culture).

3. All translations are my own, unless noted otherwise.

4. The young woman's actual name was Florence. I will retain Jacinta here as the poetry's addressee.

5. The young woman's family is absolutely opposed to the marriage. Moreno Villa will spend about three months in New York, at the end of which he will return to Madrid disillusioned and having abandoned any idea of marrying Jacinta.

6. The post had first been offered to Navarro Tomás who could not go and who proposed Moreno Villa. With characteristic modesty Moreno Villa was reluctant to assume this responsibility. He was told that this was exclusively a cultural enterprise, with no political overtones, and that his talks could deal with art or literature. He finally accepted realizing that he, like everybody else, was simply "mobilized" and therefore at the government's disposal.

7. One wonders whether, as he writes *Vida en claro* now settled in Mexico, and in spite of the ultimately positive turn of events that the poet owed to the efforts of his friend Estrada—he married his widow and had a son—the note of regret may reflect the somewhat more stringent circumstances to which he had to adapt in the sister country.

8. "Algunos de estos poemas del escritor malagueño ya habían sido publicados en el número inicial de *Hora de España* (Valencia, enero de 1937). Bajo el epígrafe *Poemas de la Guerra*, editó cuatro romances escritos en Madrid, noviembre de 1936: 'Madrid, frente de lucha,' 'Revelación,' 'Descanso de un miliciano,' y 'Frente'" (Villalba-Álvarez, 259). (Some of these poems by the writer from Málaga had already been published in the initial volume of *Hora de España* [Valencia, January 1937]. Under the epigraph of Poemas de la Guerra [Poems of War], he edited four ballads written in Madrid in November 1936: 'Madrid, frente de lucha' [Madrid, site of the fight], 'Revelación,' [Revelation] 'Descanso de un miliciano' [Rest for a Militiaman], y 'Frente' [Battlefront])."

9. "Exile" in quotes because, although his composition is situationally an exile piece, he does not yet know that exile will, in fact, be his lot.

10. Other examples that come to mind are Cernuda's long essay "Historial

de un libro" (Chart of a Book) and Alberti's memoirs in three volumes *La arboleda perdida* (The Lost Grove).

11. "Converso con vosotros" written in January 1938 reads:

1   Converso con vosotros porque estáis en mis venas,
2   en mi garganta y en mi frente.
3   Y porque yo, a mi vez, estoy viviendo
4   en el gatillo de vuestro fusil.
5   Yo voy con vuestras balas silbando
6   y recibo en silencio las que nos tocan.
7   Pego mis alas con las del buitre,
8   me aferro a los paquidermos rampantes,
9   brinco en el potro y enfilo el cañón.
10 Cuando quiero vivir converso con vosotros.
11 No hay mejores amigos,
12 mejores hermanos,
13 mejores inteligencias.
14 Cuando la incertidumbre—pena del exiliado—
15 quiere hundirme y secarme,
16 converso con vosotros.
17 Y a vosotros recurro cuando veo
18 que el curso de mi vida se ha acortado.
19 Sois vosotros, amigos infinitos,
20 los que eleváis mi caduca moral;
21 así como yo soy quien os ayuda
22 a levantar la vuestra si decae.
23 Es el pájaro quien alegra a la rama
24 y es la rama quien alegra al pájaro.
25 Es el río quien sostiene al cauce
26 y es el cauce quien sostiene al río.
27 Somos débiles y somos fuertes.
28 Por esto debemos conversar.
29 Converso con vosotros al despuntar la luna
30 y al despuntar el día;
31 cuando enmudece la ametralladora
32 y cuando bosteza el cañón.
33 Conversamos sin odios, sin alardes ni llantos.
34 En paz, como el regato y el pájaro que pasa.
35 En paz, como la muerte del que cae de un tiro.
36 Y sé que hemos de hablar hasta que un día
37 no crucen por el cielo balas, sino canciones.

[*Hora de España*, 15 (Marzo, 1938) 435–36], (1998, 615)

[I speak with you because you're in my veins, / in my throat and on my brow, / and because I, in turn, am living / in the trigger of your rifle. / I whistle along with your bullets / and receive in silence those that touch us. / I glue my wings to those of the vulture, / I fasten to crawling pachyderms, / I jump on the colt and aim the cannon. / When I want to live I speak with you. / There are no better friends, / no better brothers, / no better brains. / When uncertainty—sorrow of the exile— / wants to sink me and dry me up, / I speak with you, / and I resort to you when I see / that the course of my life has been shortened. / It is you, innumerable friends, / who elevate my flagging spirit; / as it is I who help you / to lift yours if it declines. / It is the bird that gladdens the bough / and the bough that gladdens the bird. / It is the river that sustains its banks / and it is the banks that sustain the river. / We are weak and we are strong. / That is why we must speak. / I speak with you when the moon dawns / and when the day dawns; / when the machine gun goes mute / and when the cannon yawns. / We speak without hatreds, without boasts or weeping. / In peace, like the brook and the bird that pass. / In peace, with the death of the one who's shot down. / And I know that we shall speak until one day/ not bullets but songs cross the sky.]

I wish to thank the *Residencia de Estudiantes* for permission to quote "Converso con vosotros."

12. In his poem "Despertar español" (Spanish Awakening), Jorge Guillén has some apposite lines :

> A través de un idioma
> ¿Yo podría llegar a ser el hombre
> Por fin humano a que mi esfuerzo tiende
> Bajo este sol de todos?
>
> (Guillén 1977, 17–20)

13. "The structure of the process involved reveals the two features of place that serve as guidelines for evaluating the faithfulness of the speaker. First, a true place must transform those who inhabit it in such a way that they can recognize that their acritical reliance upon their context of practice, narrative, and tradition was justified. Second, a true place will reveal the universal through the particular" (1998, 161).

Works Cited

Gadamer, Hans Georg. 1975. *Truth and method*. Trans. by William Glen-Doepel. London: Sheed and Ward.

Guillén, Jorge. 1977. Despertar español. In *Clamor*. Barcelona: Barral.

Heidegger, Martin. 1949. Hölderlin and the essence of poetry. In *Existence and being*. Chicago: Henry Regnery Co.

Jardine, Murray. 1998. *Speech and political practice*. Albany: State University of New York Press.

McIntyre, Alasdair. 1984. *After virtue. A study in moral theory*. Notre Dame: University of Notre Dame Press.

Moreno Villa, José. 1944. *Vida en claro*. México: Fondo de cultura económica.

———. 1998. *Poesías completas*. Ed. by Juan Pérez de Ayala. México: El colegio de México.

Poteat, William. 1974. Persons and places. In *Art and religion as communication*, edited by James Waddell and F. W. Dilliston. Atlanta: John Knox Press.

———. 1985. *Polanyan meditations: In search of a post-critical logic*. Durham: Duke University Press.

Ricoeur, Paul. 1992. *Oneself as another*. Trans. by Kathleen Blamey. Chicago: University of Chicago Press.

Schrag, Calvin O. 1986. *Communicative praxis and the space of subjectivity*. Bloomington: University of Indiana Press.

Taylor, Charles. 1985. *Human agency and language*, Vol. I. Cambridge: Cambridge University Press.

———. 1989. *Sources of the self: The making of the modern identity*. Cambridge: Harvard University Press.

Villalba Alvarez, Marina. 1989. Siete páginas de José Moreno Villa en *Hora de España*. In *José Moreno Villa en el contexto del '27*, edited by Cristóbal Cuevas García. Barcelona: Anthropos.

Affirmative Action: Francisco Brines's *La última costa*

Judith Nantell

Referring to Francisco Brines's 1966 *Palabras a la oscuridad* (Words unto Darkness), José Luis Cano prophetically proclaims what would become this poet's literary destiny: "Con este libro esperado, Brines se coloca hoy entre los mejores de la nueva generación poética" (With this long awaited collection of poetry, Brines nowadays takes his rightful place among the best poets in the new generation) (198).[1] One quarter of a century later, in November 1999, this poet and his poetry, inseparable as they are, were recognized by Spain's Ministerio de la Cultura for their significant contributions to and profound impact on Spanish letters. The awarding of the Premio Nacional de las Letras signals the vital importance of Franciso Brines's poetry at the close of the twentieth century and, at the same time, announces the eminent role his respected voice will have as we enter the twenty-first century.

Brines and his poetry have been celebrated by a number of critics and have been characterized with many illustrative designations over the last forty years. Cano was the first to use the denomination "poesía elegíaca" (elegiac poetry) (193), a term confirmed by Brines some years later in his 1984 *ars poetica*, "La certidumbre de la poesía" (The Certainty of Poetry): "Creo que el conjunto de mi obra, aun en los momentos en que aparece el cántico, no es otra cosa que una extensa elegía" (I believe that the whole of my work, even in the moments in which the canticle appears, is nothing other than an extensive elegy) (1984, 24). José Olivio Jiménez always has maintained this view throughout his investigations of Brines's poetry, from his first published collection to his most recent. This critic early on named Brines a poet of time, a poet who demonstrates "la más aguda conciencia temporal" (the most acute consciousness of time) (1972, 419). For Jiménez, all of Brines's poetry is a continuous, poignant, meditative elegy concerning time and the human condition (1998, 139). Jorge Manrique adds another dimension to Brines's poetry when naming him "poeta heraclitiano" (Heraclitian poet) (321). In 1997 Carlos Javier Morales bestowed on Brines the fitting title "una de las personalidades mayores en la lírica española de este siglo" (one of the major figures of Spanish lyric poetry in this century) (149). When Brines was awarded the 1999 Premio Nacional de las Letras, Miguel García Posada paid tribute to this poet in *El país* (November 24, 1999) by conferring on him what is, in my estimation, the most fitting vocative denomination of all: "el cantor de la intensidad vital" (he who sings about vital intensity). It is this aspect of Brines's poetry that I intend to investigate in my present study of his 1995 collection entitled *La última costa* (The Farthest Shore), while, at the same time, recalling other vital affirmations echoing throughout his poetry of the past four decades.

Despite the finality of human existence that the title of Brines's latest collection immediately brings to mind, the primary focus of *La última costa* is not death. Rather, it is life which this poetry celebrates and, above all, *experiencing* life or living and having lived. In his prologue to *Poemas a D. K.* (Poems to D. K.), Brines foreshadows the personal context and thematic content which years later would form the underpinnings of *La última costa*:

> La memoria, eso que al fin y al cabo nos resume, nos hace tan sólo poseedores de unos restos azarosos de nuestra vida; la poesía obra de la misma ciega manera. Llegados al final del hermoso trayecto sólo aprietan nuestras manos unos raídos y modestos esplendores. No son las atesoradas monedas del avaro, sino esa última posesión de las escasas hojas que aún cuelgan del árbol invernal. Y esto nos basta para poder decir, con entera verdad, que hemos vivido.
> (Brines 1986, 10)

[Memory, that which ultimately in the end summarizes who we are, makes us the sole possessor of what by chance are merely but a few vestiges from our life; poetry works in this same blind way. Having arrived at the end of the beautiful tale of the journey it is only then do we realize that what we clutch within our hands are but a few modest yet nonetheless resplendent remnants. These vital vestiges are not the hoarded coins of the miser, but rather they are what remains of our complete possession of what we value most, just as the last few leaves still cling to the wintry tree. And this is enough for us to state, with certainty and conviction, that indeed we have lived.]

I plan to show that in *La última costa* the reason for life is to be, to have been, and to continue to be. Living is at once existing toward death, a presence known all too well by the poet and his intimate voice speaking to us from the autumn of his own life. Yet, at the same time, living is and must be its own becoming all that it is "not yet" (*Aún no*) (Not Yet). This, as we shall see, is the most significant mode of existence displayed in all of Brines's poetry. It is, however, in *La última costa* where *being aún* becomes an insistent and driving force as well as a singular ontological mode. It is in this collection where the poetic *yo* (I) comes to understand that there is still time to live and there is still time remaining to remember having lived. Emboldened and empowered by such knowledge, Brines and his poetic *yo* now are increasingly more determined than ever before to be *and* to be fully aware of being.

Before approaching *La última costa*, however, I shall localize Brines's poetry within the critical views expressed by significant Hispanists during the last decade of the twentieth century. I shall then summarize and situate the essential themes investigated by the poet in his poetry of the last forty years. Finally, I shall turn my attention to *La última costa*, as a collection signaling new beginnings both for Brines's poetry and the readings of his poetry.

At The Turn of The Century: Critical Views

In reviewing recent critical studies of Brines's works published during the past decade, a number of distinguished critics have celebrated his poetry, its importance, and its influence.[2] José Andújar Almansa underscores the "incuestionable unidad interna" (unquestionable internal unity) of Brines's poetic production and comments: "Dicha unidad gira en torno a la presencia de un poderoso yo que, frente al vértigo del tiempo, de la muerte y de la nada, pugna por afirmarse ontológicamente en la existencia" (This unity revolves around the presence of a powerful personal "I" who, by facing the vertigo that is time, death, and nothingness, combats these by ontologically affirming himself by his very existence) (14). Francisco José Martín, in his 1998 study *El sueño roto de la vida* (The Broken Dream of Life), astutely defines the thematic essence of this poet's work in this way: "Vivir la vida con la máxima intensidad posible, es ésta una máxima que desprende de la poesía de Brines en esta hora otoñal. Lo cierto es que no nos parece nueva, si lo pensamos mejor podemos rastrearla desde los albores de su obra; pero es ahora, sin embargo, cuando adquiere su más pleno significado" (To live life with the greatest possible intensity, this is the maxim unleashed in Brines's poetry during this his autumnal hour. What is certain is that it does not seem new to us, because when we give it more thought we come to realize that there are traces of this even in his earliest poetry but it is now, however, when it acquires its most important significance) (102). Jiménez writes that one of the most salient features of Brines's poetry viewed as a collective whole is the carefully crafted revelation of his own intimate world which we soon come to realize is, ultimately, the "realidad existencial" (existential reality) of all human life understood as "la vida sin más" (life and nothing more) (1998, 34). Manrique maintains the view that Brines's work is "íntimamente reflexiva" (intimately reflexive) and that this poetry has centered on "la intensa captación de los efímeros momentos" (intensely seizing ephemeral moments) (294). In the view of Morales, Brines's poetry reveals his personal "testimony" that charts his existence. But it is more than this, as Morales correctly affirms. What we witness, as readers, is that Francisco Brines's poetry is at once a personal "biography" and also a shared human story where poetry discloses "una lección coherente, de principio a fin, sobre la grandeza y miseria de la condición humana" (a coherent lesson on, from beginning to end, the grandeur and the anguish of the human condition) (150). In the 1993 prologue to *Antología poética* (Poetry Anthology), Alejandro Duque Amusco explains that in Brines's poetry we find the thematic content of human existence which, as this critic contends, "Es el vivir del hombre ...

contemplado por el poeta sin menoscabo de su enorme variedad de aspectos y matices" (It is human life ... contemplated by the poet without in any way diminishing the vast variation found in all of its multiple aspects and its numerous gradations) (18).

As they stress the importance of Brines's work, a number of other critical voices of the past decade further uphold the commentaries quoted above. Jonathan Mayhew notes that in Brines's two most recent poetic collections, *El otoño de las rosas* (The Autumn of the Roses) and *La última costa*, we find "a serenely self-confident mastery of poetic traditions and forms" (290). Andrew Debicki's important study, *Spanish Poetry of the Twentieth Century: Modernity and Beyond*, further draws attention to *El otoño de las rosas* and to Brines's skill as a master craftsman of words and poetic traditions. Debicki explains that: "A consciousness of death, of impending annihilation, underlies the whole book. Memories of past experiences (frequently love episodes) are juxtaposed to a perception of life's evanescence. The poet skillfully fits modern referents into timeless settings and into classical poetic traditions" (194). Many of my own ideas are evident in my 1994 monograph where I explain that: "My readings of Brines's poetry point out the deconstructive and disseminative effects of language used to question the act of naming and the act of knowing by means of naming" (94). Jiménez, however, provides the overall summative description when he observes that "Desposesión y afirmación: son voces emblemáticas en el mundo poético de Brines" (Dispossession and affirmation: these are the symbolic voices within Brines's poetic world) (1998, 138).

Irreconcilable Differences in Brines's Poetry

Over the years Francisco Brines has summarized the thematic essence of his works with haunting metaphors. In one of his earliest poems entitled "Junto a la mesa se ha quedado solo" (He Remained Alone Near the Table) published in *Las brasas* (The Embers) we learn, "Ay, se muere todo, / pasa la luz, la flor, los sentimientos / se marchitan, las fuerzas van perdiéndose" (Alas, everything dies, light fades, the flower, emotions all wither, strength constantly is slipping away) (1997, 26).[3] Many of the poetic meditations found in *Palabras a la oscuridad* (Words unto Darkness) convey the transitory nature of human existence as we find in the poem "Oscureciendo el bosque" (The Darkening Forest). This is a subject that Brines would scrutinize throughout his poetic trajectory: "Es en la vida todo / transcurrir natural hacia la muerte, / y el gratuito don que es ser, y respirar, / respira y es hacia la nada angosta" (In life all naturally runs its course toward death, and the gratuitous gift that is life, and breathing, breathes and exists toward narrowing nothingness) (1997, 133). This poet's intensely personal and reflexively intimate voice always has echoed his very human understanding of temporal being. In much of the poetry of *Aún No* (Not Yet) he draws on this, revealing, as in the poem "Extinción" (Extinction), his personal lament, "Sólo soy un suspiro, que dice su extinción; / en la palabra muerte resumiré mi canto / triunfal, por verdadero" (I am merely a sigh, a sigh uttering its own extinction; in the word death I shall sum up my triumphant and truthful song) (1997, 232). In this same collection the poem "Elca y Montgó" (Elca and Montgó) discloses his sincere belief that as a poet *and* as a human being he knows that he must both write about *and* live by accepting the existential fact that is personal mortality: "agradecido, / miro con buen amor, / por la delicadeza con que hoy muero" (thankful, I watch with great tenderness the gentle way in which I am dying today) (1997, 270). Over the decades, Brines's poetry has evolved into an insistent inquiry into the uniquely human mode of being-toward-death with full knowledge of this ontological and inescapable reality as "Alocución pagana" (Pagan Allocution), another poem from *Aún no*, makes perfectly clear:

> ¿Es que, acaso, estimáis que por creer
> en la inmortalidad,
> os tendrá que ser dada?
> Es obra de la fe, del egoísmo
> o de la desolación.
> Y si existe, no importa no haber creído en ella:
> respuestas ignorantes son todas las humanas
> si a la muerte interroga.
>
> (1997, 240)

[Is it, perhaps, your opinion that by believing in immortality, it will indeed be given to you? It is an act of faith, egoism, or desolation. And if it exists, it is not important not having believed in it: ignorant answers are all the human ones when death is interrogated.]

Brines's critical questioning of personal finitude culminates in his most complex collection entitled *Insistencias en Luzbel* (Insistences on Lucifer), published in 1977. At the beginning of the second section of this poetic volume, introduced by the revealing title "Insistencias en el engaño" (Insistences on Deceit), he warns, "Nacimos inocentes; hoy, culpables. / ¿Qué significa el tiempo? Devastados. / Nacemos inmortales; hoy, mortales. / El nombre de la vida es el Engaño" (We were born innocent; today, culpable. What is the meaning of time? We are devastated. We are born immortal; today, mortal. The name of life is Deceit) (1997, 321). It is, however, in the crucial poem "Definición de la nada" (Definition of Nothingness) where Brines discloses the personal ontology underlying his view of existence exposed throughout this pivotal collection: "Lo pensáis como un frío, mas ésa es vuestra carne. / No afirma y nada niega su firme coherencia" (You imagine it to be cold, but it is your own flesh. It does not affirm and nothing negates its firm coherence) (1997, 302). Once this was understood there was no going back. Brines and his poetic *yo* now had to confront *how* to live with this painful knowledge directly and daily.

The natural world offered no solace to the poetic *yo* that viewed it as merely a reflection and extension of his own inner self, of his own death-bound existence. By always being aware of life as passage the poetic alter-ego, in much of Brines's poetry, could only witness the external world, repeating the cadenced temporality deliberately marking the course of his own finite existence. In 1966 the poem "Oscureciendo el bosque" (The Darkening Forest), published in *Palabras a la oscuridad* (Words unto Darkness), Brines had revealed a personal response: "Toda esta hermosa tarde, de poca luz, / caída sobre los grises bosques de Inglaterra, / es tiempo. / Tiempo que está muriendo / dentro de mis tranquilos ojos, / mezclándose en el tiempo que se extingue" (Everything within this lovely afternoon, of very little light fallen on England's grey forests, is time. Time that is dying within my tranquil eyes, / blending with the time that is being extinguished) (1997, 133). Some years later, however, he once again would come to realize that there is no escape from "El confín perpetuo" (Perpetual Boundary), the telling title of a poem from *El otoño de las rosas*. Finite being will always reveal itself whenever and wherever this poet recalls, attempts to recover, and sadly realizes the tragic sense of lost vitality that is his being within the world: "Las pequeñas memorias de la infancia / se han perdido; por ella fue el vivir / eterna primavera y luz de sol. / Mas dudo si ha existido. Nada queda / de lo que aquí pasó: tristeza o goce" (The little memories of childhood are forever lost; in that era living was an eternal Spring filled with sunlight. I doubt that it even existed. Nothing remains from all that once took place here: sadness or delight) (1997, 461).

At the same time, however, a number of the poems in *El otoño de las rosas* also signal a different view of human temporality. In this 1986 work, poetry begins to emerge as the poet's personal as well as shared reflection on *having been*: "Y hay, con todo, un calor de vida ya gastada, / un secreto entusiasmo de haber sido" (And there is, with everything, a warmth from life now consumed and a secret enthusiasm for having been) (1997, 385). This "secret enthusiasm" will evolve into "El pacto que me queda" (My remaining pact) (1997, 444), as another important poem from this same collection confirms. This symbolic "pact" will entail seeing the self and the self within the world, past as well as present, with distinctly new eyes: "Acógete a unos ojos, sólo jóvenes, / y descubre con ellos el mundo que perdiste. / Y que te miren luego, para ser aún del mundo" (Do welcome your new eyes, which are solely those from your youth, and do discover through them the world that you lost. And soon they will watch you, because you still are part of that world).[4] This is the prophetic perspective that will shape *La última costa*. Brines's 1995 work, after decades of struggle, finally will articulate the reconciliation of conflicting existential differences when both he and his poetic *yo* learn *how to be* and, importantly, *how to be fully*. It is in *La última costa* where Brines, after thirty-five years of self-interrogation, discovers the participatory role all human beings have in defining existence by means of living it.

Reconciled Differences and New Beginnings: *La última costa*

After receiving the 1999 Premio Nacional de las Letras (National Literary Prize) Brines explained the essence of his poetry for *El País* (The Nation) : "La elegía es una afirmación de la vida, se llora lo que no tiene, es un sentir a la vida, un abrazo a la vida:" (elegy is an affirmation of life, one laments what one does not possess, it is only by experiencing life that you embrace life). This is the personal ontology that the poet develops in *La última costa*. Here the poet explores the nature of being by charting the course of a single day in the life of his *yo*-protagonist. We witness this *yo*'s experience of dawn, midmorning, afternoon, dusk, and then nightfall. This temporal journey simultaneously follows the life stages of a human being. We thus observe within the collection a thematic evolution as well as a human lifetime from birth through childhood, then on into adolescence and adulthood, through middle-age, and finally into the symbolic *otoño* (autumn) of diminishing vitality. Temporally, existentially, thematically, and cyclically these poems take us through a personal and shared pilgrimage of self-discovery where both the poetic speaker and reader come to realize fully and to respect profoundly the remarkable and replenishing value of *being*.

The journey motif, an age-old literary *topos*, is not new to Brines's poetry which frequently has depicted human life as a trip, a road, a passage toward nonbeing. At first, *La última costa* seems to be about the mode of *being* that pervades Brines's sustained ontological and poetic inquiry of the last four decades: life as a journey of being-toward-death.[5] Both the collection's title and the final poem naming the collection readily bring to mind the voyage that is life's course: "el viaje aquel de todos a la neblina" (that trip all of us take into the mist) (1997, 533). Andújar Almansa sees the journey in this way: "Por lo que se refiere a *La última costa*, preside los poemas una imagen de bruma y la idea de un último viaje hacia esa otra orilla, personificada en un 'Hades' negro y tenebroso" (Because of all to which *The Farthest Shore* refers, the image of a deathly haze determines all of the poems and the thematic idea of a final voyage to that other coast is itself personified in a gloomy, black Hades) (54). According to this critic, the final poem represents a "helador presagio de una oscura travesía por las infernales aguas de Aqueronte" (chilling omen of a dark voyage through the infernal waters of the Acheron) (56). In Cavallo's view the collection's title alludes to "un espacio universalmente reconocible, el borde del río Estigia donde espera la barca de Caronte para llevar al hombre a su morada final" (a universally known place, that of the shore of the river Styx where Charon and his ferry wait for every human being in order to carry each across to the farther bank, the final dwelling place) (1996, 112). Luis Martínez de Mingo, moreover, indicates that here we find "hermoso y sereno senequismo, desde el que el poeta se imagina el último viaje: con la niebla, Caronte y la barcaza, porque sabe que la Vida nada sería sin la amenaza palmaria de la Muerte" (with a beautifully serene Seneca perspective the poet imagines the final journey: a dense fog, the ferryman Charon unloading and loading his skiff, because the poet knows that Life would be nothing without the obvious threat of looming Death) (20). Finally, Francisco Lucio maintains, "Viajar, pues, a la niebla, será viajar al territorio donde no existe espacio (porque tampoco existe tiempo), a la muerte, a la nada. Así concluye el libro" (To make this voyage into the dense fog is to travel to a region where space does not exist [because neither does time], toward death, toward nothingness. This is how the book of poetry ends) (66). This critic furthermore adds that when we arrive at the final lines of the very last poem in this collection we too have come to understand that "No hay salvación para la vida: el destino de todos es la muerte" (There is no salvation for the living: death is our only destiny) (66). In Lucio's view these closing lines definitively image life as a journey toward death and nothing more.

But this is not what *La última costa* is all about. It is not about endings. Rather, it is about beginnings. Brines has struggled with the finitude of human life throughout his poetic production. Many of his assumed poetic personae—from the aged protagonist of *Las brasas* (The Embers), to the cryptic ontological interrogator of *Insistencias en Luzbel*, to the voice that echoes "la estación del tiempo rezagado" (the season of residual time) (1997, 379) throughout and within *El otoño de las rosas*—have attempted to solve, each in its own way, the perplexing riddle of human mortality. In *El otoño de las rosas*, the poetic speaker initiates another kind of inquiry into human existence. This poetic voice oftentimes reveals that he is now grounded in a world that must be fully sensed in order to be appreciated. Here the speaker beckons the reader, as well as himself, *to experience* human existence and never to be deterred by being death-bound. Human existence is to be experienced wholly and passionately, as the opening poem of the 1986 work explains: "Vives ya en la estación del tiempo rezagado: / lo has llamado el otoño de las rosas. /Aspíralas y enciéndete. Y escucha, / cuando el cielo se apague, el silencio del mundo" (You now are living in the season of residual time: you have called it the Autumn of the roses. Do aspire to breathe them in and to become inflamed. And do listen, when heaven is extinguished, silence on earth) (1997, 379).

Vital experience thus replaces anguished interrogation as Brines and his poetic voice willingly begin to engage in life itself. Having come to understand personal existence in time, the first-person speaker of this collection now undertakes another poetic as well as ontological activity, that of offering sincere instructions pertaining to the urgency of seizing life. As the opening lines of "Collige, virgo, rosas" (Gather ye rosebuds while ye may) insist, "Estás ya con quien quieres. Ríete y goza. Ama. / Y enciéndete en la noche que ahora empieza, / y entre tantos amigos [y conmigo] / abre los grandes ojos a la vida / con la avidez preciosa de tus años" (You are now with whom you want to be. Do laugh and do enjoy. Do love. And do become inflamed by the night that just now only is beginning, and in the midst of so many friends [and with me] do open your vast eyes to life with that cherished voracity of your youth.) (1997, 394). [6]

In *La última costa* Brines takes this thoughtful lesson one step further. Nine years separate the publication of *El otoño de las rosas* and that of *La última costa*. Brines now has experienced the metaphoric construct that once merely served to describe an existential mode that was not his own. While telling his tale of "La dimisión del testigo" (The witness's account), Brines's poetic *alter-ego* makes this clear: "Y cómo he madurado. Bajo esta luz ya muerta / soy el otoño. Hay una luz, que es frío, / negra, negro" (And oh how I have aged. Beneath this now languid light I am Autumn. There is a light that is chillingly dark, black) (1997, 484). By contemplating, writing about, but above all living this "otoño" the poet has come to discover that mortality is only a condition for being human.[7] It is *not* the human condition. Rather, *being* is what human beings have. Being is what he *is*. Being is what he has experienced. Being is all that he has and ever will have. Being *is* his only determining existential mode and his only invigorating activity. He thus has comprehended that he and his poetic voice must embrace life in order to live. This is accomplished whenever and wherever the vital intensity of life itself infuses and replenishes his being. This poet also, finally, has come to terms with what he now realizes is a distinctly shared human mortality. He finds that he no longer is alone. The poetic voice echoing throughout *La última costa* is consoled by humanity itself and humanity's necessary and significant activity of being fully engaged in the collective act of affirming life.

What has been learned by the poet writing about this experience or the reader learning about this humanly shared ontological mode, is that the underlying imperative of *La última costa* —to be fully in the moment—only takes hold when one seizes life. The title of the first poem of this collection, "El regreso del mundo" (The return to the world) (1997, 479), thus becomes the poetic and existential prophecy for this poet's symbolic act of returning to and retaking what is now known to be his *only* task at hand in the immediate "world." Being *in* the moment must be seized and then cherished in Brines's 1995 poetic chronicle of human existence.

Heightened awareness of finite being brings with it the insistent yearning and existential urgency to live life fully here and now. *Las brasas* (The Embers), *Palabras a la oscuridad* (Words unto Darkness), *Aún no* (Not Yet), and *Insistencias en Luzbel* (Insistences on Lucifer) all reveal differing existential modes. The poetic speaker of *La última costa*, firmly grounded in being and willfully venturing forth each day from this fundamental ontological mode, the symbolic shoreline defining the basis of his life, is now intent on living feverishly each present moment and then affectionately recalling once having been. Even though this collection's title might lead us to believe otherwise, this poetry is about Life and its emergent Presence ever sensed and continually known each new day by the willful act of fully being *aún* (yet).[8]

By his very being and by deliberately and playfully engaging in living with childlike wonder and delight, the Brinesian *yo* assumes a uniquely different role whenever he positions himself to heed new life and to respond to its beckoning call as "Los espacios de la infancia" (Childhood Spaces) affirms:

> Después de una carrera sofocada
> me he tendido debajo del ciruelo,
> y olvidando de todos, contemplo el llano, abajo,
> y los naranjos quietos que llegan hasta el mar.
> La mar está calmada y la tarde en silencio.

¿Quién me llama?
Mas súbita, una abeja,
que es zumbido del mundo,
ronda las ramas bajas, y acecho su Presencia
(1997, 480)

[After a stifling journey I have stretched out under the plum tree, and in forgetting all else, I begin to contemplate what is below, the fields and the quiet orange groves extending toward the sea. The sea is calm and the afternoon enveloped in silence. Who calls to me? Suddenly, a buzzing bee within this world and hovering among the low branches emerges, and I secretly watch its Presence].

Living and absolute faith in living bring renewed strength and purpose to the voyager who now has come full circle both in Brines's poetry and also in the collection at hand. After having wrestled with insistent and daily knowledge of being-toward-death in the elusive present moment, as refrains from such poems as "Está en penumbra el cuarto" (The Room is in Shadows) (1997, 21), "Oscureciendo el bosque" (1997, 133), "Sombrío ardor" (Somber Ardor) (1997, 234), "Epitafio del vivo" (Epitaph of the Living) (1997, 337), and "Interior del paisaje" (Interior Landscape) (1997, 467) often have served to remind him, Brines initiates a decidedly new cycle in *La última costa*. This 1995 work is, in essence, a vibrant canticle to life where being is and always will be self-conceived and self-generated. A relentless, personal desire to continue to exist willfully in each emerging moment transforms this Brinesian ontology into a decisive plan of action and a rewarding existential enterprise. In *La última costa* conscious self-awareness of personal being is essential to the human experience of knowing life and living it fully. Affirmative action is required in order to participate in the "maga sorpresa / de amar aún el mundo en la mañana" (entrancing surprise of still loving the world each dawn) (1997, 479). By adhering to this guiding principle, the Brinesian *yo*, a symbolic "everyman," acknowledges that he indeed is the vigorous creator of his very own existence because, "Todo es igual a mí, todo es un mismo Dios / sólo que en mí yo vivo" (Everything is my equal, everything is a selfsame God it is only in me that I live) ("Los espacios de la infancia") (Childhood Spaces) (1997, 480). Throughout *La última costa* this staunch refusal to relinquish the fervent desire to live fully each new day leads the poetic *yo* to a sincere appreciation for the wonder that is at once being, "el mundo descubierto / y el ser, aquel asombro" (the discovered world and being, that very amazement) (1997, 481), and also having been, "La juventud del mundo, su gozoso latido, / daba en sí testimonio de mi vida" (The youthful world pulsating with joy was itself evidence of my own life) "La dimisión del testigo") (The witness's account) (1997, 484).

In *La última costa* self-narration also is required as the poetic voice records and thereby continues to provide written testimony about his being. The act of writing both confirms and upholds his role as creator and re-creator of his existence: "Destellaba el vivir, / y yo testimoniaba la existencia" (Living in a brief flash, I testified to my existence) ("La dimisión del testigo") (The witness's account) (1997, 484). In Brines's view, his self, his being human, involves a commitment to always engaging in what he now clearly views as a vitally productive process. By writing about his being, the very human poetic voice echoing throughout *La última costa* has come to learn and now is able to express the guiding principles of his existence conceived and lived as a reciprocal relationship to self, to other human beings, to the world, and to art. Self-narration in *La última costa* is self-creation and, importantly, this self-creation sustains this poet's ever-present desire to be *and* to be by writing about *being*.

Affirmation of life is not new to Brines's poetry. Years before in "La certidumbre de la poesía" (The Certainty of Poetry), Brines predicted the thematic evolution that eventually would be worked out first in the poems of *El otoño de las rosas* and then more fully in *La última costa*. He wrote that "Con la aceptación del desastre metafísico del hombre, aparece la valoración de su existencia temporal, quedando ésta entonces liberada para el goce" (1984, 19) (Along with the acceptance of the metaphysical disaster that befalls humankind, comes the valued authentication of personal temporal existence now free to experience well-being). It is this freedom to choose to indulge in life while living that defines the poetry of the 1995 collection, where Brines proclaims his "profundo amor a la vida" (profound love for life) (1984, 19). Here, *being* and poetry about *being* affirm and render meaningful personal existence. Perhaps nowhere is this more evident than in "El regreso del mundo," (The Return of the World), when the intimate first-person speaker transforms himself into and synesthetically re-experiences, if only momentarily, the child who once inhabited that other "última costa" (farthest shore) where his being began, Elca. There, at the very beginning of personal existence, this autumnal *yo*, who has imagined and imaged again and again both his and others' final, nocturnal voyage toward death, had once experienced the newness of life within and among the many "espacios de la infancia" (1997, 480). However, it is only now as the aged poetic *yo* of *La última costa* approaches that other farthest shoreline of life that he learns life's most important lesson: in order to live fully, *all* of the vital stages of human life must be experienced wholly and always with full consciousness of self-initiated and self-referential being. Human being's existential enterprise, as put forward in "Proyecto de la vida eterna" (Project for Eternal Life) is thus very straightforward: "Y después de acabar, volver al mundo / tras una corta eter-nidad, ya sosegado / volver de nuevo al mundo" (And after finishing, to return to the world after a brief eternity, and once again go back to the world now at peace) (1997, 531). Even though knowledge of nonbeing causes suffering, as this same poem reveals, "y el tiempo envejecía / no al tiempo, que es en sí siempre eterno, / sino a lo que tocaba: el mundo, / y a aquel que, por saberlo, más sufría" (and time was growing old not time, which always in itself is eternal, but rather all that time touched: the world, and that one, he who made this discovery, he was the one that suffered the most), this same knowledge vigorously instills the ardent desire to live *aún* (yet). Often this knowledge causes "weariness," as the poet discloses in "Soliloquio para que lo escuche el otro" (I Soliloquize so that the Other Might Hear): "verás cómo te cura ese cansancio / cuando te dé el sabor de que no somos" (you will see just how that weariness will soothe you when you taste that we are not) (1997, 506). At other times, however, this existential understanding vigorously instills the ardent desire to seize life and to live *aún*. Resolutely choosing *not* to forfeit life, the first-person speaker heard throughout *La última costa* recognizes that "Han tocado mis ojos el esplendor del mundo" (My eyes have been touched by the splendorous world) ("Los espacios de la infancia") (Childhood Spaces) (1997, 480). Hence, wherever each new day of personal being occurs and whenever faith in being is reclaimed and recorded, he will choose to be.

Despite "el fragilísimo presente" (the very fragile present) (1984, 41) examined in "El mendigo de lo extinguido" (The Beggar of the Extinguished) (1997, 496), or the absurdity of existence portrayed in "Metáfora de un destino" (Metaphor of Fate) (1997, 510) and "Mi hacedor" (My Maker) (1997, 528), or the never-ending search for self-identity exposed in "Reflexión sobre un incidente" (Reflecting on an Incident) (1997, 507) and "El niño perdido y hallado (en Elca)" (The lost and found child [in Elca]) (1997, 482), a sincere sense of hope pervades *La última costa*. This poetic *yo* firmly believes in the importance of *being here and now*. Both the poetic-*yo* and the reader repeatedly are encouraged to continue to seek and above all to continue to come to know and joyfully experience living, having lived, and living *aún* (yet). Perseverance is required in the "experiencias vitales" (vital experiences) (1984, 21) constituting Brines's poetry, a poetry that is and cannot be separated from his insistent affirmations of being. Experiencing life and re-experiencing it again and again through memories, through the senses, through recapturing the past in the present moment of the creation of the poem, through vital re-creation whenever poet and reader engage in "saving" and savoring "esta verdad pequeña de haber sido" (this simple truth of having been) ("Imágenes en un espejo roto") (Images in a Broken Mirror) (1997, 499), through writing the poem itself, these are all existential activities grounded in knowledge of essential being.

In *La última costa* both the personal-*yo* and his reader companion journey together from daybreak to nightfall, from beginning to end, from birth to death, from metaphoric coast to coast in the pilgrimage constituting human existence. In "Oscureciendo el bosque" (1997, 133), written some thirty years earlier, Brines offered the existential principle that is fully expressed from the vantage point of *La última costa*. This principle has shaped his entire poetic trajectory, his lifetime, and our readings of both: "Mirad con cuánto gozo os digo / que es hermoso vivir" (Do consider when I tell you with utmost delight how beautiful it is to live).[9] By comprehending that now "me queda un tiempo breve" (a brief time remains for me) ("Estos penúltimos días") (These Penultimate Days) (1997, 495), in accepting life as passage in "el viaje aquel de todos a la niebla" (that trip all of us take into the mist) as revealed in the poem "La última costa" (1997, 533), and by always paying attention to the multiple manifestations of abundant life within "el esplendor del mundo" (the splendorous world) ("Los espacios de la infancia") (1997, 480) Francisco

Brines's *La última costa*, ultimately affirms this poet's steadfast resolve to be.

Notes

1. All translations are my own.
2. The two seminal critical studies published prior to 1990 are Cano (1974) and Jiménez (1972).
3. All citations of Brines's poetry are from *Poesías completas* (1997).
4. The *carpe diem* motif is not new to Brines's poetry although it is in *El otoño de las rosas*, and then later, as we shall see, in *La última costa* where he refreshingly reinvents this age old literary theme.
5. Jiménez has noted that in Brines's earliest collections the road motif was prevalent. He explains that "La mayor parte de sus poemas se estructuran, en cuanto tales, sobre esta visión de la existencia entendida como un camino, viejo tópico de toda meditación temporalista" (The vast majority of his poems are structured around, for the most part, this vision of human existence understood as a road, as passage, an age-old literary commonplace found in meditations on temporality) (1972, 422). In my earlier "Modos de ser en *Insistencias de Luzbel* de Francisco Brines" I examine Brines's ontology (Nantell 1987).
6. Manrique (317–21) examines the *carpe diem* motif in *El otoño de las rosas*. Debicki (194) studies this theme when examining the poem "Collige, virgo, rosas."
7. The poetic *yo* in this collection is both self-referential and also the voice for all human beings engaged in existence (see Brines 1984, 42–43). Andújar Almansa observes that Brines, by recognizing and exploring his own personal existence, comes to know more fully the human condition (20). Jiménez eloquently puts it this way: "Este poeta de hoy ha elegido un héroe más modesto y cotidiano: el sencillo ser humano que es él, y que podremos ser todos" (This contemporary poet has chosen the most humble and ordinary hero: he is simply a human being, just like we all are) (1998, 135).
8. See Lucio's observations (67) regarding the use of capitalized words in *La última costa*.
9. Martín maintains that Brines's poetry discloses an understanding of being as a valued and vital adventure to be lived and enjoyed (104). See my study of the Sartrean *yo* in "Essential Existence in Francisco Brines's *La última costa*," *Anales de la Literatura Española Contemporánea* 28, no. 1 (2003): 95–113.

Works Cited

Amusco, Alejandro Duque. 1993. Espejo ciego. Prologue to *Francisco Brines. Antología poética*, 7–41. Valencia: Consell Valencià de Cultura.

Andújar Almansa, José. 2000. Una biografía poética: Sobre *Poesía completa* de Francisco Brines. *Anales de la literatura española contemporánea* 25, no.1: 13–61.

Brines, Francisco. 1984. *Selección propia*. Madrid: Cátedra.

———. 1986. *Poemas a D.K.* Sevilla: Renacimiento.

———. 1997. *Poesía completa (1960–1997)*. Barcelona: Tusquets.

Cañas, Dionisio. 1989. Introducción. *El rumor del tiempo: Antología. Francisco Brines.* Madrid: Mondadori.

Cano, José Luis. 1974. La poesía elegíaca de Francisco Brines: "Palabras a la oscuridad." In *Poesía española contemporánea: Las generaciones de posguerra.* Madrid:Guadarrama.

Cavallo, Susana. 1994. Francisco Brines. *Dictionary of literary biography. Twentieth-century Spanish poets.* Vol.134. Detroit: The Gale Group.

———. 1996. *La última costa.* Review of *La última costa,* by Francisco Brines. *A la luz.* 28, no.1: 110–14.

Debicki, Andrew P. 1994. *Spanish poetry of the twentieth century: Modernity and beyond.* Lexington: University Press of Kentucky.

Jiménez, José Olivio. 1972. La poesía de Francisco Brines (Sobre *Las brasas*). *Cinco poetas del tiempo.* Madrid: Insula.

———. 1998. Dos tiempos en la poesía última de Francisco Brines (sobre *El otoño de las rosas* y *La última costa*). *Poetas contemporáneos de España y América.* Madrid: Verbum.

Lucio, Francisco. 1995. Vida, memoria y sueño. Review of *La última costa* by Francisco Brines. *Quimera* 138 (July–Aug.): 63–67.

Manrique, Jorge. 1995. Francisco Brines. *Mundo abreviado. Lectura de poetas españoles contemporáneos.* Valladolid: Ámbito.

Martín, Francisco José. 1998. *El sueño roto de la vida (Ensayo sobre la poesía de Francisco Brines).* Alicante: Aitana Editorial.

Martínez de Mingo, Luis. 1996. La acendrada despedida de Francisco Brines. Review of *La última costa,* by Francisco Brines. *Insula* 591(March): 20–21.

Mayhew, Jonathan. 1999. Nuevos textos sagrados: Contemporary Spanish poetry and the return of the sacred. *Revista de estudios hispánicos* 33, no.2: 285–97.

Morales, Carlos Javier. 1997. La poesía reciente de Francisco Brines. (A propósito de *La última costa*). Review of *La última costa,* by Francisco Brines. *Cuadernos hispanoamericanos* 561 (March): 143–46.

———. 1998. Toda la poesía de Francisco Brines. Review of *Poesía completa,* by Francisco Brines. *Cuadernos hispanoamericanos* 573 (March): 149–52.

Nantell, Judith. 1987. Modos de ser en *Insistencias de Luzbel* de Francisco Brines. *Revista canadiense de estudios hispánicos* 12, no.1: 33–55.

———. 1994. *The poetry of Francisco Brines: The deconstructive effects of language.* Lewisburg: Bucknell University Press.

El País (Madrid). 1999. No. 1300 (24 November).

A Chronological List of Francisco Brines's Poetry

1960. *Las brasas.* Madrid: Ediciones Rialp. Rev. ed., Valencia: Fomento de Cultura.

1965. *El Santo Inocente.* Madrid: Poesía para Todos. Republished as *Materia narrativa inexacta,* in *Poesía, 1960–1971: Ensayo de una despedida.* Barcelona & Madrid: Plaza y Janés, 1974.
1966. *Palabras a la oscuridad.* Madrid: Ínsula.
1971. *Aún no.* Barcelona: Ocnos, 1971; Barcelona: Llibres de Sindera.
1974. *Poesía, 1960–1971: Ensayo de una despedida.* Barcelona & Madrid: Plaza y Janés; enlarged as *Ensayo de una despedida, 1960–1977.* Madrid: Visor, 1984.
1977. *Insistencias en Luzbel.* Madrid: Visor.
1984. *Selección propia.* "La certidumbre de la poesía." Madrid: Cátedra, 13–53.
1985. *Poemas excluidos.* Sevilla: Renacimiento.
1986. *El otoño de las rosas.* Sevilla: Renacimiento.
1986. *Poemas a D. K.* Sevilla: El Mágico Íntimo.
1995. *La última costa.* Barcelona: Tusquets.
1997. Ensayo de una despedida. *Poesía completa (1960–1997).* Barcelona: Tusquets.

Gloria Fuertes's Last Words: *Mujer de verso en pecho*

Douglas K. Benson

THE POETRY OF GLORIA FUERTES HAS ALWAYS PRESENTED SPECIAL concerns for the literary critic. Difficult to categorize, without any apparent thematic organization or conventional artistic matrix, her work converges with and diverges from that of the most innovative groups of the Spanish postwar period: Postismo (Postism); the "social" or "realist" generation of Alonso, Otero, and Hierro; the second postwar generation of 1956–70; and even the "novísimos" (the newest ones) of the 1960s and 1970s.[1] She is now most commonly associated with the second postwar generation of José Angel Valente, Claudio Rodríguez, and Angel González, with their quest for a "poetry of discovery" and a "renewed emphasis on style and poetic language" (Debicki 1994, 101–4).

At the same time, critics have noted with increasing frequency, since her first book in 1950, her role as a pioneer in creating texts based on the ludic juxtaposition of discourses taken from traditional and modern culture, subverting the personal and social situations and experiences so characteristic of postwar "social" poetry rather than using them referentially. José Manuel Caballero Bonald and Francisco Ynduráin observed these phenomena early on, but only in the last two decades have they been examined in detail, especially by Nancy Mandlove, Margaret Persin, Sylvia Sherno, Andrew Debicki, and Peter Browne.

Thus, the relationship between Fuertes's "word" and the "world" represented by this word is often a tenuous, fluid one. Her texts undercut conventional referentiality while at the same time feinting with bits and pieces of known discourses and meanings. This trend, seen very early in her work, was continued by a few other poets of the second postwar generation in the 1960s as well as by the *novísimos* (newest ones), but with a key difference noted by Debicki:

> Whereas the older writers had used their poetry to examine and reconstruct, artistically, personal experiences and themes in a search of self-discovery, the *novísimos* began by avoiding the personal and the anecdotal, sought their referents in prior literary and cultural texts, and constructed linguistic and formal structures to reflect their themes. (1994, 137)

Debicki's characterization of the *novísimos* could apply to much of Fuertes's poetry from the very beginning, although at first glance she appears to create texts similar to those of her contemporaries. While she never abandoned the colloquial matrix of her work, she anticipated the metapoetic bent and the high-culture "masking" of the poetic self manifested by the *novísimos* (Jiménez, 26; Debicki 1994, 138–40; Benson 2000, 219).

Fuertes's poetry has always been accessible to both the educated and everyday reader, in spite of the fact that her texts juxtapose a wide range of erudite and popular sources to create a voice that is absolutely "unmistakable," in the words of Luis Antonio de Villena in *El Mundo* on November 28, 1998, the day after her death. To date her artistic mode has also proven inimitable; she pledged fealty to no single movement, and she created none. This is partly due to the fact that few poets possess her sensitive "feel" for so many colloquial, commercial, official, and literary sources and registers from so many historical periods. Her multivoiced approach to poetry, however, helped create a redefinition of the genre (Debicki 1982, 100–101; 1994, 117) that became widely accepted by the early 1960s, and for which she was quite popular in the two decades after that. Nine editions of her *Obras incompletas* (Incomplete Works) appeared between 1975 and 1984.

In recent years, critics have turned to the tenets of postmodern theory to help explain the ways in which Fuertes achieves her effects (Persin 1997, 18–19; Browne, 161–65). Some of these theoretical insights appear to clarify certain aspects of her work, but many categorizations do not fit as well (Debicki 1994, 102–3, 117; Benson 2000, 212–13). Linda Hutcheon and Marjorie Perloff define the postmodern text in terms of two fundamental ideas: first, that the past can only be known by means of its texts instead of through its situations or "historico-political context"; and second, that no element of the past nor of the present, from popular or "high" culture, can be subverted without first "installing" it in transparent, obvious ways. This process in turn highlights both the limitations and "countercurrents" as well as the perspectives dramatized by those elements, together with the basic human concerns they carry with them (Hutcheon, x, 3, 5, 41, 44; Perloff 1988, 6).

Fuertes's poetry appears to be transparent and naive at first glance, but as many critics have noted, it rarely turns out to be that way (Miró, 6; Long, 7; Debicki 1994, 116–17; Browne, 17, 108). Her poems demand a reader conversant with both "high" and popular culture, but also one who is comfortable walking the quicksand of voices, speakers, situations, and structures that are characteristic of her peculiar brand of postmodernity. It is precisely the fusion of languages, genres, and conventions that creates a paradox without resolution; that is, a semiotic field of multiple voices that refuses to resolve its contradictions, as Hutcheon notes (x, 43–44). Ralph Cohen sees in postmodern procedures not a lack of depth nor the dearth of a historical perspective, not a disappearance of the centers of the traditional genres nor the "death of the subject," as Jameson asserts (2–10, 15–17), but rather the great discovery of our time: "Combinations [of genres] present not merely the procedures of scientific and literary inquiry, but serve to illustrate the procedures by which they conceal antagonisms, prejudices and disunity" (Perloff 1988, 16). Put another way, the meticulous dissection of artistic and social conventions by means of their juxtaposition with others that do not correspond to them, reveals what those conventions were able to hide due to their familiarity and invisibility within their original context, and allows them to be contemplated in a more informed way in the new context of the poem. Of course, all this requires more work and attention on the part of the reader than the text more traditionally defined as "poetic," but the aesthetic experience can be equally satisfying and compelling.

The poetry of Fuertes appears to correspond to some aspects of this characterization. Since 1950 the rich mixture of voices, in the manner of Bakhtin's *heteroglossia*, the exuberant pilfering and recycling of texts from all times and social classes, and the consistently ironic treatment of traditional narrative and poetic structures (as well as of Fuertes herself as a literary character) have served to undercut the conventional integrity and uniqueness of the poetic voice and the monolithic center of omniscience as described by Hutcheon (10–11), to call into question the nature of the *order* implicit in any systematic plot, in Perloff's terms (1985, 158), and to examine the inability of language to represent any totalizing reality. Yet her texts celebrate the democratic, liberating nature of language and its ability to reveal unexpected facets of that same reality.

Almost always, then, we find that in Fuertes's texts what appears to be a known quantity at the outset, often a commonplace or cliché, turns out to be camouflage for other realities that, in turn, change our perception of the entire text (see the works of Mandlove and Persin) and defy closure. In addition, the realities suggested by Fuertes's texts are difficult to visualize, unfolding much like the play of words and ideas in baroque *conceptismo* (conceptism) (Benson 2000, 213–14). In this way the poet can maintain considerable distance between speakers and readers, as is the case with many postmodern texts, because it is almost impossible to determine a single recognizable, consistent poetic voice and to "place" the situation. Her personal and social concerns nevertheless ooze through the cracks of her porous structures to take shape in the subsequent concretizations carried out by her readers. The chorus of familiar voices and the supposed "autobiographical" elements also work to cancel out this objective posture, to create an illusion of interpersonal and thematic familiarity and determinacy that belies the ironic stance of postmodernity and often appears to resemble social or testimonial poetry (Benson 1994). The illusion is a powerful one, drawing readers toward what seems to be an obvious conclusion which is then withdrawn at the last minute to reveal the subterfuge and the resultant indeterminacy. Her texts thus fit Debicki's characterization of the postmodern text as "necessarily plurisignificant or indeterminate," and yet do not seem quite to fit either the postmodern aesthetic nor his characterization of the second postwar generation as "grounded in individual experience and philosophical meanings," still reflecting "some quest for closure" (1994, 133).

Thus, in multiple ways, the relationship between Fuertes's "word" and the "world" (both the everyday world and the literary world) is one of mutual attraction and repulsion: the fusion of conventional poetic discourse with other professional and colloquial ones; the illusion of poetic distance and social solidarity, the appearance of referentiality undercut by her ever-changing voices, structures, and speakers; the mimicry of "high-culture" metapoetic texts and the masking of the poetic voice(s) subverted and exposed by everyday reality and even vulgarities, and above all her vision of language as confining and oppressive, and at the same time as liberating and limitless in its power to discover.

Fuertes's last book, *Mujer de verso en pecho* (Woman with Verse in Breast), published in 1995, just three years before her death, presents ample evidence that her indomitable spirit of social and artistic rebellion, her multivoiced approach to poetic creation and expression, her delight in the construction of ambiguities, and her stunning verbal virtuosity had not diminished with time. Like her earlier books, *Mujer de verso en pecho* is largely unorganized, uneven in quality, wide-ranging in theme, and often utterly unsettling and compelling. Her readers will recognize immediately how she divided the book into thematic sections, something that she had not done since *Cómo atar los bigotes al tigre* (How to Tie the Tiger's Moustache) in 1969, but that the titles of these sections do not always correspond with the poems themselves. Many "social" texts, for example, are far from the section titled "Haced sólo una zona, a ver si de una vez la paz se asoma" ("Poemas a la paz") (Make just one zone, to see if once and for all peace appears [Poems to peace]). Love poems are scattered throughout, rather than being collected in the section titled "El amor tiene vocación de santo, pero no pasa de mártir" ("Poemas de amor") (Love has the vocation of sainthood, but never gets beyond martyrdom [Poems of Love]). The witty titles of those sections also subvert traditional convention. The effect is that of paying homage to the canon, the literary "world," while at the same time questioning and undercutting it.

Many of Fuertes's poems, such as the poem entitled "Diablito de mi guarda" install the convention to be dissected right into the title:

> **Diablito de mi guarda**
> Inquieta compañía,
> líbrame de mal
> de noche y de día.

Tú puedes.
No digo que te vayas
digo que te quedes.
Diablito de mi guarda,
te comprendo y te comprendería
(en el fondo quieres ser
mi ángel de la guarda
y por eso le envidias).
Diablito de mi guarda
misteriosa compañía,
nadie te quiere
nadie te estima.
Por eso haces el mal
para hacerte notar.
Diablito de mi guarda
estar solo
es tu infierno . . .
Si vienes a visitarme,
te peinaré los cuernos.

(1995, 33–34)

[**My Little Guardian Devil**
Restless company,
deliver me from evil (illness)
by night and by day.
You can do it.
I'm not telling you to leave
I'm telling you to stay.
My little guardian devil,
I understand you and I would understand you
(deep down you want to be
my guardian angel
and that's why you envy him).
My little guardian devil
mysterious company,
no one loves you
no one values you.
That's why you do evil
to make yourself noticed.
My little guardian devil
being alone
is your hell. . . .
If you come visit me,
I'll comb your horns.]

The popular colloquial inversion of "mi ángel de la guarda" (my guardian angel), evoked a century ago by Angela Carballino as "mi demonio de la guarda" (my guardian demon) in Miguel de Unamuno's *San Manuel Bueno, mártir* (51) (Saint Emmanuel the Good, martyr), takes on a new dimension with the diminutive, which suggests that this "diablito" is perhaps younger and more mischievous than usual. As the poem progresses, he also seems to diverge from the image of the maleficent "demonio" who plagues our everyday lives.

Following a common strategy in Fuertes, the first strophe takes the words of the title in a different direction. The Golden Age and biblical language conventions ("inquieta compañia" [restless company], "líbrame de mal" [deliver me from evil]) create an abrupt change of register and tone which evoke something more stylized, similar to the language of moral, mystic, or even love poetry of the sixteenth century. The reader encounters the first twist of logic: if the "diablito" is to deliver the speaker from evil, he cannot himself be that evil. By the end of the first strophe, however, the reader is beginning to hear another voice, that of children's nocturnal prayers, in the easy assonant rhyme and the childlike repetition of the phrase "de noche y de día" (by night and by day). The text already has begun to implement the logical and linguistic inversions typical of Fuertes, and the reader is no longer on solid ground.

In line 5 the text continues with the familiar, childlike register and tone, "Tú puedes" (You can do it). By now the reader is faced with the paradox of how one of Lucifer's creatures can carry out this particular request and why the speaker and "diablito" seem to know each other so well. Examples come to mind of the medieval personifications of death or the more abstract, grotesque monsters of Dámaso Alonso and Pedro Salinas, all addressed as "tú" (you, familiar). The "diablito" seems to be a more welcome visitor than those, but no less mysterious.

The colloquial discursive mode of the third strophe adopts a convention more appropriate for a situation involving friends or family members on a visit, or perhaps an admonition to a child: "No digo que te vayas / digo que te quedes." (I'm not telling you to leave / I'm telling you to stay). The repetition of "digo que" (I'm telling you) appears to maintain the childlike language and tone, but the peremptory tone suggests a shift toward the language of an adult. At the same time, the strophe creates another conceptual inversion of expectations in this context. How can a "diablito" deliver her from evil if he stays?

By the fourth strophe the text clearly has taken on the type of language that adults use with children, in a new context that evokes the effects of sibling rivalry and envy. In fact, the framework of the entire poem has changed to dramatize an adult's awareness of the perspective of a child who feels marginalized by his family or his society, and to further demythify the convention of the guardian angel. The "diablito" feels himself to be in competition with a more "favored" child: "mi ángel de la guarda" [my guardian angel]. The next two strophes broaden and deepen this new meaning, evoking his feelings of abandonment and the indifference with which people treat him.

The conventional psychological insight of the sixth strophe is so unexpected in the context of the "diablito" that it creates a comic effect. Readers will recognize in professional psychiatric and sociological diagnoses, in the media, in our children, and even in ourselves this universal motivation for bad behavior: "Por eso haces el mal / para hacerte notar" (That's why you do mischief / to make yourself noticed). As always in Fuertes, the comic moment has its Pierrot or Charlie Chaplin side, alluding to correlative situations outside the text. The "diablito" has much in common with disabled children, or short children, or children from a lower social status, or children from a "different" racial or ethnic group. The notion of "el mal" has taken another twist, and the reader is perhaps obliged to return the term to its more conventional meaning of "evil" and "mischief," but now with broader implications and motivations.

The final strophe further humanizes this son of the underworld, condemned to eternal solitude. For the first time the text determines the gender of its speaker more precisely as well. The action of "combing his horns" evokes graphically the pleasure mothers receive from combing their daughters' hair, as a gesture of their affection and a tactile expression of their spiritual bond. For the first time the "diablito" has someone who can love him, despite his external appearance and his reputation as a troublemaker. As Ellen Engelson Marson notes, "If for Gabriel Celaya poetry was an 'arm to transform the universe,' for Gloria Fuertes it is a warm 'embrace' to cure the universe" (201). Fuertes herself has said that she wants to be "Santa Ladrona de Penas" (Saint Thief of Griefs) (1984, 270).

As we return to the poem, it becomes clear that the "diablito" context does not dramatize a relationship with the underworld or with a specific child at all, but with the marginalized beings of the world. The first part of the poem, with its abrupt changes of language and register, its juxtapositions of different voices from past and present, serves as a form of camouflage, as it cloaks meanings which would be overly sentimental and obvious if declared outright. A vivid portrait of the maternal instinct emerges, rather like that of Gabriela Mistral, a mother for the world. Another meaning emerges as well; the speaker needs the "misteriosa compañía" (mysterious company) as much as he does her: "líbrame de mal / de noche y de día" (deliver me from evil / by night and by day). They share the same "mal" (illness): loneliness.

The notion of solidarity, then, appears to bring closure to the text. But the restlessness of the diablito ("inquieta compañía" [restless company]), coupled with the mere idea of a little devil sitting still while someone combs his horns as if he were "a girl" and the logical absurdity of the entire image, works against the carefully crafted illusion of this peaceful, maternal scene. "Te peinaré los cuernos" (I'll comb your horns) would more likely drive him off than bring him in. The speaker, despite her best intentions, is oblivious to the creature's needs and concerns; yet the particular way in which Fuertes has structured her "word" makes her both believable and appealing in her good intentions and human frailties. In fact, the speaker, to counteract her loneliness, has imagined a relationship with a fantastic creation of her own making who is allowed no voice in the matter and to whom she cannot relate. The relationship is an illusion, as is the entire situation. The conversation and the "home" to which he is being invited, and even his presence ("si vienes a visitarme" [if you come visit me]), which through Fuertes's conventional discourses had appeared to take on referential meaning, do not exist anywhere in the text itself. The different voices and registers that the poem installs become themselves subverted, part of Fuertes's subversion of language itself, as Browne has noted in another context (65–67). The "word" and the "world" converge and diverge, oscillating back and forth as the reader progresses. None of these conventions, linguistic or social, finally comes to dominate, instead refusing to resolve their own contradictions. At the same time, it is impossible to ignore the seeming allegory of familial and social injustice, and so the reader experiences the sense of closure as if it were real.

The illusion of autobiographical and social realism through the cunning manipulation of language and of reader expectations can be seen even more clearly, albeit in a very different context, in the untitled poem that directly follows "Diablito de mi guarda" in *Mujer de verso en pecho*:

> En la evolución del hombre hay más inteligencia y menos
>   fuerza.
> También los animales domésticos de hoy
> son más inteligentes que los de hace dos mil años.
> El mono de hace setecientos mil años
> fue nuestro más cercano antepasado.
> Hemos surgido del mundo animal
> y no hay más.
> Dios no nos impone creer
> que todo fue hecho de una vez.
>
> (1995, 35)

> [In the evolution of man there is more intelligence and less force.
> Even today's domestic animals
> are more intelligent than those of two thousand years ago.
> The monkey of seven hundred thousand years ago
> was our closest ancestor.
> We have come from the animal world
> and that's all there is to it.
> God does not demand that we believe
> that everything was done all at once.]

Although the gender of the speaker is never indicated, the voice of a professor of biology can be clearly perceived in the initial declaration. Nonetheless, that voice is almost immediately undercut by the imprecision of the second half of the first line, where the reader might have expected something like "there are many elements to consider," followed by a list of factors. The second sentence, without presenting any scientific criteria or evidence, heads off in another direction dealing with the evolution of "animales domésticos" (domestic animals), which, in turn, begins to unnerve and provoke in the mind of the reader a series of questions: Does this "lecture" deal with evolution or with deliberate breeding, hybridization to produce the traits most congruent with the wishes of human beings? How is this "inteligencia" (intelligence) in domestic animals measured, by the reduction in their use of the "fuerza" (force) already mentioned, or by their obedient character, or by their potential for the entertainment of their masters and their children?

The two subsequent lines do not offer much consolation, although on the surface the language continues to resemble that of faculty in the natural sciences. In truth, however, lines 4 and 5 form a non sequitur, cleverly disguised as information that comes directly from the "canon" of evolution science, even to the extent of replicating the "date" of the earliest known replacement of *homo erectus* by *homo sapiens*. They appear to contradict the preceding lines through their de-contextualization of the conventional order of argumentation: if human beings and animals have evolved, why do we have our "más cercano antepasado" (closest ancestor) in prehistoric times? There is another mirage: the "date" in this text does not refer to human beings, but to the monkey from seven hundred thousand years ago. The following sentence expresses the same idea, but the language changes abruptly to another much more dogmatic one. The phrase "y no hay más" (and that's all there is to it) appears to thoroughly negate the possibility of another *prima causa* in human life and in the creation of the world.

Given these pseudoscientific reversals, when the reader arrives at the word "Dios" (God) in the next-to-last line, so out of place in a discussion of evolution, he or she might expect to read some variation on the irrelevance of God, some version of the existentialist notion of "God is dead." In its place appears the affirmation of another canon, the religious one, which appears to support and extend the previous conceptual framework, that everything evolves slowly and inexorably, even with the help of God. The language and transparent meaning seem to allude to the Book of Genesis, which informs us that the creation of the world and of humans was carried out over six days. At the same time, general knowledge of the biblical convention does not coincide with the rest of the poem, because many Jews and Christians believe that when God had concluded, he had also finished, that is, that there would be nothing left to "evolve." The reader's confusion is discursive in part and results from the fact that the person who has heard language similar to that of line 8 ("Dios no nos impone creer" [God does not demand that we believe])—from a priest, minister, or rabbi—expects a different ending, perhaps something like, "Dios no nos impone creer / que somos perfectos" (God does not demand that we believe / that we are perfect). The text says that, more or less, but with language that comes from another, more colloquial source.

We have here the core of the debate between creationists and evolutionists. Nevertheless, upon closer examination of the parts of the poem, it becomes clear that what appears to be rational argumentation, in spite of its more dogmatic aspects, is in reality made up of five disconnected declarations from different voices and contexts, each one in turn only partially realized and linked structurally to the others so that they appear to be related: evolution with social positivism, today's domestic animals with prehistoric ones, animal prehistory with human genetics, genetics with existentialism, and a sermon or admonition with a colloquial saying used under pressure: "Mira, no todo fue hecho de una vez" (Look, everything wasn't done all at once). It all was, in effect, an illusion of logical thought, with a desperate cliché thrown in at the end. Now, when the reader returns to the text, he or she begins to doubt human evolution rather than being convinced of its truth. Is there in fact "más inteligencia y menos fuerza" (more intelligence and less force) in today's world, with its impersonal long-distance bombardments, its electric torture racks controlled by computers, its genocide, hunger, and consumer-driven exploitation of human and natural resources on a scale never seen before? When "evolved" humans are compared to domestic animals and with the monkey from seven hundred thousand years ago, the balance does not come out in our favor: "hemos surgido del mundo animal / y no hay más" (we have come from the animal world / and that's all there is to it). The world may be finished, but humans are not yet there.

This poem uses a series of pseudoscientific and pseudophilosophical language bits and pieces, but also a "typical" postmodern structure, that is, a juxtaposition of elements and discourses disconnected on the surface. Through its cracks, the reader experiences a hair-raising realization: evolution, for all its efficacy in explaining biological changes in the plant and animal worlds, is largely camouflage for what has not changed in human beings except in the most superficial ways. The "evolution" of technology could be considered in the same light. And yet, through the play of language, the dramatization of these voices foregrounds important myths in our social and educational makeup. We cannot help but sympathize with the speaker and his incongruous "proofs" of that which cannot be proven.

Through the ingenious manipulation of her discourse fragments, Fuertes has managed to create a text that is transparent in its obvious intention to support a certain point of view about evolution, but that in reality refers to another context which is completely outside the poem, in the awareness of its readers, and with which she maintains neither distance nor objectivity. The "postmodern" structure in which a central poetic voice dissolves completely into a series of discursive clichés, communicates a social attitude not typically associated with postmodernism. Even the specifics of that attitude, however, are not clearly determined in the poem, and a number of alternate interpretations could be as easily defended.

In "Diablito de mi guarda" the move toward closure is undercut by the misunderstandings of the speaker herself and the absurd nature of the situation, though linguistic inversion helps support the indeterminacy. In the poem about evolution, it is the interplay and mutual subversion of discourses that makes the conceptual framework difficult to assemble and resolution impossible to achieve. In both, however, the notion of social injustice works its way out of the words to reject indifference and objectivity. Fuertes's "word" dramatizes, evokes, and questions known situations from the world without ever referring to them in conventional ways.

On the same page of the book another poem brings under study the relationship between the natural and human worlds:

> La Naturaleza es toda arte.
> Es bello ver a un elefante
> en la selva haciendo el elefante
> y no bailando un vals con tu-tú de organdí en el circo.
> Las mariposas nocturnas son más grandes
> y las borracheras.
>
> (1995, 35)

[Nature is all art.
It's beautiful to see an elephant
in the jungle playing the part of (making) the elephant
and not dancing a waltz with an organdy tutu in the circus.
Nocturnal butterflies are larger
and drunken binges.]

The language of the initial speaker brings to mind a lecture by a naturalist at a zoo, or perhaps on safari. And again, his or her gender is never specified. By the second line the speaker's idealism has become rather theatrical: "Es bello ver a un elefante/ en la selva . . ." (It's beautiful to see an elephant/ in the jungle . . .). At precisely this moment the illusion is undercut by another, more colloquial mode of discourse which produces a somewhat comic effect: "un elefante . . . / haciendo el elefante" (an elephant . . . / playing the role of an elephant). In one sense, the sentence refers to play-acting or mimicry, except that here it is not a child or an actor who plays at being an elephant, only the elephant itself. The beautiful, "natural" scene is staged. In another sense "haciendo el elefante" (making the elephant) refers to the reproductive act, often witnessed in zoos by puzzled children; this reading, too, serves not to support the speaker's lofty intention and language but to subvert it.

Line 4 utilizes the same colloquial language to equally comic effect, but also returns validity to the initial speaker's argument—animals do not belong in artificial environments like the zoo or the circus, but in their natural habitat. The succinct, efficient structural fusion of two conventional registers of voice and two reversals of simultaneous yet contradictory ideas in three lines of poetry calls attention to a sophisticated, highly self-conscious form of mannerist poetic expression, one that avoids the strict antithesis/paradox lines of Golden Age *conceptismo* (conceptism) and which draws on nonliterary sources, but which creates similar effects for the reader. Now, clearly, the image of elephants "making elephants" in a natural setting is the favored one. If we remove the phrase "haciendo el elefante" (making the elephant), however, the entire first strophe becomes more dogmatic, more trite, and far less poetic.

The illusion of closure does not last long. The fifth line appears at first to continue the study of "natural" animal life, but the relationship to elephants (which are not known to be nocturnal) makes no sense. A comparison based on size (compared to diurnal butterflies?) also leads nowhere, because the second half of the sentence is missing. The illusion of a declaration of scientific truth by an "expert" in such matters once again leads us by means of subversion of language, register, and tone to another situation, and in all likelihood to another speaker entirely. The protection offered by darkness is shared by nocturnal butterflies, which are less likely to be attacked than diurnal ones (though the image can also refer to streetwalkers, male or female), and by people drinking to forget the images that daylight brings. This ironic last voice could not be more different from the idealistic first one; the location has suddenly changed as well. The final image of a person seeking to escape the commodification of the natural world by drowning his or her anguish in the man-made distillation of a natural product is a telling one. Which is the true speaker of this poem? Which is favored, the idealist or the drunk?

The first three poems, taken deliberately from only two pages of *Mujer de verso en pecho*, demonstrate how Fuertes brings together very different conceptual frameworks using a variety of strategies and drawing on many different discourse types, with no apparent connection. An argument could be made that her themes here all come from late-twentieth-century activist concerns, though her texts' refusal to resolve their own contradictions and to determine specific stances makes that argument more difficult to support. Two short final examples from other parts of the book serve to illustrate her peculiar treatments of conventional themes: the autobiographical and the metapoetic.

Autobio
En mis ratos de ocio a veces,
busco trabajar para ganar,
busco tiempo para perder.
Me encanta perder el tiempo
dando vueltas a un pensamiento
dando vueltas a un "tío-vivo"
o a una amiga muerta.
(1995, 98)

[In my leisure moments at times,
I seek work to earn (gain),
I seek time to waste (lose).

I love to waste (lose) time
turning over in my head a thought
riding a merry-go-round (a live fellow)
or a dead (female) friend.]

The speaker opens with a conversational "formula" in a discussion of pastimes. The two contradictory examples that follow depict a very different situation, however, that of a person who has neither time nor money for "ocio" (leisure). Each is a popular cliché which makes no sense in this new context and in combination. The structures and wordplay, on the other hand, do mimic a familiar poetic convention, that of Golden Age antithesis, paradox and, in the following lines, parallelism. Readers who notice the convention can expect to have the paradoxes resolved in the last lines of the poem, as sonnets and *redondillas* (quatrains) conventionally did.

The second half of the poem does comply with the reader's conceptual expectation, by indicating three appropriate activities to pass the time in moments of leisure, and by providing the anticipated "desengaño" (eye-opener) as well. However, it does not offer the closure that might be expected from the *conceptista* (conceptist) structure. Instead, the three activities characterize (at least) three different speakers and situations. The first ("dando vueltas a un pensamiento") depicts an intellectual given to the life of the mind. The second ("dando vueltas a un 'tío-vivo'") abruptly undercuts the preceding line by suggesting a child's excitement on a "tío-vivo" (merry-go-round) or that of a sexual encounter. The third phrase ("o a una amiga muerta") pulls back the cape to reveal an older speaker, ever more alone as her life progresses. In this new context, the verb "ganar" (gain; earn; win) suggests (but does not determine) several possible interpretations: working to earn money, as opposed to women's work in the home, which is not typically remunerated; working to earn one's livelihood to resolve the problems of seasonal work or unemployment; or working to "win out" over nostalgia or the implacable effects of time. The speaker may be looking for "tiempo para perder" (time to waste) because she can never rest, or because she does not wish to have free time on her hands; she remembers too much when she is not otherwise occupied. Each interpretation evokes a different situation with its corresponding speaker: divorce, widowhood, abandonment. The happy memories of her childhood, of a lost love, or of her intellectual life with her friends, now dead, as suggested in lines 5 to 6, are diminished by her nostalgia for them. Perhaps, then, she hopes to "trabajar para ganar" (work to triumph) over that nostalgia; certainly for these reasons she finds it difficult to find time simply to "perder" (waste). But it is hard to be certain; the relationship between these "words" and the everyday world as well as the referential linguistic world is again brought into question.

The function of the conventional autobiography is to set out the most desirable details of the author's life to explain what brought that person to his or her present situation, and often to establish a preferred version of the events. Typically the autobiography is written from the perspective of old age, and this example complies with that convention. On the other hand, this "autobiography" provides no concrete detail about any specific person's life, except in the version that each reader creates as he or she assembles the conventional but indeterminate fragments into a possible interpretation. Even then, the "autobios" of Fuertes contain less of her life story than that of her readers; they are pre-texts offered through the voices of her speakers so that readers can create their own histories. Brian Morris noticed this peculiarity in 1991: "If we are familiar with the self-portraits that artists and other poets have executed, we should use caution in reading those of Fuertes, whose purpose may be to intrigue as much as to inform, to confuse as much as to communicate" (68).

Metapoetry also takes its own form in the poetry of Fuertes:

> **Accidente**
> Pétalos de amapola sobre el asfalto.
> Las navajas se hunden en los pechos.
> No se encuentra al adolescente herido.
> La luna lo sabe todo.
>
> (1995, 80)

> [**Accident**
> Petals of poppy upon the asphalt.
> Knife blades sink into chests.
> The wounded adolescent cannot be found.
> The moon knows all.]

It is difficult to read this poem and not be struck by its mimicry and mockery of Lorca's "Sorpresa" (Surprise), "Reyerta"

(Quarrel), and "Romance de la luna luna" (Ballad of the Moon Moon). The strategies and use of images and metaphors, of synecdoche and metonymy, and the fusion of the human world with the natural and cosmic ones (in which all being responds to the senseless, self-instigated death of marginalized people) are unmistakable. And yet a few details, a few "words," make clear the fact that we are in another, urban world: "asfalto" (asphalt); "no se encuentra al adolescente herido" (the wounded adolescent cannot be found). It is the same timeless "Reyerta" (Quarrel), "Romans against Carthaginians" in Lorca's terms, but now in the streets of the city in an encounter between gang members. The reader's sudden realization is powerfully managed. The text subverts some of the mythic quality of Lorca, in part because the last line mocks the ominous grandeur of Lorca's moon, but it has just as great an impact in its communication of the tragedy. One "unmistakable" voice is partially transformed into another, yet neither dominates. At the same time, the metapoetic text, conventionally removed from the everyday world, is hauled right back into it.

Fuertes created variations on this type of metapoetic text during her entire career (Benson 2000, 217), paying homage to the vision of poets that she admired, while simultaneously undercutting the monolithic nature of their vision, revealing the limitations of language to express reality, and at the same time joyously celebrating its power to do just that. By "masking" her speaker as Lorca and making transparent reference to the nature of poetic creation, she achieves many of the effects of the *novísimos* while maintaining the accessibility of her poems and the power of her concern for the marginalized.

Not all of the poems in *Mujer de verso en pecho* manifest this complexity, though they do act out her curious blend of solidarity and ironic objectivity. Some communicate their experiences more directly and are more clearly designed to be "poetry for the people," which in turn, she often hoped, might create a "people for poetry" (Marson, 197). Fuertes had many reading (and listening) publics (González Rodas, 17) and she wrote for all of them. Despite the "naiveté" of some of the book's texts, she would have been delighted to see them become an entryway into poetry for a day-laborer, a maid, or a young couple sitting in a bar. An admiring José Luis Cano noted that these very people regularly interrupted their "caricias y coloquios" (caresses and colloquies) to listen to an impromptu Fuertes recital (17). To borrow a phrase from Virginia Woolf and Sylvia Sherno (1990), her world was in no uncertain terms "a room of her own."

Gloria Fuertes blazed her own artistic path: comic and dead serious, sophisticated and accessible, inclusive rather than exclusive. The thematic and technical contradictions which result from a reading of the many critics who admire her work, including those listed in the Works Cited, only bring us to a broader appreciation of the many ways in which her texts undercut and extend our notions of poetry. To the end, her unique vision of herself, of life and of the poetic enterprise provided her the means—a "word of her own"—to map out a kaleidoscopic, wondrous world for her readers.

Notes

1. Unless otherwise noted, all translations in this text are my own. Also, I wish to express my appreciation to Cátedra for permission to quote Fuertes's poems.

Works Cited

Bakhtin, Mikhail M. 1981. Discourse in the novel. In *The dialogic imagination: four essays,* edited by Michael Holquist and translated by Caryl Emerson and Michael Holquist, 259–434. Austin: University Press of Texas.

Benson, Douglas K. 1994. Tres calillas en la posmodernidad y la poesía española de la posguerra. *Siglo XX/20th Century* 12: 69–85.

———. 2000. La voz inconfundible de Gloria Fuertes, 1918–1988: poesía temprana. *Hispania* 83: 210–221.

Browne, Peter E. 1997. *El amor por lo (par)odiado: la poesía de Gloria Fuertes y Angel González.* Madrid: Pliegos.

Cano, José Luis. 1991. *Vida y poesía de Gloria Fuertes.* Madrid: Torremozas.

Debicki, Andrew P. 1982. *Poetry of discovery: the Spanish generation of 1956–1971.* Lexington: University Press of Kentucky.

———. 1994. *Spanish poetry of the twentieth century: modernity and beyond.* Lexington: University Press of Kentucky.

Fuertes, Gloria. 1984. *Obras incompletas.* Madrid: Cátedra.

———. 1995. *Mujer de verso en pecho.* Madrid: Cátedra.

González Rodas, Pablo. 1981. Introducción. In *Historia de Gloria.* Madrid: Cátedra.

Hutcheon, Linda. 1988. *A poetics of postmodernism. History, theory, fiction.* New York: Routledge.

Jameson, Fredric. 1991. *Postmodernism, or, the logic of late capitalism.* Durham, NC: Duke University Press.

Jiménez, José Olivio. 1992. Fifty years of contemporary Spanish poetry (1939–1989). *Studies in twentieth century literature* 16: 15–41.

Long, Ada. 1984. Introduction. In *Off the map: Selected poems by Gloria Fuertes,* edited and translated by Philip Levine and Ada Long. Middletown, CT: Wesleyan University Press.

Marson, Ellen Engelson. 1993. Gloria Fuertes. In *Spanish women writers: a bio-bibliographical source book,* edited by. Linda Gould Levine, Ellen Engelson Marson, and Gloria Feiman Waldman, 194–210. Westport, CT: Greenwood.

Miró, Emilio. 1973. Sola en la sala. *Ínsula* 324: 6.

Morris, C. Brian. 1991. Strategies of self-effacement in three poems by Gloria Fuertes. *Mester* 20: 67–76.

Perloff, Marjorie. 1985. *The dance of the intellect: studies in the poetry of the Pound tradition.* Cambridge: Cambridge University Press.

———, ed. 1988. *Postmodern genres.* Norman: University Press of Oklahoma.

Persin, Margaret H. 1987. *Recent Spanish poetry and the role of the reader.* Lewisburg, PA: Bucknell University Press, 119–136.

———. 1997. *Getting the picture: the ekphrastic principle in twentieth-century Spanish poetry.* Lewisburg, PA: Bucknell University Press. 89–113.

Sherno, Sylvia R. 1990. Gloria Fuertes's room of her own. *Letras femeninas* 16: 85–99.

Unamuno, Miguel de. 1996. *San Manuel Bueno, mártir y tres historias más.* 6th ed. Madrid: Espasa-Calpe. Colección Austral.

Ynduráin, Francisco. Prólogo. *Antología* 9–45.

Radical Musicality and Otherness in the Poetry of José Angel Valente

Linda D. Metzler

> Cuando, en el camino hacia la escritura, percibimos un ritmo, una entonación, una nota, algo que es, sin duda, de naturaleza radicalmente musical, algo que remite al número y a la armonía, la escritura ha empezado a formarse. Escribir exige, ante todo, del oído una gran acuidad.
> —José Angel Valente,
> "Cómo se pinta un dragón"
> (1995, 12; 1997, 23)

> [When, on the path toward writing, we perceive a rhythm, an intonation, a note, something that is, without doubt, of radically musical nature, something that reverts to numbers and to harmony, writing has begun to shape itself. Writing requires, above all, great acuity of the ear.]

Immersing myself anew in the work of José Angel Valente, I was struck by the musical sounds my mind's ear heard as I read certain poems: their lyric fulfillment—that mysterious process whereby the word of the poet becomes the reader's world[1]—seemed to depend in no small measure on sonorous and rhythmic language. Sensing the relation of musical sound to something essential in Valente but uncertain what it was, I culled the critical literature for insights. A few critics drew a connection between Valente's poetry and music, but they did so with little elaboration and in the context of studies that stressed other aspects of his work.[2] Other critics noted, but usually only in passing, the importance of rhythm in certain poems.[3] Only Santiago Daydí-Tolson, in a perceptive 1980 essay, discussed in detail the poet's use of sonorous language, signaling what he called "la resonancia rítmico-acústica" (rhythmic-acoustic resonance) as a key expressive strategy in poems from *Punto cero* (107–18). Considering selected poems in light of Daydí-Tolson's insights into resonance and ideas about poetic rhythm, sound, and otherness contributed by Octavio Paz, Robert Hass, and Robert Pinsky, my paper finds that Valente's predilection for sonorous and rhythmic language is intimately bound up with the poet's search for the existential and linguistic "other." I show that Valente's musical poems portray as one the lyric subject's search for harmonious release in an "other"—a beloved, poetry, nothingness—and the striving of poetic language to renew itself in the sonority and rhythmic articulation of song.[4]

In *Los efectos de la resonancia en la poesía de José Angel Valente*, Daydí-Tolson considers rhythmic-acoustic resonance within the framework of a larger discussion of resonant expressive strategies that he finds central to Valente's poetic creation. Key components of rhythmic-acoustic resonance in Valente, Daydí-Tolson observes, are rhymes, repetitions, syntactic parallelisms, anaphora, alliteration, and free combinations of traditional meters (109). For Daydí-Tolson, however, resonance in Valente is a question not only of sound but also of meaning: just as rhythm and sound resonate in readers' auditory perception of the poem, so also do "resonant" images, symbols, idiomatic expressions, speaking voices, and anecdotes "echo" in their understanding.

In the same work, Daydí-Tolson finds that the multiple techniques of resonance employed by Valente have in common "el establecer relaciones y sugerir correspondencias entre elementos textuales, o entre éstos y otros del contexto cultural y lingüístico común al poeta y sus lectores" ([the effect of] establishing relationships and suggesting correspondences among textual elements, or between these and others drawn from the cultural and linguistic context shared by the poet and his readers). In analyses of selected poems, Daydí-Tolson shows how such strategies influence our reception of meaning by simultaneously heightening emotion and highlighting key ontological concepts; in so doing, these techniques help readers fuse experience and knowledge into a complex synthesis irreducible to component parts. As Daydí-Tolson says, "El poema no comunica una idea, sino la actitud de un hablante que sintetiza lo abstracto de la concepción ontológica y la experiencia emotiva concreta" (The poem does not communicate an idea, but rather the attitude of a speaker that synthesizes the abstract nature of the ontological conception and the particular emotional experience) (109).[5]

Daydí-Tolson's article serves as a valuable point of departure for my own inquiry in its specific clarification of the link between sound/rhythm and the synthesis of meaning in Valente's poems. It is helpful as well in its broader suggestion that interwoven resonant strategies lead readers to perceive the correspondences underlying apparent differences in things, experiences, people, and ideas. But interestingly Daydí-Tolson, even while using such musical terms as "ecos," "ritmos," "correspondencias," "resonancia," "relaciones sonoras," and "armónica correlación," stops short of drawing explicitly the connection between Valente's poetry and musical sound—a connection that Valente himself eloquently affirms in the aphorism quoted at my paper's beginning.[6]

Following the poet's aphoristic lead and guided by the textual evidence of his poems, I will argue that Valente's work pursues a radical musicality not just of form but also of content. I will suggest moreover that this pursuit manifests itself as a search for otherness encompassing both language and the self. At the level of language, I will show that Valente imbues his poems with otherness by musically modulating words and phrases with an ear to their sonorous, rhythmic, and sensorial potential when given voice and breath by the reader. Recurrent and varying sounds in pleasing play, expressive silences, rhythms that alternately swell and subside,[7] and syntax in creative relation to line ending consistently inform the linguistic otherness of Valente and condition the reader's auditory experience of his poems in such a way as to make it verge on song.

But just as Valente's poems portray a quest for otherness that unfolds musically at the level of language, so too do they depict a search for otherness that unfolds musically at the level of the self. They show lyric subjects, in ardent pursuit of a transcendent harmoniousness, abandoning the self and seeking merger with a desired "other": a divinity, someone beloved, poetry, death/nothingness. Helping to render conceptually accessible to the reader these otherwise elusive transports of the self are such stylistic devices as the overlapping of first- second- and third-person speaking voices, unfurling prepositional phrases that call disparate things into relation, and the use of cascading analogies that powerfully portend the underlying identity of different modes of being.[8]

In the analytical section soon to follow, I study the interlocking musical searches for ontological and linguistic otherness in Valente and consider their consequence for us as readers. But first I turn, for useful theoretical insights into the nature and function of poetic rhythm and sound, to poets Octavio Paz, Robert Hass, and Robert Pinsky. Following different paths of reflection, the three come to conclude that rhythm and sound, inflected by the human desire to transcend temporality, hasten poets and readers toward an experience of otherness.[9]

Octavio Paz, in the essay "El ritmo" from *El arco y la lira*, hails rhythm as the constitutive element of the poetic phrase: "[L]a unidad de la frase, lo que la constituye como tal y hace lenguaje, no es el sentido o dirección significativa, sino el ritmo" ([T]he unity of the phrase, that which constitutes it as such and makes it into language, is not the meaning or the significative thrust, but rather the rhythm) (51). Rhythm, in Paz's idea, is fundamentally connected to the poet's desire-inflected search for something "other": "El ritmo provoca una expectación, suscita un anhelar . . . El ritmo engendra en nosotros una disposición de ánimo que sólo podrá calmarse cuando sobrevenga 'algo'. Nos coloca en actitud de espera. Sentimos que el ritmo es un ir hacia algo, aunque no sepamos qué pueda ser ese algo" (Rhythm provokes an expectation, arouses a yearning . . . Rhythm engenders in us a spiritual disposition that can only be calmed when "something" ensues. It places us in an attitude of waiting. We feel that rhythm is a going toward something, although we don't know what that something may be) (57). Paz locates in rhythm's identification with human temporality its power to thrust us toward the unknown in multiple guises: "[E]l ritmo es inseparable de nuestra condición . . . es la manifestación más simple, permanente y antigua del hecho decisivo que nos hace ser hombres: ser temporales, ser mortales y lanzados siempre hacia 'algo,' hacia lo 'otro': la muerte, Dios, la amada, nuestros semejantes" ([R]hythm is inseparable from our condition . . . it is the simplest, most permanent and ancient manifestation of the decisive fact that makes us be men: to be temporal, to be mortal and launched always toward "something," toward the "other": death, God, the beloved, our fellow beings) (60).

Robert Hass, in two essays from *Twentieth Century Pleasures*, also ponders the connections among rhythm, desire, temporality, and the experience of otherness. Arguing for the psychological basis of rhythm's power, Hass signals pleasure and satisfaction in recurrent rhythms as one of the infant's first and most formative experiences: it is through events' predictable recurrence that the infant comes to know his identity in the world. In Hass's words, "[W]hat is fresh in [children] is that they still experience the power of repetition, from which our first sense of the power of mastery comes" (56). Hass speculates, "[T]hinking this is going to happen and having it happen might be, then, the authentic source of the experience of being, of identity, that word which implies that a lot of different things are the same thing" (57).

Considering how rhythm engages readers, Hass discerns three phases. The first is our attention to and apprehension of rhythm, during which "we are pattern-discerning animals . . . We attend to a rhythm almost instinctively, listen to it for a while, and, if we decide it has no special significance for us, we can let it go; or put it away, not hearing it again unless it alters, signaling to us . . . that something in the environment is changed." According to Hass, our attentiveness to rhythm—"wakeful, animal, alert"—is "the first place to which we are called by the first words of any poem or story" (112).

The second phase is our experience of "recurrent and varying sound." Hass points out that here "[w]e move from attention to pleasure, from necessity to a field of play . . . The effect is hard to describe. Interplay, weaving, dialogue, dance: every phrase that comes to mind is a metaphor" (113). He says, "Repetition makes us feel secure and variation makes us feel free" (115). Consequently, as we perceive rhythmic patterns and variations, we paradoxically feel both "the desire for merger, union, loss of self and the desire for freedom, surprise, singularity" (116). These contradictions in response are what makes "the relation between repetition and variation in art dialectical and generative" (117).

Hass's third phase is our achievement of a sense of closure, the completion of a pattern. Of this phase, Hass says, "Many things in the world have rhythms and many kinds of creatures seem to be moved by them but only human beings complete them. This last phase, the bringing of rhythmic interplay to a resolution, is the particular provenance of man as a maker" (118). For Hass, "what hovers behind all this, I would guess, is a wish. Formally, the completion of a pattern imitates the satisfaction of a desire, a consummation," one which leads to a "a voluntary abandonment of the self" (1984, 119), an assumption of "otherness" akin for Hass to orgasm or death.

Like Paz and Hass, Robert Pinsky seeks to understand why poetry's rhythm and sound have the power to move us beyond the merely personal. Pinsky says that "poetry's cadences and its patterns of like sounds ... [embody] the deep, ancient links that join memory, human intelligence, culture, and the sound of spoken language." But Pinsky foregrounds a dimension of poetry mentioned only in passing by Hass and not discussed at all by Paz: the physicality of the act of reading: "In the particular physical presence of memorable language we can find a reminder of our ability to know and retain knowledge itself: the 'brightness wherein all things come to see'" (116). In Pinsky's idea, we avail ourselves of the self-transcendent knowledge that the poem imparts through memorable language made physically manifest in the act of reading. And, in Pinsky's view, poetic sound brought alive by readers links not only the individual reader and the poem, but also past, present, and future readers: " ... [T]he technology of poetry ... evolved for specific uses: to hold things in memory, both within and beyond the individual life span; to achieve intensity and sensuous appeal; to express feelings and ideas rapidly and memorably. To share those feelings and ideas with companions, and also with the dead and with those to come after us" (9).

Pinsky's conviction that the poem connects readers to something "other" through sound is grounded in his view of poetry as "a vocal, which is to say a bodily, art. The medium of poetry is a human body: the column of air inside the chest, shaped into signifying sounds in the larynx and the mouth" (8). According to Pinsky, poetry has among the arts "a special intimacy ... because ... the medium is not an expert's body, as when one goes to the ballet: in poetry, the medium is the audience's body. When I say to myself a poem by Emily Dickinson or George Herbert, the artist's medium is my breath. The reader's breath and hearing embody the poet's words. This makes the art physical, intimate, vocal, and individual" (8).[10]

Paz believes that poetry's rhythm, in expressing human temporality, arouses an expectation of an unknown "other"; Hass posits that rhythm is psychologically dialectical and generative, enticing readers alternately to affirm the self and to relinquish it in merger with something other; and Pinsky says that audiences avail themselves of the poem's otherness through sound rendered in hearing and breath. Together these form a loose theoretical framework for the readings of particular poems that I offer in the next section of my paper. Reflecting a compositional principle that Valente himself seems intuitively to embrace, my readings divide each poem into three sections—sections clearly heard although not necessarily formally demarcated. The first presents the poem's speaker and an existential "other" in elusive relationship and, through familiar syntax and engaging rhythms and sounds, elicits our visceral and psychic complicity in what we do not rationally grasp. The second complicates the relation of the speaker to the "other" and, through the variation and intensification of established syntactic, rhythmic, and sonorous patterns, heightens our expectation that a revelation will be produced. The third, marked by a return to syntactical regularity and by greater sonorous and rhythmic intensity/gravity, ushers us toward both a rhythmic resolution and an existential merging of the speaker and an existential "other." Tracing these three phases in four Valente poems, I hope to illuminate the musical process whereby readers, embodying in breath and hearing the poem's songlike sound and rhythm, appropriate for themselves the lyric subject's experience of harmonious merger with an "other."[11]

I begin with Poem XXX from *El fulgor* (1984), one of Valente's most musical compositions. My analysis aims to show how readers, enacting the poem's songlike language, partake vicariously of the speaker's fusion with an elusive "other":

> Venías, ave, corazón, de vuelo,
> venías por los líquidos más altos
> donde duermen la luz y las salivas
> en la penumbra azul de tu garganta.
> Ibas, que voy
> de vuelo, apártalos, volando
> a ras de los albores más tempranos.
> Sentirte así venir como la sangre,
> de golpe, ave, corazón, sentirme,

sentirte al fin llegar, entrar, entrarme,
ligera como luz, alborearme.
(Valente 1995, 178)

[You came, bird, heart, in flight,
you came through the highest liquids
where light and saliva sleep
in the blue penumbra of your throat.
You were going, I'm going
in flight, avert them, flying
at the level of the earliest dawns.
To feel you come like blood,
suddenly, bird, heart, to feel myself
feel you finally arrive, enter, enter me
weightless as light, suffuse me with dawn.]

In the poem's first stanza, as the lyric speaker addresses the interlocutor ("ave, corazón"), whose mysterious "coming" he recalls, alluring rhythms and sounds draw us toward visceral and psychic complicity in an existential relation we cannot yet fathom. Familiar hendecasyllable lines, with predictable beats largely on even-numbered syllables, enlist us in embracing the unknown: attending to this well-known rhythm,[12] feeling it inflect our hearing and breath, we let down our psychological guard and embrace the desire for merger with something beyond ourselves that Paz and Hass identify as one response to poetic rhythm. Reinforcing this response is the incantatory effect exercised by certain reiterated consonant and vowel sounds—the *v*'s of "venías," "ave," "vuelo," and "salivas"; the *i*'s, the *a*'s, and the *u*'s that receive rhythmic stresses. Syntax, too, helps lure us toward a visceral and psychic complicity in what we cannot logically apprehend: flowing from the second line to the stanza's end without the disruption of punctuation, it creates in us a literally breathless anticipation that something will be revealed. In this stanza, familiar rhythms, sounds, and syntax—imprinting themselves on our body and in our psyche—keep us reading in the hopes of a revelation: we may not get the meaning, but we trust what we hear to get us there.[13]

The second stanza immerses us in an existential and acoustic uncertainty that both unsettles and entices. Shifts in word choice ("venías" becomes "ibas"), in verb tense ("ibas" becomes "voy"), and in point of view (second person cedes to first) blur the distinction between speaker and interlocutor, while sonorous/rhythmic variations with respect to the patterns of the first stanza beguile our hearing and belabor our breath. Hearing the gathering frequency of *v/b* sounds, or the way in which vocally open stressed *a*'s and *o*'s increasingly supplant the more vocally constricted *i*'s and *u*'s of the first stanza, we feel a subtle intermingling of disquietude and exhilaration. Rhythmic changes determined by altered stress patterns, metrical form, and syntax agitate our breathing and heighten our anxiety as well: the word "Ibas," stressed on the first syllable, gets the stanza off to a more emphatic rhythmic start than was supplied by the preceding stanza's syntactically parallel "venías." The ensuing dactylic rhythmic period stands out in expressive contrast to the poem's trochaic beginning; the first stanza's consistently hendecasyllabic metrical pattern gives way in the second to lines of 5, 9, and 11 syllables. Syntax, rather than flowing uninterrupted as it did in the first stanza, here is broken up by commas within the lines ("de vuelo, apártalos,"[14] volando) only to verge precipitously over line endings ("que voy/de vuelo"; "volando/a ras"). Small wonder that, hearing ourselves read, we feel breathless, excited, apprehensive.

In the poem's third stanza, speaker and interlocutor who verge toward fusion as readers—rendering in hearing and breath a crescendo of rhythm and sound—are led toward a kindred transcendence.[15] The stanza's single utterance derives its considerable rhythmic, sonorous, and existential urgency from a series of counterpoised infinitives that evoke, on the one hand, the lyric speaker's sentient receptiveness ("sentirte," "sentirme," "sentirte") and, on the other, the interlocutor's active coming ("venir," "llegar," "entrar," "entrarme"). We feel the expressive pull exerted by the endings of these infinitives; on them fall many of the stresses that inflect the stanza with its compelling trochaic rhythm ("Sentirte así venir," "sentirte al fin llegar, entrar, entrarme"). They enact a sonorous back and forth between the vocally constricted *i* sounds and the more vocally open *a* sounds that underlines the erotically charged human contending. Commas strategically placed throughout make us pause to take quick successive breaths even as the hendecasyllables' rhythm lures us forward, heightens our excitement, and intensifies our hunger for revelation. By the time we reach the end of line 10 we are as eager for breath and for release from building sound as we are for ontological closure. Line 11 provides the release we seek. Saying its initial phrase, "ligera como luz," we sense impending metaphysical lightness even as we hear rhythmic accents grow sparser, consonant sounds less harsh, and vowel sounds (the stressed *e* and *u*) less weighty. But not until we intone the poem's final word—the grammatically transgressive "alborearme"—does full relief suffuse us. Saying it, we exhale with a sigh, overtaken simultaneously by the word's euphonious beauty and its metaphorical aptness: we hear it echo the earlier "albores" and fulfill the crescendo of ending-stressed *a*'s of line 10, even as we behold the speaker's transmutation in the element of light linked with the interlocutor throughout the poem.

Like Poem XXX, Poem XXXV (also from *El fulgor*) portrays in musical language an experience of union that eludes our rational understanding: the lyric interlocutor's body is drunk by a bird. If the "pájaro" of this poem evokes in some vague way the "ave" of the earlier poem, and if both poems speak to us emblematically of poetry's capacity to overtake and transform us, this is no coincidence. Valente, echoing San Juan de la Cruz, recurrently identifies birds with the songlike essence of poetry:[16]

> La aparición del pájaro que vuela
> y vuelve y que se posa
> sobre tu pecho y te reduce a grano,
> a grumo, a gota cereal, el pájaro
> que vuela dentro
> de ti, mientras te vas haciendo
> de sola transparencia,
> de sola luz,
> de tu sola materia, cuerpo
> bebido por el pájaro.
>   (Valente 1995, 183)[17]

[The appearance of the bird that flies
and returns and that alights
on your chest and reduces you to grain,
to curd, to cereal drops, the bird
that flies inside
of you, while you turn into
sheer transparency,
into sheer light,
into your sheer substance, body
drunk by the bird.]

The poem's first three lines serve, existentially as well as sonorously, as an introduction. As they trace the bird's appearance and his incipient complicity with the interlocutor, they draw us into the scene through continuous syntax and leisurely rhythms and sounds that subtly intensify. The first line unfolds unhurriedly: its relaxed hendecasyllabic rhythm and serene tone seem simply to call us to attend to a natural scene. More metrically compressed, the second line invites us to experience a slight sonorous and rhythmic intensification : the first stressed syllable ("vuel") repeats the last (invariably) stressed syllable of the preceding line ("vue") but is more rhythmically emphatic; while the stressed *po* of "posa" establishes a sonorous link to the first line's "aparición" and "pájaro." The third line is a rhythmically and sonorously intensifying hendecasyllable that discloses the bird in disquieting metaphorical relationship to an unidentified second-person interlocutor: the bird is poised on his chest and is reducing him to grain! Reading this line—a line inflected with more rhythmic stresses than was the first hendecasyllable—we hear "pecho" echo the foregoing *p*'s as well as the introduction of a compelling new sound, the guttural *gr* of "grano." Lured by continuous syntax to try to inflect these lines with unbroken breath, we feel ourselves grow a bit breathless.

In the poem's second section (lines 4–6), the bird—no longer poised "on" the interlocutor but flying "within" him—intensifies its reduction of him to "otherness." Readers are summoned to more agitated breathing and greater emotional unrest by intensified rhythm and sound, syntactic disruptions, and metrical alterations. We hear, for example, the disquieting rhythmic and sonorous density of line 4's four rhythmic accents, of which the first two fall on syllables inflected with the harsh *g* sounds ("grumo" and "gota") that echo the previous line's "grano." Syntactic changes—the use of commas within lines, consistently more abrupt enjambments—introduce a changed rhythmic intensity that alternately slows down and speeds up our articulation of sounds and our breathing. Finally, the appearance of metrical lines of different length (11, 5, 9) also lends instability to our vocal rendering of this section.

In the poem's last four lines, as metaphor renders the interlocutor's body definitively "other," syntactical parallelisms, reiterated sounds, and more gravely inflected rhythms enlist readers in assuming viscerally a process the mind alone can not fathom. Echoing the poem's earlier three-part utterance ("a grano/a grumo, a gota"), lines 7 to 9 configure three syntactically parallel prepositional clauses that describe the interlocutor becoming successively "transparencia," "luz," and "material." Reading these phrases, we take more frequent breaths in order to accommodate the commas that separate them. And, even as we are compelled by their syntactic similarity, we hear sonorous differences. While in each line the adjective "sola" underlines with sonorous and rhythmic force its etymological suggestion of reduction to oneness, in lines 7 and 8 the adjective's resonant first syllable receives the first rhythmic accent. Whereas in line 9—due to the interposition of the stressed tu—it receives an expressive extra-rhythmic second accent. The four strongly stressed syllables in this nine-syllable line make us feel the line's metaphysical weight—as does, at the end of the same line, the section's only enjambed word "cuerpo."[18] Reading the poem's last line we render the sonorously vigorous *b*'s of "bebido" and the dramatic rhythm of the thrice-invoked "pájaro," and we register in our flesh the emphatic finality of the interlocutor's merger with the bird.

At first glance "Silos," (*La memoria y los signos*, 1960–1965), seems as distinct in matter and manner from the poems just discussed as it is distant in time of production. While the other poems depicted subjective inner landscapes and used natural images only as metaphors, "Silos" comes into focus with abundant descriptive detail, a particular Spanish landscape.[19] But my reading suggests that, like the first two poems discussed, "Silos" moves readers through musical language to apprehend in hearing and breath an experience of existential otherness or insight. Embodying the poem's rhythms and sounds, we come to assume the poet's vision of an arid landscape become one with timeless human suffering.

> Silos.
> La luz.
> La Yecla: el socavado
> corazón de la piedra
> o la ascensión del aire.
> Arriba
> el agrio son quebrado de los grajos.

Y en lo alto la tierra,
sola desde la altura,
capaz, enorme, terca, hasta lo lejos.
La extensión de la tierra.
La mano, la matriz, el silo, el hondo
clamor rojizo de la tierra oscura,
de la tierra solar.
Amenazada
raíz, jamás vencida,
bajo un sol de injusticia.
Pesa la luz. Gravita el eje ardiente
sobre el pecho del hombre,
sobre su sorda servidumbre
y el seco llanto de los siglos.
                    (Valente 1980, 204–5)

[Silos.
The light.
La Yecla: the sunken
heart of the stone
or the ascent of the air.
High up
the bitter broken sound of the grackles.
And up above the land,
Alone (seen) from the heights,
capable, huge, stubborn, off into the distance.
The land's extension.
The hand, the womb, the silo, the deep
red clamoring of the dark land,
the solar land.
Threatened
root, never vanquished,
under a merciless sun.
The light bears down. The burning axis gravitates
over the breast of man,
over his echoless servitude
and the dry weeping of centuries.]

    The poem's opening sequence (lines 1–7) evokes, in third person and in language largely non-metaphorical, the poem's lyric subject: the arid high plain of Silos. Throughout this section, readers are called to unperplexed contemplation of an imposing natural scene not just by the relative neutrality of tone and of language but by unhurried rhythms and pleasant, reassuring sounds. As we say the poem's opening line, for example, we hear punctuation and spacing slow down our rendering of the regular rhythmic flow of the hendecasyllable. Enhancing our impression of rhythmic leisureliness in this section are syntactical and breath units that generally coincide with the end of metrical lines, as in the section's last three lines. (Exceptional is the single rhythmically intensifying instance of enjambment at the end of line 1.)

The leisurely recurrence of unlike and like sounds throughout this first section helps to sustain our pleasure and sense of psychic expansiveness in reading.[20] Reading line 1, for example, we may be aware of hearing four different vowels in the four syllables that receive rhythmic stresses (*i, u, e,* and *a*), the last more vocally open than the first. And we register with some degree of pleasure the more obvious subsequent reiteration of open vowel sounds (*a*'s and *o*'s) in syllables that get rhythmic stresses ("el *a*grio s*o*n quebr*a*do de los gr*a*jos"; "cap*a*z, en*o*rme, terc*a*, hasta lo lejos"). Other sonorous correspondences—the half-rhymes of "corazón"/"ascension," "socavado"/"quebrado," "grajos"/"lejos" —act on our ear as we read as well, lulling us into a state of quiescent receptiveness. Our expectation of something "other" is quickened by an intensification felt at the levels of meaning and of sound in the section's last three lines (5–7), a single grammatical utterance. Here, culminating an intensifying series of references to height ("ascension," "arriba," "en lo alto"), we find invoked for the first time the key noun "tierra"—a word echoed sonorously and rhythmically by the succeeding "altura" and "terca." Almost without our noticing it, line 7 begins to confer upon this solitary "tierra" a human otherness ("capaz" and "terca") that succeeding lines will more fully embody.

In the second section (lines 8–13), shifting syntactical patterns, overtly metaphorical language, and intensifying rhythms and sounds summon us to richer emotional complicity with a landscape rendered ever more human. If "la tierra" arose in section 1 as syntactically and metaphysically independent, here— where the word is repeated three times—it stands in subordinate syntactic and metaphysical relation to the encroaching "other." Just as it is the object of a preposition in each utterance, so is it overshadowed by metaphors denoting human presence: "La mano, la matriz, el silo, el hondo / clamor rojizo de la tierra oscura/de la tierra solar." Rhythmic tensions and the play of like and unlike sounds make us feel a heightened anxiety: the breaking up of hendecasyllabic lines 9 and 11 with commas and a period slows our reading down, even as the rhythmic implacability of the hendecasyllables—each marked by an enjambed final adjective ("hondo," "Amenazada")—exerts a forward pull. From line 9 through the end of line 13, a new sonorous pattern—the pairing of open and closed vowels in successive stressed syllables ("la mano, la matriz," "el silo, el hondo" "clamor rojizo", "tierra solar", "amenzada /raíz", "jamás vencida", "un sol de injusticia")—renders our reading more agitated and intensifies our expectation of revelation.

As we read the poem's final section (lines 14–17), emphatic rhythms and repeated sounds inflect our hearing and breath, lending visceral force and emotional intensity to the metaphysical revelation of the landscape's merger with its human other. In the section's opening utterance ("Pesa la luz"), an explosive bilabial *p* underlines the syntactic prominence of the poem's first verb; and strong rhythmic stresses on the first and fourth syllables bring into sharp sonorous relief the *e* of "pesa" and the *u* of "luz," making the metaphysical weight of these words more manifest. Reaching the period at the end of this utterance, we briefly pause, but are pulled toward the line's second utterance by our hearing's anticipation of the hendecasyllable's rhythmic completion—a completion constituted by the clause "Gravita el eje ardiente." Restating the meaning of "Pesa la luz," this clause sonorously reinforces it as well: the opening *gr* sound is as harsh in its way as the *p* was in "pesa," and the stressed *e*'s of "eje" and "ardiente" carry through on the *e* of "pesa." From this formulation the poem's last three lines, which are parallel prepositional phrases, flow with syntactical inevitability and sonorous/rhythmic gravity toward the poem's conclusion. In line 15, as "pecho" echoes the previous line's "pesa" in both sound and rhythm, we register in our hearing and breath the landscape's usurpation by human presence and in lines 15 to 17, the rhythmic and sonorous prominence of open vowels in nouns evocative of human presence ("hombre", "sorda" "llanto) calls us to the same awareness. But, most dramatically, in the poem's last two lines a crescendo of *s* sounds provokes our disquietude and summons our expectation of the poem's resolution. Key to this resolution at the level of rhythm and sound but also of meaning is the invocation at the poem's end of the word with which it began. Intoning "Silos" a second and final time, we hear its rhythmic/sonorous difference. Now it is a rhythmic accent subsumed within the line's invariably stressed tenth syllable rather than falling on the emphatic first syllable. The word's sonority is subsumed within all the foregoing *s*'s, causing the reader to grasp the word's metaphysical difference: Silos, no longer pure landscape, has been subsumed by human pathos.

Like "Silos," the following poem, an elegiac work from Valente's posthumously published *Fragmentos de un libro futuro*,[21] depicts a natural scene that becomes suffused with human pathos. Readers, rendering its musical sounds in hearing and breath, viscerally experience poetry's capacity to mark human passage from existence to oblivion.

> El amarillo, el verde, el encendido
> rojo sólo para morir
> bajo el tendido velo del otoño.
> La luz no está en la luz, está en las cosas
> que arden de luz tenaz bajo la lluvia.
> Nada tiene más fuego en sus entrañas
> que la melancolía ardiente de esta hora.
> Nada tiene más fuego que la ausencia.
> ¿Llorar?
> Lloradme nunca.
> Me he perdido
> con el aire en las bóvedas tan bajas
> de un cielo que, piadoso, me disuelve.
> 							(Valente 2000, 71)

> [The yellow, the green, the flaming
> red only to die
> under the thrown veil of fall.
> The light is not in light, it is in things
> that burn with light tenacious under rain.
> Nothing has more fire within its core
> Than the ardent melancholy of this hour.
> Nothing has more fire than absence does.
> Cry?
> Cry for me never.
> I've lost myself
> with the air in the so-low vaults
> of a sky that, merciful, dissolves me.]

In the poem's first section (lines 1–3), an impersonal speaker invokes in quick succession the colorful splendor of fall ("El amarillo, el verde, el encendido/rojo") and the inevitability of its demise ("sólo para morir"). As we render aloud these lines, subtle sounds and rhythms underline the metaphorical opposition between presence and absence, engaging our emotional responsiveness and priming us for revelation. The first line's relative rhythmic gravity is infused with an incipient sonorous and metaphysical intensity. Its first rhythmic stress—delayed until the fourth syllable—falls on "amarillo," heightening the auditory impact of the vowel-rhyming "encendido" that receives the line's last stress and sonorously underlining both words' metaphorical evocation of fall's brightness. Line 2, depicting the "death" of fall's brightness, alters our auditory experience while dramatically redefining the existential prospect. In contrast to the ascending pitch with which we read the first line, we inflect the second with a tonal descent that concludes at the end of line 3. While punctuation slowed down our reading of the first line, punctuation's absence in the formally foreshortened second line speeds us up, hastening our arrival at the sonorously and metaphysically powerful infinitive "morir." Rhythmic accents in the second line (falling on syllables 1, 3, 5, and 8) are more numerous and emphatic than those of the first line and more sonorously arresting (the first two fall on *o*'s). In line three, the words "tendido" and "velo" echo the first line's "amarillo," "encendido," and "verde," but they connote an existential somberness in striking contrast to the "burning" evoked by the latter.

The poem's next section (lines 4–8) immerses us in a meditation of ever more explicit human import in which light and fire are suffused with their metaphorical and ontological opposites: nothingness, melancholy, and absence. Fluctuating rhythms and dialectical plays of sound underline the grammatical tension between negative and affirmative utterances; the metaphorical tension between fire and nothingness, and the metaphysical tension between presence and absence. Rhythmic stresses throughout this section are more numerous, emphatic, and metrically irregular than those of the previous section, and they tend to fall on words—often repeated—that possess both sonorous and metaphysical weight. In lines 4 and 5, for example, we hear rhythmically stressed and sonorously expressive *u*'s and *a*'s contend as the speaker reflects dialectically on the nature of light ("La luz no está en la luz, está en las cosas/que arden de luz tenaz bajo la lluvia").[22] And in lines 6 and 9, where the speaker shows nothingness to be infused with fire, we hear stressed *a*'s alternate rhythmically with stressed *e* sounds: "Nada tiene más fuego en sus entrañas" and "Nada tiene más fuego que la ausencia." Assuming the visceral, emotional, and metaphysical weight of these words, we feel engulfed in temporal anguish.

But from the thrall of temporal anguish the poem's conclusion, in sound and in meaning, would free us. When in lines 9 to 11, a lyric speaker turned suddenly personal enjoins us not to cry for him and then evokes his own "merciful" dissolution, we inflect in our breath and hearing rhythms that swell only to subside, syntax at first slowed down by punctuation and then continuous to the point of breathlessness, and sound that invokes and then frees itself from patterns of previous sections. The ninth line's poignant appeals to readers ("¿Llorar? Lloradme nunca") are underlined with a resolute trochaic rhythm, punctuation, and spacing that slow down our reading, and re-invocation of the sonorous tension between stressed *a* and *u*. But as the speaker portrays his dissolution in the long sentence that unfurls from "Me he perdido," our reading is inflected with syntactic, rhythmic, and sonorous changes. Rendering aloud the syntactically continuous prepositional phrases, we feel ourselves grow breathless, we hear rhythmic stresses get sparser, and we hear unfamiliar sounds intensify. Most resonant of all, even as it is freighted with existential pathos, is the poem's antepenultimate word "piadoso." Saying this word with the emphasis its isolation by commas demands, we hear its percussive *p* inflect our breath, its strong syllable *do* echo sonorously and rhythmically the *bo* of "bóveda," and its *s* compel us with sibilant sound. As we say the poem's final word, "disuelve," we hear its attenuated vowel and consonant sounds echo in brief sympathy with the stronger sounds of "piadoso" before fading, along with the speaker, into silence.

I set out in this essay to explore the essence and expressive thrust of the musical sounds I heard when reading certain Valente poems. I hoped to learn how resonant words might help to produce an experience of insight so compelling as to alter the reader's world. My investigation owes a debt to the work of Santiago Daydí-Tolson, who identifies the phenomenon of rhythmic-acoustic resonance as a key to the creation of emotion and ontological meaning in Valente's poetry.[23] But I have gone beyond Daydí-Tolson's conclusions to suggest that rhythm and sound lie at the heart of a radical musicality present in Valente as a search for the ontological and the linguistic "other": Valente's most musical works show poetic subjects in harmonious merger with existential "others" even as they portray language taking on the rhythmic and sonorous attributes of song. I have sought to illuminate this process and its consequence for readers by studying selected poems in light of ideas about rhythm, sound, and otherness advanced by Octavio Paz, Robert Hass, and Robert Pinsky. Most useful have been Paz's insight that poetic rhythm is a magnet, taking time-bound readers ineluctably toward an existential "other"; Hass's notion that rhythm's psychological power—a power harking back to our first experiences of identity—propels us toward the poem's self-transcendent insight; and Pinsky's view that the reader's body, rendering the poem's sound, is the poet's medium in forging meanings that transcend time and self. My analyses have shown that Valente's musical poems draw readers harmoniously to assume an existential otherness—that of a beloved, that of nothingness, that of poetry itself—by prompting them to perform in hearing and breath rhythms and sounds that make poetic language verge on song.

To the motif of song Valente returned time and again throughout his work, always identifying it with a cherished if elusive poetic ideal. The last poem of *Fragmentos de un libro futuro*, a haiku written only weeks before the poet died, evokes song's plenitude and, once more, the speaker/interlocutor's fusion with a songbird:

> Cima del canto.
> El ruiseñor y tú
> Ya sois lo mismo.
> (Valente 2000, 102)

> [Summit of song.
> The nightingale and you
> Now are the same.]

Readers, embodying Valente's poems in hearing and breath, themselves surely are fused with the radically musical words and world of an enduring *cantor*.

Notes

All translations are my own.

1. In the introduction to *The Given and the Made,* Helen Vendler states an assumption that my paper shares: "the purpose of the lyric, as a genre, is to represent an inner life in such a manner that it is assumable by others." Vendler sees "the lyric [as] a script written for performance by the reader—who, as soon as he enters the lyric, is no longer a reader but an utterer, saying the words of the poem *in propia persona,* internally and with proprietary feeling" (xi).

2. María Zambrano, in "La mirada originaria en la obra de José Angel Valente" (The Originating Look in the Work of José Angel Valente) says that Valente's poetic word "en un acto único se ofrece y se retira, tal como en los cantos litúrgicos sucedía, y así como también en los recitativos de ciertas óperas" (in a single act offers itself and withdraws, just as happened in liturgical chants, and also as in the recitatives of certain operas) (39). José Teruel Benavente, in "En la extensión vacía de la memoria: un itinerario por la poesía de José Angel Valente" (The Empty Extension of the Memory: An Itinerary Through the Poetry of José Angel Valente), says, "El poeta apela a un lenguaje transparente/virginal capaz, como la música, de revelar el fondo" (The poet draws on a transparent/virginal language capable, like music, of revealing the depths) (167). And José M. Cuesta Abad, in "La enajenación por la palabra (Reflexiones sobre el lenguaje poético en Valente)" (Enchantment by Word: Reflections on Poetic Languages in Valente) says that the poem "Arietta, Opus 111, from *Interior con figuras (Interior with figures)* "ejemplifica el proceso de identificación de la palabra poética con una materia creadora e intraspasable que al fin se asimila a la esteticidad pura, absolutamente formal de la música" (exemplifies the process of identification of the poetic word with a creative, irreducible substance that finally merges with the pure, absolutely formal aestheticity of music) (9).

3. Père Gimferrer en "El rigor" speaks of Valente's "admirable sentido del ritmo" (admirable sense of rhythm) (3). Jonathan Mayhew, analyzing the poem "Graal," from *Mandorla,* speaks of the poet's "play with sound" and observes that the poet's "evocation of primordial biological rhythms is strongly suggestive of Kristeva's *chora,* her term for a 'semiotic,' pre-linguistic, maternal space" (128–29). Sylvia R. Sherno, in "José Angel Valente: From the Dark Centre to the Limits," points to the expressive use of "contrapuntal rhythms" in the poem "El angel," from *A modo de esperanza* (163).

4. I am indebted for this insight to an idea expressed by Theodor Adorno in "On Lyric Poetry and Society": "language's chimerical yearning for the impossible becomes an expression of the subject's insatiable erotic longing, which finds relief from the self in the other" (53).

5. Another essay by Daydí-Tolson, "*Breve son*: Clave interpretativa de la obra poética de José Angel Valente," applies the concept of "resonancia" to a study of the poems of the volume named in the title.

6. In two interviews, Valente comments on the importance of music to his poetic creation. In a 1984 interview with Martín Arancibia, he says,

> "yo he llegado a la música más tarde que a la pintura, pero he recibido de ella un inagotable caudal. He aprendido mucho de la mutua potenciación de la música y la palabra en Schoenberg y, sobre todo, en ese

lugar de la aventura creadora moderna que es para mí el *Wozzeck* de Alban Berg. Los rastreadores de influencias pueden circular por canales estrechos e incomunicados. No prestan mucha atención a estas cosas. Sin duda, yo he sido profundamente modificado por la escucha de ciertos compositores, como Varese o Webern."

[I have come to music later than to painting, but I have received from it an inexhaustible inspiration. I have learned a lot from the mutual potentiation of music and the word in Schoenberg and, above all, in that space of the modern creative adventure that for me is *Wozzeck* of Alban Berg. Influence seekers can inhabit narrow and isolated channels. They don't pay much attention to these things. Without a doubt, I have been profoundly modified by listening to certain composers, like Varese or Webern.] (86)

And in a 1998 interview with Nuria Fernández Quesada, he says, "mi poesía... nace en gran parte de la música. Por ejemplo, *Tres lecciones de tinieblas* arranca de la audición de Francois Couperin, y de una infinidad de lecciones de tinieblas de todas las épocas... Además, he escrito sobre la música de Beethoven, sobre todo el Beethoven de las últimas sonatas y de los cuartetos, que me ha influído... Recientemente he terminado el texto de una ópera sobre Giordano Bruno que ha compuesto Mauricio Sotelo y que se estrenará en el 2000, año en que se cumple el cuarto centenario de su muerte en la hoguera.

[my poetry... is born in large part from music. For example, *Tres lecciones de tinieblas* grows from listening to Francois Couperin, and a large number of *lecciones de tinieblas* from all periods... In addition, I have written about the music of Beethoven, especially the Beethoven of the late sonatas and of the quartets, which has influenced me... Recently I have finished the text of an opera about Giordano Bruno which Mauricio Sotelo has composed and which will have its debut in 2000, the year in which the four hundredth anniversary of his death at the stake will be commemorated.] (145)

The exhaustive Valente bibliography contained in *Anatomía de la palabra* [Anatomy of the Word] includes a section entitled "Bibliografía musical" (Musical Bibliography) which lists instrumental and vocal performances of Valente's poems set to music by such composers as Santiago Lanchares, Francisco Luque, and Mauricio Sotelo (246–47).

    7. The compelling rhythmic character of Valente's musical poems stems in part from the poet's mining of the rich polyrhythmic potential of traditional metrical lines. He is particularly drawn to the hendecasyllable, a line designated by Navarro Tomás "el metro más complejo de la poesía española" (115). That Valente deliberated on the question of rhythm in Spanish poetry is shown by this quote from a 1999 interview with José Andrés Rojo. "Unamuno... (v)io como la poesía española se había metido en lo que él llamaba 'el ritmo tamborilesco'. Habla literalmente de una poesía 'en la que el compás mata al ritmo'.

Yo, por mi parte, he buscado siempre ese ritmo interior que había encontrado en Wordswoorth (sic) o Coleridge. Y esas lecturas de Unamuno fueron también para mí muy importantes" (Unamuno . . . (s)aw how Spanish poetry had become mired in what he called "the drum-like rhythm." He speaks literally of a poetry "in which the beat kills the rhythm." I, on the other hand, have always sought that interior rhythm that I had found in Wordswoorth (sic) or Coleridge. And those readings from Unamuno were also for me very important) (54).

8. Suggestive in this regard is the reply of baritone Richard Porterfield of the New York-based *a capella* group Lionheart to a question I posed after the group's performance in Columbus, Ohio, in February 2001: "When is poetry musical?" "Poetry is musical for me when it makes me see one thing in terms of another," Porterfield said.

9. Valente himself links desire, rhythm, and union with another in his essay "Verbum absconditum" (*Variaciones sobre el pájaro y la red*), a commentary on San Juan de la Cruz's "Canciones de la esposa" (211).

10. F. Amittai Aviram, in *Telling Rhythm: Body and Meaning in Poetry*, regrets the "trend in Western poetry toward the effacement of the bodily pleasure experienced in the regular, musical rhythm of meter" (3). He proposes "to view meaning in poetry as representing, allegorically, aspects of the power of the poem's own rhythm to bring about a physical response—to engage the reader's or listener's body, and thus to disrupt the orderly process of meaning. In this way, meaningful content in poetry paradoxically represents something that itself is outside of meaning" (5).

11. Inquiry into the "other" as a phenomenon encompassing both language and the self has shaped much contemporary critical theory. The term, formulated in psychoanalysis, is given extensive treatment by Lacan (see Anthony Wilden's essay, "Lacan and the Discourse of the Other), enters into the feminist theoretical writings of Simone de Beauvoir, Cixous, Irigaray, and Kristeva (see Toril Moi's *Sexual Textual Politics*), and is imported into postcolonial theory by such writers as Homi Bhabha (see his "The Other Question: Stereotype, Discrimination and the Discourse of Colonialism."

12. Navarro Tomás notes, "En líneas generales es posible apreciar que el ritmo trocáico sugiere serenidad y equilibrio y que el dactílico, por el contrario, indica exaltación y vehemencia" (Along general lines it is possible to observe that trochaic rhythm suggests serenity and equilibrium and that dactylic rhythm, on the other hand, indicates exaltation and vehemence) (15).

13. Here I follow Pinsky, who speaks of "an audible web so attractive to me that I feel willing to trust the meaning, even while I can't quite get it, because the sounds have so much conviction and appeal" (80).

14. "Apártalos" (Avert them) is an intertextual reference taken from San Juan de la Cruz's "Canciones de la esposa." In San Juan's work it is an invocation uttered by "la esposa" at the moment when she sees the eyes of the beloved upon her. Valente comments on the "carga de significación" (weight of signification) and the "extrema belleza" (extreme beauty) of this utterance in "Verbum absconditum" (*Variaciones sobre el pájaro y la red*, 213).

15. Readers intoning these words perhaps experience an emotion kindred to the "*jouissance* of semiotic motility" spoken of by Toril Moi in characterizing the thought of Kristeva (170).

16. Nowhere does Valente do so as transparently as at the end of "Las condiciones del pájaro solitario," in *La piedra y el centro*, where he affirms "(la) libertad esencial de la obra, cuya definición mejor acaso fuese predicar de ella las cinco condiciones del pájaro solitario, según las declaró Juan de la Cruz ... *La primera, que se va a lo más alto; la segunda, que no sufre compañía, aunque sea de su naturaleza; la tercera, que pone el pico al aire; la cuarta que no tiene determinado color; la quinta que canta suavemente*" ([t]he essential freedom of the work, whose best definition would be perhaps to state about it the five conditions of the solitary bird, according to how Juan de la Cruz declared them ... *The first, that it goes to the heights; the second, that it cannot bear company, even if it is of its own kind; the third, that it sets its beak to the air; the fourth that it has no determined color; the fifth that it sings softly*) (21).

17. Readers may hear Valente reading this poem on the CD which accompanies the text *La voz de José Angel Valente: Poesía en la Residencia*.

18. Pinsky says that "there is a kind of philosophical or metaphysical weight that the tension of enjambment emphasizes" (48).

19. Situated to the south of Burgos, Silos is home to the monastery Santo Domingo de Silos. La Yecla, nearby, is "una profunda y estrecha garganta excavada en los espesos bancos de calizas que caracterizan el relieve de las Peñas de Cervera" (a deep and narrow gorge dug in the thick limestone banks that characterize the topography of Peñas de Cervera) (Rivero, 6).

20. Pinsky observes, "In different ways, and in varying degree, the sounds of words are similar and different. This simple fact, almost embarrassingly obvious to note, provides the basis for a tremendous part of poetry's power" (87).

21. In October 2001, *Fragmentos de un libro futuro* received the Premio Nacional de Poesía awarded by the Spanish Ministry of Culture.

22. In "La rima en la poesía última de Vicente Aleixandre," Miguel A. Márquez refers to "la fuerte tendencia a vincular la vocal *u* con los contenidos oscuros, lúgubres y fatídicos, observada en diversas manifestaciones de la poesía española, desde el *Polifemo* de Góngora a la obra de los poetas de la Generación de '27'" (the strong tendency to link the vowel *u* with dark, lugubrious and prophetic meanings, observed in different manifestations of Spanish poetry, from Góngora's *Polifemo* to the work of the poets of the Generation of "27") (352).

23. For suggested readings and critical commentary on this essay, I am grateful to Kenyon College friends and colleagues James Carson, Jennifer Clarvoe, Juan De Pascuale, Sheila Jordan, David Kridler, Carlos Piano, and Clara Román-Odio.

Works Cited

Adorno, Theodor W. 1992. On lyric poetry and society. In *Notes to literature*, vol. 1, edited by Rolf Tiedemann and translated by Shierry Weber Nicholsen. New York: Columbia University Press.

Arancibia, Martin. 1984. Palabras y ritmos. *Quimera* 39-40: 83-95.

Aviram, Amittai F. 1994. Telling rhythm: Body and meaning in poetry. Ann Arbor: University of Michigan Press.

Bhabha, Homi. 1994. The other question: stereotype, discrimination, and the discourse of colonialism. In *The location of culture.* New York: Routledge.

Cuesta Abad, Jose M. 1995. La enajenación por la palabra (Reflexiones sobre el lenguaje poético en Valente). In *El silencio y la escucha: José Angel Valente,* edited by Teresa Hernández-Fernández. Madrid: Cátedra; Ministerio de Cultura.

Daydí-Tolson, Santiago. 1980. Los efectos de la resonancia en la poesía de José Angel Valente. In *The analysis of literary texts: Current trends in methodology,* edited by Randolph Pope. Ypsilanti: Bilingual Press.

———. 1983. *Breve son*: Clave interpretativa de la obra poética de José Angel Valente. *Hispania* 66: 376–84.

Fernández Quesada, Nuria. 2000. Entrevista. In *Anatomía de la palabra. José Angel Valente,* edited by Nuria Fernández Quesada. Valencia: Pre-textos.

Gimferrer, Père. 1994. El rigor. *Insula* 570–71: 3.

Hass, Robert. 1984. *Twentieth century pleasures.* New York: Ecco.

Márquez, Miguel A. 2000. La rima en la poesía última de Vicente Aleixandre. *Hispanic review* 69: 337–53.

Mayhew, Jonathan. 1991. El signo de la feminidad: Gender and poetic creation in José Angel Valente. *Revista de estudios hispánicos* 25: 123–133.

Moi, Toril. 1985. *Sexual/textual politics.* New York: Routledge.

Navarro Tomás, Tomás. 1973. *Los poetas en sus versos: Desde Jorge Manrique a García Lorca.* Barcelona: Ariel.

Paz, Octavio. 1970. El ritmo. *El arco y la lira.* Mexico, D.F.: Fondo de Cultura Económica.

Pinsky, Robert. 1998. *The sounds of poetry.* New York: Farrar, Straus, Giroux.

Rivero, Enrique del, ed. 1997. *Espacios naturales de Burgos.* Burgos: Patronato de Turismo de Burgos.

Rojo, José Andrés. 1999-2000. "José Angel Valente: Mi lema es nadar contra corriente." *Espacio/espaço escrito: Revista de literatura en dos lenguas* 17–18: 53–56.

Sherno, Sylvia. 1989. José Angel Valente: From the dark centre to the limits." *Revista canadiense de estudios hispánicos* 14: 161–73.

Teruel Benavente, José.1993. En la extensión vacía de la memoria: un itinerario por la poesía de José Angel Valente. *Revista hispánica moderna* 46: 157–78.

Valente, José Angel. 1980. *Punto cero: Poesía 1953–1979.* Barcelona: Seix Barral.

———. 1995. *Material memoria: Trece años de poesía: 1979–1992,* rev. ed. Madrid: Alianza.

———. 1997. *Notas de un simulador.* Madrid: La Palma.

———. 2000. *Fragmentos de un libro futuro.* Barcelona: Galaxia Gutenberg.

———. 2001. *La voz de José Angel Valente: Poesía en la residencia.* Madrid: Publicaciones de la Residencia de estudiantes. Contains CD.

Vendler, Helen. 1995. *The given and the made.* Cambridge: Harvard University Press.

Wilden, Anthony. 1968. Lacan and the discourse of the other. In *The language of the self: The function of language in psychoanalysis,* edited by Jacques Lacan and translated by Anthony Wilden. Baltimore, MD: Johns Hopkins University Press.

Zambrano, María. 1981. La mirada originaria en la obra de José Angel Valente. *Quimera* 4: 39–42.

Old Photographs, New Views: Interpretation and Creation in Atencia's *A orillas del Ems*

ANITA M. HART

SEEING RICHNESS IN THE DETAILS OF DAILY LIFE AND CAPTURING these visions in words, Spanish poet María Victoria Atencia writes imaginative poems that explore layers beneath the surface of visible reality. Her works often show a link between concrete elements of existence and larger human issues, and her poetry frequently uncovers connections between the self and the other.[1] Atencia, awarded the Premio Nacional de la Crítica in 1998 and the Premio Luis de Góngora in 2000, is known for her carefully crafted poetry in more than fifteen books and anthologies—including *Marta & María* (Martha & Mary) (1976), *Compás binario* (Binary Time) (1984), *Paulina o el libro de las aguas* (Pauline or the Book of Waters) (1984), and *La pared contigua* (The Adjoining Wall) (1989).[2] The recent collections *Las contemplaciones* (Contemplations) and *A orillas del Ems* (On the Banks of the Ems) appeared in 1997. Atencia's poems reveal a thoughtful gaze that both engages and enhances reality. Her work recalls Claudio Rodríguez's position that poetry is born of a participation that the poet establishes between reality and his or her experience of it, through language. This participation is an unusual way of knowing (Ribes 1969, 87). Atencia's participatory process of discovering multiple levels of reality—at times creating a new consciousness—exemplifies José Angel Valente's claim that every poem is "un conocimiento 'haciéndose'" (knowledge in the making, in process) (Ribes 1969, 158). Her poems offer readers an evolving, deepening view of daily existence and human experience.

In one of her recent works, Atencia transports herself and her readers to a world beyond her own. The collection of poems titled *A orillas del Ems* (On the Banks of the Ems), written around 1985 and published in *Litoral's* special issue *El vuelo. María Victoria Atencia* (The Flight. María Victoria Atencia) (1997) was inspired by photographs of people and places in the small German town of Telgte dating from the end of the nineteenth century and the beginning of the twentieth. Atencia chose these photographs from the book *Telgte in Erinnerung: Für Bewohner und Freunde Einer Kleinen Stadt* (Telgte in Remembrance: For Residents and Friends of a Small Town), by Renate Kruchen, published in Germany in 1984. A gift to the poet from her son Álvaro when he was studying in Germany, this book attracted Atencia's attention as she observed images from the past in a culture different from her own. In *A orillas del Ems*, which includes Atencia's poems and selected photos from *Telgte in Erinnerung* on facing pages, she often gives voice to the unidentified people in the photographs, allowing them to speak of themselves and their circumstances. As the poet looks at another time and place, she uses the photographs as a point of departure for her own creation, thus interpreting the past and constructing another reality, a new reading, through her words. The poetry generates connections between the past and the present, the visual and the verbal, the other and the self. In this collection of poems "the word" in a sense expands "the world," producing multiple perspectives as Atencia resurrects a past reality, creates a vivid present moment, and occasionally anticipates a future time subsequent to the period captured in the photographs.

I think of photography as capturing a present moment, which immediately becomes a moment in the past. As I examine Atencia's poetry, it is meaningful to consider what Roland Barthes tells us of the photographic art. In his essay "Rhetoric of the Image," Barthes opines that photography "establishes not a consciousness of the *being-there* of the thing (which any copy could provoke) but an awareness of its '*having-been-there*'" (1977, 44). Following this line of thought, he elsewhere claims that the photograph testifies to "the fact that this object has indeed existed and that it has been there where I see it" (1981, 115). In Barthes's view the essence or *noeme* of photography is "That-has-been" or "the Intractable" (1981, 77). For him, photography is not a "copy" of reality, but rather "an emanation of *past reality*." As he explains, "From a real body, which was there, proceed radiations which ultimately touch me" (1981, 88, 80). Claiming that the photograph produces in him "an astonishment which endures and renews itself," Barthes continues, "this astonishment, this persistence reaches down into the religious substance out of which I am molded. . . . Photography has something to do with resurrection" (1981, 82). Further, he emphasizes a connection between himself and the people and objects photographed: "I am the reference of every photograph" (1981, 84). Critic Nancy Shawcross explains that for Barthes photography "becomes a potential forum to transform or animate the spectator into becoming the novelist, the artist, the witness" (65). Barthes claims that the photograph "possesses an evidential force" or "evidential power" (1981, 88–89; 106), which Shawcross describes as "the potential to resurrect the subject in the mind of the viewer" (65). Atencia's collection of poetry brings together photographs and poems that give life and energy to a variety of subjects—men, women, and children—who are resurrected in the minds of the poet and her readers.

The initial poem of *A orillas del Ems* invites readers to enter another place and time as the first-person speaker (whom I associate with the poet) finds herself intrigued by a house on the cover of a book of photographs. From the beginning, the poem "La casa" (The House) demonstrates the involvement of this poet-speaker in the past reality that she encounters in the visual images:

> Me adentraba por ella—ante mí en la cubierta del libro—,
> en su planta cuadrada y un silencio en sus muebles que adivino o invento:
> podría pintarla como cuando era niña y abrir con una cuchilla sus ventanas,
> porque ella era mi mundo inserto en otro mundo de intimidad discreta
> que yo invadía y daba a los demás.
> Lo que en ella pasaba—un perro, una bombilla—me resultó feliz.
>
> (IV)

> [I went deeper into it—before me on the cover of the book,
> into its square floor and a silence in its furniture that
> I guess or invent:

I could paint it as when I was a girl and open its windows
with a large knife,
because the house was my world inserted into another
world of
discreet intimacy
that I was invading and giving to the rest.
What was happening in it—a dog, a light bulb—I
found to be agreeable.]

With the verb "Me adentraba" (I went deeper) and the imperfect tense suggesting a process of entering the house on the cover, the poem opens by focusing on the poet-speaker's viewpoint and participation. The phrase "un silencio en sus muebles" (a silence in its furniture) shows that the house has been vacant for a period of time and hints that the poet-speaker probably examines a home whose residents no longer exist. The words "podría pintarla como cuando era niña" (I could paint it as when I was a girl) recall Atencia's statement that she had an early interest in painting (Ugalde 1991, 4) and suggest that she can identify with the period that the house represents. A hint of tension enters the poem with the phrase "abrir con una cuchilla sus ventanas" (open its windows with a large knife), as if the poet-speaker were piercing a veil to reveal another world, perhaps entering and violating someone else's space. She acknowledges her act of invasion and her reading of the past reality, which she offers to readers. The phrase "era mi mundo" (it was my world) indicates connections to be made between the poet-speaker as spectator and the world she observes. In one of the poems, as we shall see, she is a participant who walks into the past. In several pieces she offers a view of what may have been happening; in other poems she allows the photographed subjects to express themselves. The closing line of "La casa" leaves behind any hint of invasion and underscores a felicitous relationship between the poet-speaker and the past reality she interprets.

The photographs reproduced in *A orillas del Ems* and the poems that follow "La casa" take readers-viewers on a tour of the small German community where people, places, and objects are captured in the photographs, sometimes in carefully arranged poses and occasionally without any deliberate structuring of the scene. Atencia observes people of different ages—young, middle-aged, and old—and a variety of circumstances—including work and leisure—as she offers an imaginative reading of the reality "that-has-been," in Barthes's terms. For Barthes, "Photography is a kind of primitive theater, a kind of *Tableau Vivant*, a figuration of the motionless and made-up face beneath which we see the dead" (1977, 32). Atencia's poems, placed on the left-hand page and linked to the photographs on the right-hand page, generate new views of this *Tableau Vivant*. The poetry exposes the complementarity of life and death, as well as the ambiguity of presence and absence, as the pieces blend together the past, the present, and the future.

With the title focusing on a river, the collection *A orillas del Ems* captures the life and vitality symbolized by water and documented by photographs that stop the daily activities for a moment to invite viewers to take a close look. In a sense Atencia resurrects these scenes, revitalizing the residents and interpreting their situations. The poem "Lavandera" (Washerwoman) accompanies a photograph with the caption "Der Waschplatz an der Ems um 1900" (Washing place on the Ems about 1900) (Kruchen n.p.), showing women washing clothes on the banks of the Ems:

> De rodillas, en el tablón anclado o en la margen del Ems
> junto al nivel del agua,
> puedes mojar, enjabonar la ropa, golpearla,
> restregarla en la piedra con un compás idéntico de claridad
> y aroma,
> torcerla y retorcerla para que el chorro añada mayor espuma
> al río;
> puedes llorar, cantar, callar en tanto que renuevas
> el blanco de una sábana que supo del sudor del amor o el de
> la muerte
> que ahora, ardor y frío, se diluye contigo río abajo.
>
> (XXVI)

> [On her knees, on the anchored plank or on the banks of the Ems
> next to the level of the water,
> you can wet and soap the clothes, beat them,
> scrub them on the rock with an identical beat of brightness
> and scent,
> twist them and wring them so that the stream of water will add
>   greater foam
> to the river;
> you can cry, sing, be silent as long as you renew

the whiteness of a sheet that knew the sweat of love or of
death
that now, burning and cold, dissolves with you downstream.]

The poem and the photograph not only capture a moment in the woman's workday but also bring up many human themes, including the connections between life and death. Atencia's poem, in which the poet-speaker addresses the woman as "tú" (you), features verbs picturing the woman's actions in the process of cleaning: "puedes mojar, enjabonar la ropa, golpearla, restregarla . . . torcerla, retorcerla" (you can wet and soap the clothes, beat them, scrub them . . . twist them, wring them). Along with these infinitives, others show the woman's alternatives for expression or silence as she works: "puedes llorar, cantar, callar" (you can cry, sing, be silent). Her task is to recover the whiteness and brightness of a sheet, which bears the traces of many life experiences. In the poem, "una sábana" (a sheet) has caught the sweat of both love and death. Here "la sábana" can be interpreted metaphorically as a page on which life stories are written, erased, and rewritten. These histories find representation in the terms "ardor" (heat, burning) suggesting the passion of a relationship, and "frío" (cold), relating to death. The physical traces of these life events are laundered, ultimately merging with the water and flowing down the river.

In the final line the poet-speaker, after focusing on the actions of the washerwoman, leads readers to another level of meaning. With the phrase "se diluye contigo" (dissolves with you) the poem indicates in an understated fashion that the woman's own life story is also flowing and will ultimately pass away. The photograph of "la lavandera" may serve to remind the poet-speaker that her present existence, too, with both "ardor" (burning) and "frío" (cold), will end. Here the link between the poet-speaker as observer and the subject of the photograph is a one-sided conversation capturing a moment in a washerwoman's day, interpreted by the witness, who may be viewed as the poet. The visual and the verbal aspects work together to make this past reality a present time experience for readers and viewers, reminding us that some traces of our stories will disappear and that others may remain for some other witness to ponder.

Atencia's poem "Lavandera" brings to mind other works of Spanish poetry and art. The poem recalls Claudio Rodríguez's piece "Alto jornal" (High day's wages), with its focus on simple, honest daily work and its connection with larger issues of life and with the eternal. Rodríguez's lines "y cuando / se ha dado cuenta al fin de lo sencillo / que ha sido todo, ya el jornal ganado" (and when one has finally realized how simple everything has been, indeed the day's wages) (Ribes 1969, 105) might well apply to the efforts of the washerwoman along the banks of the Ems. She perhaps returns home content, acknowledging the spiritual nature of humble work, as does the unnamed subject of "Alto jornal" (Ribes 1969, 105). The poem "Lavandera" also reminds readers of Jorge Manrique's "Coplas por la muerte de su padre" (Stanzas on the Death of his Father) with the lines "Nuestras vidas son los ríos / que van a dar en la mar, / que es el morir" (Our lives are the rivers that run into the sea, which is death) (Manrique, 70). In Atencia's poem, both observer and observed will experience a passing and a merging with something beyond the self. Further, the poem recalls a painting by Velázquez, *La vieja cocinera* (The Old Cook), with its emphasis on the dignity of the woman who is performing her daily tasks. Velázquez, interested in the moment and immediate reality, often painted unpretentious people and real things, elevating them to the level of the immortal. Similarly, Atencia's "Lavandera," accompanied by the photograph of the washerwoman along the banks of the Ems, reflects the theme of the relationship between the everyday and the eternal. The poem captures a consciousness of a life "that-has-been," in Barthes's terms. For Barthes, "each photograph always contains this imperious sign" of his "future death" (1981, 100). Atencia's poem offers a similar sign. The photograph has led to a connection between the viewer and the subject of the photograph, one being a part of present reality observing the past and the other a participant in a past time that finds its way into the present. Readers are witnesses of both. The poet-speaker, through her verbal picture of "la lavandera," leads readers to larger issues of reality, the temporality of life that is moving toward death and the validity of the present moment as part of the eternal, themes reflected in the works of poetry and painting mentioned above.

Work is again the focus of Atencia's "El pregonero" (The Town Crier), a poem in which the first-person speaker is a town crier who announces significant as well as insignificant matters to the citizens. His photograph, like that of the woman in "Lavandera," attests to the fact that he is an entity "that-has-been," resurrected here by a viewer who offers her own interpretation of the town crier's self-assessment. The poem relates well to Barthes's claim that "Every photograph is a certificate of presence" (1981, 87). Atencia's poem offers an imaginative perspective on a presence now past:

> Por costumbre comienzo a la puerta de casa, y bien puede decirse
> que es un ensayo general de lo que debo repetir durante todo el día.
> De manera que agito la campana y convoco a mis nietos
> hasta que me rodea su parva en mitad de la calle,
> resignados a oír lo que el alcalde quiere que en la ciudad se sepa,
> lo que quiere el comercio y yo voy pregonando:
> las cosas que se venden o se compran, se pierden o se
> encuentran y el premio por su hallazgo.
> Ellos no entienden bien todo lo que les digo. Y a veces yo tampoco,
> con tantos años ya en este mismo empleo.
>
> (XXIV)

> [By habit I begin at the door of the house, and it could well be said
> that it's a general rehearsal of what I have to repeat
> all day long.
> Thus I ring the bell and call together my grandchildren
> until their innocence surrounds me in the middle of the street,
> resigned to hear what the mayor wants to be known in the city,
> what business wants and I go announcing;
> the things that are sold or bought, or lost or
> found and the reward for their recovery.
> They don't understand well everything I tell them. And at times I don't either,
> with so many years in this same job.]

The photograph from *Telgte in Erinnerung* captures the aging man with his grandchildren surrounding him to hear his first announcement of the day. In Atencia's poem the adjective "resignados" (resigned), describing the children, suggests a bit of routine and monotony in his message, as do the phrases "las cosas que se venden o se compran, se pierden o se / encuentran" (the things that are sold or bought or lost or found). The end of the poem brings a shift to the town crier's analysis of the children's less than total understanding of his words and his own lack of comprehension. This personal slant reflects a questioning of self, work, and meaning in language, an attitude that may well be the blending of the poet's view with that of the town crier. The perspective offered in the final lines leads readers to confront similar questions of meaning, facing the issue of language that is often inadequate for expression and sensing that work can become routine and incomprehensible "con tantos años ya en este mismo empleo" (with so many years in this same job). With the photograph and this poem, spectators and readers are conscious of the person's "having-been-there," having gathered his grandchildren around him as his first audience of the day, and having gone about his work with a hint of skepticism. The visual and verbal images reflect a past time, quite different from the present days of newspapers, 24-hour television news, and electronic communication. At the same time, the shift in the last two lines allows readers to see another layer of reality behind the visible appearance of the town crier. The poem "El pregonero" generates a questioning of words, meaning, and occupation; it also hints that this uncertainty is understood and accepted.

Both the poems "Lavandera" and "El pregonero" show Atencia's interpretation of the circumstances of people captured in photographs going about their daily responsibilities. Another poem that offers a reading of the individual in the world of work is "Jefe de estación" (Stationmaster), which ends with a revealing comment by the first-person speaker, who in this poem is the stationmaster. The man, who in the photograph stands erectly outside the train station, relates that his control over the coming and going of the trains brings admiration from passengers, including a specific woman on the 2:30 express who captures his interest. He celebrates the sound of a whistle, which signifies his authority and fills him with pride: "—un orgullo de / jefe— / que llega a persuadir a mis vecinos y que a mí me persuade" (a pride as boss—which comes to persuade my neighbors and even myself) (XIV). With a hint that his self-esteem is a construction resulting from the requirements of his work, the last line of "Jefe de estación" looks behind the reality of the stationmaster presented in the photograph and in the opening lines of the poem to discover a more humble character who suggests that external presentation—his job performance—has created his internal perspective. The final line gently undercuts the stationmaster's earlier enthusiasm and pride, but the ending shows that he has accepted the impression of validity and importance in his work.

Although the poem "Posan cuatro ancianas" (Four Mature Women Pose) differs from "El pregonero" in that it does not have a first-person speaker, this poem similarly offers both an interpretation of what the photograph shows and also a conjecture about what lies behind the visible past reality. Atencia's poem accompanies an image of four traditional older women photographed in fine clothes, all wearing striking white collars and dark dresses. The poem begins with an interrogative: "¿Por qué fueron creciendo sus narices?" (Why were their noses growing?) (XXVIII) Does the question suggest that the women seem to be telling a lie, appearing too perfect to reflect their existence? Whatever the implication, this disjunction underscores the interweaving of different times, with the photo of past reality and the gaze of a present-day viewer. After the question, the poem leads readers to doubt the illusion: "Pretenden / confundirnos sus crenchas divididas y el lujo de sus ropas, / sus erguidos asientos, el ganchillo o labor para beneficencia" (Their divided hair and the luxury of their clothes, their upright seats, the crochet work or charity work attempt to confuse us). Behind the appearance of good taste and decorum lies the probable hidden reality that the poet would not forget: "Se olvidaron de todo, del empuje de los años vehementes, / las guerras, el servicio y su tráfago, los niños / y las razones nunca compartidas...." (They forgot everything, the strain of the difficult years, the wars, the service and toil, the children and the reasons never shared....) The women's material finery only partially conceals the fragility of their physical and mental selves. Featuring the "magníficas señoras en su papel Habsburgo" (magnificent women in their Hapsburg role), the poem expresses curiosity about the reality behind the photograph, encouraging readers to consider the women's experiences that would otherwise remain unexpressed and unnoticed.

The photographs of the citizens of Telgte and Atencia's poems in *A orillas del Ems* capture the lives of people of all ages and circumstances. In addition to the pieces that offer the poet's creative reading of the lives of adults from Telgte who are engaged in work or other commitments, several selections focus on young adults and children pursuing their activities. Whereas the poems on adults often bring to light issues in their lives—past or present—that lie behind the reality captured by the camera, the poems centering around young people often explore another layer of existence, some aspect of the future that they could not know at the point in the past when they were photographed. For example, the poem "Pareja" (Couple) celebrates the present and hints at the future of a young couple dressed for their wedding. With a look at the photo of the two, the speaker in the poem compares the bride to a work of Rosenthal porcelain. In contrast to her beauty and elegance, the groom appears "serio en exceso" (excessively serious) and yet at the same time he catches the viewer's attention because of his stance: "parece asomar su cabeza sobre un cuerpo que no es / exactamente el suyo" (his head seems to appear over a body that is not exactly his own) (XXX). This twist, reflecting the scrutiny and curiosity of the observer, breaks the illusion of the photo to accentuate the overlapping realities of a past existence and a viewer belonging to a later time. The touch of gentle humor may show the man's discomfort or tension as he stands in formal dress before the camera on this occasion. The closing lines of the poem celebrate the anticipated happiness to be found in this relationship, but the ending reminds readers of the difficulties that also characterize the human experience: "Juntos van a afrontar momentos de intensa luz—las luces / enceguecen más que las sombras mismas— / y largas, largas horas de apacible penumbra" (Together they are going to face moments of intense light—lights are more blinding than shadows—and long, long hours of gentle darkness) (XXX). The dualities of light and darkness are complementary: they exist in relationship. Readers looking at the photograph and reading "Pareja" progress through a poem that begins with a celebration of the bride's appearance and dress, continues with a good-natured dig at the rigid groom, and concludes with a reflection on the inevitable existence of pain within a life of love. Atencia's piece, with its shifts in focus and the conclusion that points to larger issues of human life, recalls Valente's claim that every poem is knowledge in the making.

"Joven con bicicleta" (Young Man with Bicycle), another poem on the perspective of a youth whose future is yet to be experienced, presents a first-person speaker, a young man who is delighted that his bicycle allows him to gain freedom from his immediate surroundings. At the same time, the words of the poem bring to light the circumstances of his life that touch him greatly, tying him closely to the world that he escapes for a brief outing. Atencia gives voice to the young man, offering multiple perspectives, both his awareness of the experience of the moment and a consciousness of the future that he could not know at the time of the photograph:

> El manillar fundido dice el calor de mis manos asiéndolo
> con un fuego que penetra el cartón y llega a vuestra época.
> Tengo al fin lo soñado: avanzo sobre ruedas, ya soy un triunfador
> que recorre los húmedos campos aspirando su aroma,
> caracol sucesivo del verde tras la lluvia.
> Los atentos del otro lado podréis ver la brillante cadena que me cruza el pecho,
> la gorra de visera que fue moda entonces,
> mas, tal vez, no el amor que ya se despertaba asombrando mis ojos;
> la cara de manzana de Gretchen a la hora del recreo,
> los disgustos de Herr Professor con su vara severa.
> Algo mío poseo en el campo que cruzo:
> un mundo que no sueño sino que tomo y alzo y que muevo a mi gusto,
> hechura de mis manos guiando, de mis pies al pedal,
> mientras van agotándose los días de anteguerra.
>
> (XVI)

> [The cast handlebars take on the heat of my hands, burning with a fire that penetrates the cardboard cover and arrives at your age.
> I have at last what I have dreamed of: I move forward on wheels, already I'm
> a victor
> who travels over the humid fields breathing their aroma,
> successive snail of green after the rain.
> You observant ones on the other side will be able to see the brilliant chain that

crosses my chest,
the cap with visor that was in style at the time,
but, perhaps, not the love that was already awakening, astounding
my eyes;
Gretchen's apple face at the recess hour,
the displeasure of Sir Professor with his severe rod.
I possess something of my own in the field that I cross:
a world that I don't dream about but rather that I take and lift
    and move
at my pleasure,
a creation of my hands guiding, of my feet on the pedal,
while the days before the war go slipping away.]

The opening lines introduce a first-person speaker, the young man pictured on his bicycle in the accompanying photograph, who is aware that his activity and energy can be observed by others. The words "el calor de mis manos" (the heat of my hands) and "un fuego" (a fire) capture the vitality the youth enjoys, as well as an enthusiasm that present-day readers perceive. These lines recall Barthes's claim that the radiations proceeding from photographs ultimately touch the observer.[3] Atencia's poem creates an unanticipated perspective that represents a departure from the usual observation of the individual in time. Here it is the person from the past who expects viewers of the future to see his adventure. The poem works to capture the intensity of the young man's feelings of triumph and freedom when his dream becomes a reality: "ya soy un / triunfador" (Already I'm a victor), choosing his own direction, winding his way through the countryside. In a strange comparison, the triumphant youth becomes a snail that emerges after the rain to cut a path through the green earth. He celebrates options and multiple ways to proceed through life.

In the section of the poem that begins "Los atentos del otro lado" (You observant ones on the other side), the first-person speaker addresses those of a future time (on the other side of death), pointing out the chain he proudly wears across his chest and the stylish cap with visor, both obvious in the photograph. Atencia's poem contrasts this observable reality with what lies behind or beneath the exterior, the young man's experiences as uncovered by her interpretation: love, a girl's face, the displeasure of a teacher. The poet gets behind the photograph to create and reveal hidden feelings. The final lines of the poem highlight the reality embraced by the character who generates his own world. The assertion that he possesses something truly his own and the first-person verbs "cruzo" (I cross), "no sueño" (I don't dream), "tomo" (I take), "alzo" (I lift), and "muevo" (I move) intensify his experience and his conscious effort. The phrases "a mi gusto" (at my pleasure), "hechura de mis manos" (creation of my hands), and "mis pies al pedal" (my feet on the pedal) focus on the individual, his choices, and his control. The sobering last line of the poem provides a context not actually known by "Joven con bicicleta"—the days preceding World War I. The understated ending contrasts the young man's sense of freedom and pleasure with a future world of war and destruction that is not yet part of his reality. Is there a chance that he died in the war? Blurring the lines between past, present, and future as the young man looks back at himself and converses with viewers, the poem allows readers to see him from multiple angles as he hints at both his lack of knowledge of the future and his later understanding of the difficult times ahead.

"Las tres gracias" (The Three Graces), another poem featuring youth at play, interprets the experience of three young women posing for the camera in swim attire, offering their response to being photographed. The photo in the book *Telgte in Erinnerung* provides the caption "Bademoden 1904" (Bathing style 1904), along with the names of the three: Valerchen and Paula Hardensett and Lisbet Klostermann (n.p.). In Atencia's poem the three adolescents, who must have reminded her of the mythological characters descended from Zeus and Hera or Eurynome, become first-person speakers who voice their memory of slight discomfort and indifference:

> La sensación penosa no supimos borrarla, aunque sólo los brazos
> y las piernas mostrábamos con aquel bañador azul y aquel gorro ridículo.
> Tan jóvenes, no habíamos perdido aún la noción de las cosas
> e ignorábamos el gozoso desnudo que del amor se viste. Eso vino más tarde.
> Pero entonces, al mirar nuestra imagen sentimos un pudor

invencible:
ni siquiera pensábamos en nadie al ponernos delante de la máquina.

(VI)

[We didn't find out how to erase the sad feeling, although we showed only arms
and legs, with that blue swimsuit and that
ridiculous bathing cap.
So young, we had not already lost the notion
of things
and we didn't understand the happy bareness that is dressed in love. That
came later.
But then, looking at our image we felt an unconquerable modesty:
we didn't even think about anyone as we positioned ourselves before the
camera].

Atencia's piece presents the young women as if they had moved forward in time, looking at their photo and remembering themselves dressed in a blue swimsuit or a ridiculous cap on that particular occasion. The scene recalls Barthes's reference to the "evidential power" of the photograph and its ability to resurrect the subject in the mind of the viewer. One viewer is, of course, the poet. In this poem the subjects also become viewers: the adolescents of the past and the "nosotras" (we) of a later point in time are merged. The three comment on their youth and their swimwear, which actually revealed very little of their bodies. They were too young, the poem tells us, to know experiences of life and love that would come in the future. The notion of uncovering oneself contrasts with the fairly well covered bodies of "las tres gracias" (the three graces). Atencia's poem captures the nonchalance the three demonstrate in the photograph: "ni siquiera pensábamos en nadie" (we didn't even think about anyone). Like the bicycle rider, they did not know what would come later in their lives.

Another poem that interprets the reaction of those in the photograph is "Heinrich und Clärchen" (Henry and Clara), featuring two children dressed especially for the occasion and solemnly posing for the event. They are the speakers in the poem who remember their experience of facing the camera, which the children's eyes see as a threatening insect of wood: "Tenemos angustias, es cierto, mi hermanito y yo. / Hoy nos pusieron las ropas de domingo / y a lo oscuro nos llevaron de la mano. / Opaco es el cristal con que estuvo fijamente mirándonos / aquel amenazante insecto de madera" (X) (We are anxious, it's true, my little brother and I. Today they dressed us in Sunday clothes and took us by the hand to darkness. Opaque is the lens with which that threatening wooden insect stared at us fixedly). The present tense verbs of the first part of the poem show the children recounting their adventure and their concern. The final part of the piece, with preterite verbs, shifts the children's involvement to remembering the past to which they belong: "Rozarnos a escondidas nos mantuvo en silencio / hasta que al fin volvimos a la casa querida / donde en el perchero colgaba el traje de marinero de / Heinrich / y mi gorra de lazo pendiente a la derecha, / frente al cartón roído por los peces de plata / y el olor a nosotros, distancia y naftalina" (Touching secretly kept us in silence until finally we returned to our beloved home where on the hanger hung Henry's sailor suit and my hat with ribbon trailing on the right, facing the cardboard eaten away by silverfish and the smell of ourselves, distance and mothballs) (X). The poem generates ambiguity and a play of perspectives, making the children spectators who see themselves as "that-has-been" or "having-been-there." They observe that their clothes are hung near a box eaten away by silverfish and that their scent, along with that of mothballs, reflects a distant time. Atencia's poem allows the children to appear as both past and present reality, both tensing for the threatening camera and recalling the experience, which was partially understood, from a later point in time. They could not know that a poet would interpret them as looking back from the future to remember the past event and their reaction.

Also focusing on youth, the poem "La niña" (The Child) differs from "Joven con bicicleta" (Young Man with Bicycle), "Las tres gracias" (The Three Graces), and "Heinrich und Clärchen" (Henry and Clara) in that from the beginning it establishes a connection between the first-person poet-speaker and the child who is addressed, the "tú" (you). "La niña" is based on a photograph in *Telge* that bears the identification: Inni Stumpe 1927 "Mein erster Schultag" (My first day of school) (*Telge in Erinnerung* n. p.).

Atencia's poem blurs the lines of differentiation between the viewer and the young German girl:

> La niña de trenzas y flequillo, de babero y maleta a la
> espalda,
> en la que me enseñaron a reconocerme las fotos de los míos,
> hoy, frente a mí, en este cuaderno aparece.
> Coincidencia feliz: de esa criatura vine
> para llegar a ella tras de un largo camino.
> Te lo ruego: sigue tú misma, o vuelve y disfruta de tus
> padres aún jóvenes,
> la borrega y el agua en el cauce de piedra. No te preocupes:
> soy una de esas señoras que se encuentran a veces de visita
> en las casas
> y cuyo nombre no vuelve a recordarse.
>
> (XXXII)

> [The child with braids and bangs, with smock and bookbag on her
> shoulder,
> the one in whom I recognize myself from photos of my family,
> today, in front of me, appears in this notebook.
> Happy coincidence: from this creature I came
> to arrive at her after a long trip.
> I beg you: go ahead or return and enjoy your
> youthful parents,
> the lamb and the water in the river bed. Don't worry:
> I am one of those women who are found visiting
> in homes
> and whose name is not remembered again.]

The poet-speaker, claiming to see a bit of herself in "la niña," creates an ambiguous blend and separation of identities between the two with the phrase "de esa criatura vine / para llegar a ella tras de un largo camino" (from this creature I came to arrive at her after a long trip). She addresses the child, encouraging her to carry on with her life or to enjoy the variety of her existence, everything from her young parents to a young lamb to water in a river bed. The child should not be concerned about the older woman who appears before her. Here the poem creates a reversal in which the viewer sees "la niña" as able to observe the poet-speaker as present in that past moment. Or, from another perspective, the poet-speaker inserts herself into the child's reality, walking in to visit, as so many women did. "La niña" is the "emanation of past reality," as Barthes explained the subject of a photograph, and in Atencia's poem the child engages the poet-speaker with her look. She has an effect on the viewer, who recognizes herself in the child and contemplates her own passage from youth to old age. The photo of Inni Stumpe and the poem "La niña" offer visual and verbal images that indicate a blending of presence and absence as they capture the vitality of the young girl on her first day of school and at the same time suggest that the child is a past entity who may no longer be alive. The poem ends as the poet-speaker reminds herself that she may be forgotten. In the future she will be the unknown and the unrecognized: "una de esas señoras que se encuentran a veces de visita / en las casas / y cuyo nombre no vuelve a recordarse" (one of those women who are found visiting in homes and whose name is not remembered again). Just as she entered the book in the initial poem "La casa," she departs from the scene in "La niña," leaving her words for readers to contemplate.[4]

Atencia's *A orillas del Ems* offers a multitude of faces, stories, poses, actions, and reflections. The photographs that serve as a basis for the poetry "resurrect the subject in the mind of the viewer," in Barthes' words. They inspire Atencia as poet to be the witness and the storyteller, creating her version of the theater or *Tableau Vivant* that Barthes sees in photography. The visual and the verbal aspects work together to give readers a picture of people living in community. The poems retrieve the past and tell it as present, with hints of the future, occasionally with the viewer's consciousness that someday she will be part of the past. Conversing with and through others, the poet reveals details about their lives, often uncovering hidden layers of existence and frequently connecting self and other. Atencia establishes a participation with the reality she observes, as Rodríguez has claimed that poets do, offering her vision or generating a possible scenario. The photographs and the poems transform us as readers into witnesses of a slice of humanity along the banks of the Ems decades ago. Although the individuals may have disappeared, the fact of their "having-been-there" remains, thus affirming the ties between life and death. Atencia's interpretation of a past world in *A orillas del Ems* calls to mind the role of language as presented in the final lines of Jorge Guillén's "Sospecha de foca" (Seal Suspected): "A la realidad ya toca / Con su potencia el lenguaje" (Language already touches reality with its power). For Andrew

Debicki, Guillén's poem provides "a commentary on how poetry weaves beauty from reality" (1994, 131). In a unique way Atencia's poems, offering new views of the circumstances captured in the photographs, create yet another reality, one that complements and enlivens the photographs. Here "the word" expands "the world," with multiple, shifting perspectives. The people of Telgte, visually immortalized by the camera and verbally interpreted by the poet, come alive.

Notes

This work was supported in part by funds provided by the University of Nebraska at Kearney Office of Graduate Studies and Research / Research Services Council. I wish to thank María Victoria Atencia for showing me the book *Telgte in Erinnerung* as we conversed about her life and work. I am grateful to *Litoral: revista de la poesía y el pensamiento* for permission to quote poems by Atencia. All translations are my own.

1. In recent scholarship on Atencia's work, Sharon Keefe Ugalde explains that Atencia's poetry is distinguished by her ability to make moments of insight and transcendence seem eternal as well as by her inclination to reveal a fusion of the self with the other (1998, 14–15). Biruté Ciplijauskaité, pointing out the dualities that other critics have studied in regard to Atencia's focus on daily reality and spiritual or abstract directions, emphasizes that the poet's works feature a constant juxtaposition of two worlds, two points of view, and two emotions as well as the use of dialogue and a search for the essences (1998, 43–44). For Andrew Debicki, Atencia often uses poetic strategies that transform particular events or elements of reality so that they acquire wider meanings (1998, 57, 63).

2. Unless otherwise noted, all translations to English in this text are my own.

3. In a similar vein, Susan Sontag claims that the photograph "is a part of, an extension of that subject" (155).

4. I wish to thank Professor Martha LaFollette Miller for her observation that with the first poem, "La casa," and the last one, "La niña," Atencia frames the other poems with two pieces in which she enters the book and then ultimately departs.

Works Cited

Atencia, María Victoria. 1997. *A orillas del Ems. El vuelo. María Victoria Atencia*. Málaga: Litoral.

Barthes, Roland. 1977. *Image / music / text*. Trans. Stephen Heath. New York: Hill and Wang.

———. 1981. *Camera Lucida: Reflections on Photography*. Trans. Richard Howard. New York: Hill and Wang.

Ciplijauskaité, Biruté. 1998. El compromiso alado de María Victoria Atencia. In *La poesía de María Victoria Atencia: Un acercamiento crítico*, edited by Sharon Keefe Ugalde. Madrid: Huerga & Fierro..

Debicki, Andrew P. 1994. *Spanish poetry of the twentieth century: Modernity and beyond*. Lexington: University Press of Kentucky.

———. 1998. La transformación artística del referente en Marta & María, Los sueños y el mundo de María Victoria Atencia. In *La poesía de María Victoria Atencia: Un acercamiento crítico*, edited by Sharon Keefe Ugalde. Madrid: Huerga & Fierro.

Kruchen, Renate. 1984. *Telgte in erinnerung: Für bewohner und freunde einer kleinen stadt*. (Telgte in remembrance: For residents and friends of a small town.) Harsewinkel, Germany.

Manrique, Jorge. 1970. Coplas por la muerte de su padre. In *Spanish poetry from its beginnings through the nineteenth century: An anthology*, edited by Willis Barnstone. New York: Oxford University Press.

Ribes, Francisco, ed. 1969. *Poesía última*. Madrid: Taurus.

Shawcross, Nancy M. 1997. *Roland Barthes on photography: The critical tradition in perspective*. Gainesville: University Press of Florida.

Sontag, Susan. 1977. *On photography*. New York: Farrar, Straus and Giroux.

Ugalde, Sharon Keefe. 1991. Conversación con María Victoria Atencia. In *Conversaciones y poemas: La nueva poesía femenina española en castellano*. Madrid: Siglo Veintiuno.

———, ed. 1998. Presentación. La palabra atenciana en el umbral. In *La poesía de María Victoria Atencia: Un acercamiento crítico*. Madrid: Huerga & Fierro.

Writing the Book of Life: Ana Rossetti's *Punto umbrío*

MARTHA LaFOLLETTE

ONE OF THE STRONGEST THREADS OF CONTEMPORARY THOUGHT has been the questioning of the relationship between signs and things. In overturning the assumption that experience precedes its capturing in words or pictures, Oscar Wilde's conceit that "Life imitates Art far more than Art imitates Life" (20) anticipated a line of thinking that extends from Saussure to the present day. According to Terry Eagleton, the defining feature of the "'linguistic revolution' of the twentieth century" is the "recognition that meaning is not simply something 'expressed' or 'reflected' in language: it is actually *produced* by it" (60).[1] For poststructuralist poets and their readers, cognizance of the unbridgeable gap between words and things has created problems but has also brought opportunity. Along with skepticism and creative self-doubt has emerged considerable creative freedom. Ana Rossetti's important volume of poetry *Punto umbrío* (Shadowy Point)—published in 1995 and ten years in the making—reflects her awareness of the impossibility of finding presence or groundedness through the written word, as well as a profound ambivalence toward the search for transcendent meaning, even in relationships. Ultimately, however, her book has a positive message: she opts for courage in the face of doubt and gives herself over to life's experiences and to the artistic potential of the written word. At the same time, she endows her word with a political significance that gives her work the force of action.

In *Punto umbrío* Rossetti intensifies and deepens her exploration of many of the issues that appeared in the writings she published in the 1980s and 1990s.[2] Before embarking on an analysis of this significant addition to her *oeuvre*, a review of some characteristics of her previous works is in order. A variety of poetic and narrative texts (often characterized by an erotic sensibility that caught the attention of critics in Spain and abroad) embody Rossetti's intense consciousness of the gap between words and things. Sometimes this awareness assumes the form of undecidability, produced when textual clues point to two competing or alternative interpretations. The arresting poem from *Dióscuros*[3] identified as "Uno" (One) (Rossetti 1987, 68) exemplifies this phenomenon. The text apparently evokes a childhood memory and thus suggests the act of witnessing, as does the event narrated: a girl observing the actions of her brother. But in simultaneously activating two diverse meanings of a particular phrase ("ardiente esperma" can signify both burning candle wax and "burning" sperm) the text calls into question the possibility of fixed meanings behind verbal constructs. The double meaning, in fact, seems to generate the text, which then becomes a linguistic artifact whose relationship with actual events is impossible to determine. The protagonist's name, Anna, coincides with yet differs from that of the poet, which reinforces the notion of the double nature of language as both truth and lie. In another poem, the well-known "Chico Wrangler"(Wrangler Boy), Rossetti plays with her reader in a similar fashion. Here the object of the speaker's desire bifurcates into both a person and an advertising photograph, perceived simultaneously through the speaker's eyes and the photographer's lens.

In some senses, the two examples cited above, "Uno" and "Chico Wrangler," call into question Mirella Servodidio's 1992 reference to Rossetti's poetry as "(t)he flesh become word," a phrase that seems to suggest some kind of correspondence between the two elements.[4] According to Servodidio, in Rossetti's "double voiced discourse of desire," "the ligatures between the literal and the metaphoric, between eroticism as an act of the imagination and as an act of the flesh are everywhere apparent" (318; 326). The indeterminacy of Rossetti's texts makes it possible to argue equally as well that Servodidio's ligatures are also gaps—gaps between experience and its representation that in her poetry are "everywhere apparent."

In the works that led up to *Punto umbrío*, Rossetti pointed to the lack of coincidence between world and word not only through creating undecidable texts but also through her intertextual appropriation of the master narratives of the Western tradition. Through the constant intrusion of these master narratives into situations that are framed as the stuff of conventional lyric poetry (the unique, evanescent, emotional experience of the lyrical voice), Rossetti acknowledges the conditioning of human perception by language and confirms Northrop Frye's dictum that literature is made out of other literature. Among the master narratives that play foundational roles in Rossetti's works are the fall from Eden, martyrdom in various forms, and Christ's crucifixion. Additionally, the experience of her poetic speakers is often mediated by specific literary predecessors. One such case, "Homenaje a Lindsay Kemp y a su tocado de plumas amarillas" (Homage to Lindsay Kemp and his Headdress of Yellow Feathers) (Rossetti 1987, 47–48) offers Rossetti's interpretation of a transvestite rendition of Wilde's recasting of Salome's version of the Dance of the Seven Veils. This text creates a kind of closed-circuit or house-of-mirrors *mise en abime* of textual renderings.

Mediation through master narratives and literary citations is related to another type of doubling found in Rossetti's poetry, that of ekphrasis. In enlightening studies on this topic, Margaret Persin and María Inés Zaldívar have noted the centrality of visual elements in Rossetti's poetry. Indeed, some of the master narratives she incorporates into her work are among the prime subjects of Western religious art.[5] In dealing with these eclectic cultural borrowings, however, Rossetti's poetry has always embodied both tradition and rupture.[6] Time and again she has written both with and against the grain of the patriarchal master narratives and the voices of previous writers.

Not surprisingly, Rossetti's consciousness of the fictional nature of experience (that is to say of meaning-making as an approximation conditioned by linguistic and artistic models) led her to a fascination with the theatrical and to various types of involvement with theater. As a child, she was intrigued by her grandmother's trunk filled with old-fashioned clerical and military costumes, as well as by liturgical events and spectacle (Ugalde 153–55). As an adult, she has maintained many connections with the theater, writing plays and librettos as well as performing.[7] Her theatrical approach to self-presentation is apparent in some of her photographs, in which she poses *à la Dietrich*. Yet at the same time, she views herself as primarily a spectator in life: "[A]nte todo y sobre todo soy espectadora. Todo lo miro desde el palco" (154)—(Above all I'm a spectator. I view everything from the box seat). While Rossetti's combination of theatricality with spectatorship may seem paradoxical, in reality it is not as contradictory as it might seem. Writer and reader, actor and spectator, operate in a fictional milieu created by various types of language and at a remove from any unmediated experience of reality.

In many works leading up to *Punto umbrío*, Rossetti incorporated her personal theatrical bent into her writings, often portraying human behavior as following social and/or literary scripts. When Ugalde commented on the dramatic nature of many of her poems, the poet described them as "embriones de guiones" (embryonic scripts). Both of her novels, *Plumas de España* (Feathers of Spain) (1988) and *Mentiras de papel* (Paper Lies) (1994), deal with performers (and with sex roles). Rossetti based her art in these works on the premise that human behavior involves the adoption of roles given to us with our language (whether that language be verbal or visual). Like her texts with no decidable meaning, her characters live out their life stories by adopting various fictional personae. She frequently presents language, sexuality, and gender in theatrical terms. Experience, in these writings, becomes tainted by, infused, and fused with fiction. Theatricality relates to the lack of coincidence between words and things; paradoxically, our lives imitate and partially coincide with those of our models, leaving us forever unable to access experience without mediation. Although erotic love in literary and mystical tradition often signifies union and ineffability, in Rossetti consciousness of the impossibility of union is also ever-present. In titling her novel *Mentiras de papel*, she highlights not the essential truth of art but the essential lie, perhaps alluding as well to Oscar Wilde (a major influence for Rossetti) and to his assertion that "Lying, the telling of beautiful untrue things, is the proper aim of Art" (23).

As my references to gender roles suggest, Rossetti's works exhibit a confluence between the sexual subject and the writing subject. As Zaldívar points out, writing permits women to liberate themselves from the historical patriarchal pattern in which the female was simply "a text/object written by men" (24). Zaldívar sees in Rossetti's works the following alteration in the conventional pattern: "(L)a relación sujeto poseedor y objeto poseído se reemplaza por una relación en la cual, más que hablar de un sujeto poseedor y de un objeto poseído, tiene que hablarse de roles o papeles intercambiables entre sujeto/objeto poseedor/poseído" (The relationship possessing subject and possessed object is replaced by a relationship in which, rather than speaking of a possessing subject and possessed object, one has to speak of roles that are interchangeable between subject/object, possessor/possessed) (83). Zaldívar's terms recall the duality of Rossetti/actor and Rossetti/spectator, as well as the fundamental role of the imagination in her works, rightly pointed out by Servodidio.

As a continuation of Rossetti's earlier work, *Punto umbrío* incorporates the constellation of characteristics found in those works, including undecidability, eclectic appropriation of master narratives and literary allusions, theatricality, and destabilization or erasure of the distinction between erotic subject and object. Yet the volume differs from Rossetti's earlier volumes of poetry in various ways. In *Punto umbrío* the confluence between writing and the erotic subject continues, but emphasis shifts somewhat. A more reflective mood replaces what Servodidio saw as the "ravenous sexual energy," the "physicality and jouissance" of Rossetti's poetry (318), and for that reason the *writing* subject, in relation to gender roles, becomes at least as important as the erotic subject position. Much as Zaldívar notes the interchangeable nature of roles of subject and object in earlier works (the novelty being the female's assumption of the role of subject), here the speaker—pointedly identified neither as masculine nor as feminine—appropriates a full register of discourse that goes beyond one gender.[8] In earlier works, Rossetti's speakers assumed what was a male prerogative by turning men into the object and by expressing sexual desire, while she as poet appropriated the patriarchal master narratives to her own use. Much as in those writings Rossetti expropriated masculine sexual/textual terrain—through the gaze—here she expropriates masculine discourse terrain, through employing images of warfare, politics, and weaponry.[9] Many of her images call to mind cinematic clichés. Thus while she evoked fashion photography in certain earlier poems, here she makes a case for women's access to perhaps the most powerful collective vocabulary of our times, that of film. It is not coincidental that the protagonist of *Mentiras de papel,* the novel she was working on at the same time she was writing *Punto umbrío,* is a female model who becomes a filmmaker. The self-assertion that in earlier books took the form of narrated situations or incidents (as in "Marinero en tierra" [Sailor on Land]), or of a female voice that shocked readers by assuming male prerogatives, here takes the form of refusal of the gendered voice, of the appropriation of masculine spheres of discourse, and of identification with male poets through intertextuality. Thus in *Punto umbrío* Rossetti takes the political import of her poetic art one step further.

Other differences between Rossetti's previous works of poetry and *Punto umbrío* include the comparatively greater narrative unity of the latter work and its more introspective tone. As she herself has suggested, in earlier volumes Rossetti created miniscripts—poems that presented contextualized dramatic situations. Here, on the other hand, the volume as a whole tells a story, with individual poems forming part of the sequence. (Like *Mentiras de papel, Punto umbrío* tells a story of setbacks and determination.) The volume's narrative unity reminds us that, much more so than some other poets, Rossetti is a teller of tales, as her varied production, including stories, children's books, novels, plays, and librettos, confirms. But although she continues her storytelling in *Punto umbrío,* Rossetti permits her speaker much more introspection than in earlier works, where "the relation to the self" was "one of exteriority" and the "interiority of her poetic subjects . . . largely foreclosed by scrupulous avoidance of a confessional or self-questioning mode" (Servodidio, 320). A personal journey emerges from the twenty-nine poems of the collection, though the reader must infer most of the anecdotal significance. The work's opacity, as well as the need to read the poems sequentially, makes the book more challenging than Rossetti's previous works. Ironically and paradoxically, the poet who has worked to fully liberate the voice of the female erotic subject dons a veil when dealing with emotionally intimate topics.

The poet opens *Punto umbrío* with three poems headed by Roman numerals I, II, and III. The twenty-six poems that follow, neither titled nor numbered, form the main body of the volume.

Elsewhere, in a detailed exposition of the story line of *Punto umbrío*, I identified poems I, II, and III as evocations of three important life stages that the speaker has left behind: childhood, adolescence, and young adulthood (see Miller "Continuidad y ruptura" [Continuity and Rupture]). The remaining twenty-six poems convey, despite a lack of contextualization and enigmatic language, the story of a love affair in midlife, which the speaker approaches encumbered by memories, his/her personal history, and fear.[10] The affair's eventual failure does not destroy the spirit of the speaker. By the end of the volume, s/he manages to put his/her struggle into the context of the human condition, which demands the realization, as Rossetti put it in an interview, that "la principal esencia de la vida es que termina" (the principle essence of life is that it ends) (Ugalde, 157). Ultimately the speaker embraces life on its own terms (with death inseparable from the life principle associated with the erotic). Life and love are self-consuming, yet the speaker of *Punto umbrío* ends up giving him/herself up to the intensity of experience nevertheless. John Wilcox noted the similarity of this giving oneself up to life with a master narrative that has fascinated Rossetti from the beginning—that of martyrdom, noting that "(I)n the final poem . . . , the speaker offers herself up to love, like a lamb to the slaughter, and like a mystic to her goddess."

In addition to being an amorous autobiography that portrays love as a kind of martyrdom, the book relates the tale of the author's sacrifice as she performs the writing process in creating her poems. Despite inevitable failure caused by the treason of words and thus the impossibility of coincidence, the author consummates her own love affair with the word in an almost sexual act that, although doomed to failure, represents a noble effort. The book not only tells a story but in itself is an event—a significant action carried out by the poet.

The linguistic richness of the poems of *Punto umbrío* precludes a detailed analysis of the entire work. I will therefore limit myself, first, to a discussion of five poems that present the speaker's initial situation and reveal his/her existential dilemma, and second, to a brief examination of the speaker's situation in the two final poems, after love's failure. The first of these six poems begins with an admonition. The emotionally deadened speaker cautions him/herself against amorous involvements:

No quieras de hoy más que, dócil, el día
cumpla su plazo.
Que vaya, al vivir, siendo.
Lejos de las conjunciones de los horóscopos que no
predecirán la belleza ni impedirán su destrucción.
Lejos de los sentimientos y sus ataduras que determinan
las conjugaciones de las sílabas.
Del tiempo sacudido y convulso donde no hay otro
ahora que en el imperativo del deseo.
Del arrepentimiento y la nostalgia que se inscriben en el
tiempo imperfecto de la memoria.
Lejos del imán de las ambiciones y del reclamo de los
sentidos que pertenecen al futuro inmediato de la
tentación.
No, no quieras de hoy más que, enamorado, el día, al contemplarse, se conciba, se nutra y, por sí mismo, muera.
Que en sí se reconozca y se perciba
lejos de las conjuraciones de los astros y de las abjuraciones
de los verbos,
lejos de esta irresistible rebeldía que, sin embargo,
embarga.

(19)

[Don't wish more from today than that the day, docile,
Complete its term.
That it continue, as it lives, to be.
Far from the conjunctions of horoscopes that won't
Predict beauty nor impede its destruction.
Far from feelings and their bonds that determine
The conjugations of syllables.
From shaken and convulsed time where there's no other
Now than in desire's imperative.
From the regret and nostalgia that are inscribed in the
Imperfect tense of memory.
Far from the magnet of ambitions and the call of the
Senses that belong to temptation's immediate future.
No, don't wish from today anything more than that, enamored,
   the day,
Contemplating itself, conceive of and nurture itself, and by
   itself, die.
That in itself it recognize itself and perceive itself
Far from the conjurations of the stars and the abjurations
Of verbs,

Far from this irresistible rebelliousness that, nevertheless,
Arrests.]

The speaker makes a strong case for a posture of passive renunciation. When desire takes over, he/she cautions, the now becomes the need to satisfy that desire, which in turn gives way to consummation as regret, nostalgia, and memory (lines 10–11). Rossetti's repeated use of technical terms related to grammar underscores the confluence of language and eroticism. Speaking of "conjugaciones" (conjugations) and "sílabas" (syllables), she counterposes the imperative mood of desire to what comes later—the inevitable imperfect tense when consummation is only a memory. The phrase "las conjunciones de los horóscopos" (the conjunctions of horoscopes) (an acoustic parallel to "las conjugaciones de las sílabas" [the conjugations of syllables]) suggests that although the language of the zodiac may seem to point to a love that is in the stars, astrological predictions are deceptively incomplete. Because of the link between the zodiac and words, established through the parallel construction, the falsity of the horoscopes also taints with untruth the language alluded to in the phrase "conjugaciones de las sílabas." Double meanings reinforce the reader's uncertainty. Do the "conjunctions of horoscopes" imply conjoining, or merely grammatical categories? Do feelings determine "conjugaciones," or vice-versa? And which meaning of "conjurar" does the reference to "las conjuraciones de los astros" (the conjurations of the stars) invoke—"ligarse con otro, mediante juramento, para algún fin" (to join with another, through a vow, for some purpose), "conspirar, uniéndose muchas personas o cosas contra alguien, para hacerle daño o perderle" (to conspire, with many persons or things uniting against someone, in order to do him or her harm or ruin him) or "invocar la presencia de los espíritus" (to invoke the presence of spirits) (*Diccionario de la Real Academia Española*, 21st ed.). Surely one should avoid entanglements, the speaker avows, suggesting they are dangerous and illusory. Yet he/she clearly undermines his/her own message of skepticism and restraint by what s/he does rather than what s/he says, that is, by reveling in the very description of what s/he cautions against. S/he spends eighteen of the twenty-one lines of the poem drawing our attention to the compelling nature of love, with its "tiempo sacudido y convulso" (shaken and convulsed time), its magnetism and temptation, its irresistible pull. In contrast to the vitality of entanglements in lines 4–21, the renunciation of the first three lines is highly insipid. In characterizing the desire for carnal knowledge as an "irresistible rebeldía" (irresistible rebelliousness), the speaker further undermines the conviction of his/her warning and foreshadows events to come by hinting to the reader that indeed s/he will give in to temptation.[11] This fascination with the proscribed is consistent with opinions Rossetti expressed about her early religious education in her interview with Sharon Keefe Ugalde:

> La visión del paraíso, tal como nos la han puesto en el catecismo, y hasta en Milton y en Dante, es un paraíso estático, inerte y muerto. Contrastaba con el infierno, para cuya descripción se llenaba páginas y páginas. Tenías 5.000 torturas, 5.000 formas de pasártelo mal, siempre excitantes y terroríficas. Cuando llegaban al cielo, se quedaban sin palabras, porque ya no pasaba nada. El tenerlo todo, el estar plena de todo, es de verdad una visión del paraíso que no puedo concebir. Si el paraíso es así, ¿para qué quieres la eternidad? ¿para qué quieres un minuto? El ver diariamente que todo es inmutable, inmodificable e inmovible, es un paraíso eterno que da angustia. (162–63)

> [The vision of Paradise, the way they presented it to us in the catechism, and even in Milton and Dante, is a static, inert, and dead Paradise. It contrasted with Hell, for whose description they filled pages and pages. It had 5,000 tortures, 5,000 ways of having a bad time, all of them exciting and terrifying. When they got around to Heaven, they had no words left, because there was no longer anything happening. Having everything, being full of everything, is truly a vision of Paradise that I can't conceive of. If Paradise is that way, why would you want eternity? Why would you want one minute? To see every day that everything is immutable, unchangeable, and immovable is an eternal Paradise that produces anguish].

The fourth of the unnumbered texts, "Permanecer en las sombras" (To remain in the shadows), begins a new phase in which the speaker exists in a liminal state, where his/her attempt at renunciation and withdrawal conflicts with the imminent irruption of temporality in his/her life:

> Permanecer en las sombras, al hilo del
> insomnio, hasta que la atención penetra en la noche.

En el tejido compacto de la noche.
En el uniforme, apaciguador e inmóvil tejido de la noche.
Y distinguir su trama, hebra a hebra.
Y vislumbrar la luz que, emboscada, se oculta.
Que, sin embargo, deja averiguar las pulsaciones
sofocadas del acecho.
La luz que, inevitablemente, se cierne.
A qué espera para soltar su relámpago, rápido y
brillante como una vena abierta.
A qué para, con su detonación, hacer que lo oscuro
retroceda, se comprima, se disuelva, se absorba debajo
de las cosas y se alargue tras ellas, marcando—una tras
otra—las horas a su alrededor.
A qué espera para descubrir tanta variada y alterable
realidad.
A qué, para trasmutar el reposo en geometría, distancia, iris, diferencia . . .
perturbación.

(21)

[To remain in the shadows, following the drift of
insomnia, until attention penetrates the night.
The compact fabric of the night.
The uniform, calming, and immobile fabric of the night.
And to distinguish its weft, thread by thread.
And to make out the light that, lying in ambush, hides,
which, nevertheless lets one verify the stifled
throbbing of stalking.
The light that inevitably hovers.
What is it waiting for in order to release its lightning bolt,
  rapid and
brilliant like an open vein.
What, in order, with its detonation, to make what is dark
  recede,
grow compressed, dissolve, be absorbed
beneath things, and go away after them, marking—one
after another—the hours around it.
What is it waiting for in order to uncover so much varied
  and changeable
reality.
What, in order to transmute repose into geometry, distance,
iridescence, difference . . .
disturbance.]

Essentially a paradox, the poem explores the speaker's situation in terms of the polar opposites of night and day, light and darkness. Rossetti portrays the speaker as alone at night in bed, safe in the cocoonlike comfort of a seemingly unchanging state of suspension. The "uniforme, apaciguador e inmóvil tejido de la noche" (uniform, calming, and immobile fabric of the night) that envelops him or her is in some senses shroudlike, but its positive connotations include the evocation of swaddling clothes as well. Light, even though invisible, lies concealed within the night that, in a temporal universe, implies its inevitable return. Indeed, the day arrives as imposingly as when God said "Let there be light," terrible, grandiose, and awe-inspiring, as night shrinks away as if withered by the presence of a magical or divine power. Yet paradoxically, the coming to life (by leaving the stasis of the cocoon) means facing danger and death, something the text has prepared us for through the sinister connotations of the reference to light as ready to ambush ("emboscada" [ambush], "pulsaciones / sofocadas del acecho" [the stifled / throbbing of stalking]). When the day comes, the awestruck speaker affirms, it will "soltar su relámpago, rápido y brillante como una vena abierta" (release its lightning bolt, rapid and / brilliant like an open vein). The overtones of suicide suggest a very Rossettian notion: that to choose life means also to choose death.

Rossetti's poem is fully in line with elements of traditional symbology. According to J. E. Cirlot, most symbols of life also evoke death. The night Rossetti portrays evokes both death (immobility) and life (germination). The arrival of day is linked to blood ("vena abierta" [open vein]), a substance clearly associated, paradoxically, with both life and death. Cirlot also points out the causal link traditionally attributed to light in bringing about "differentiation and hierarchical order" by replacing the primordial darkness that precedes differentiation and connects with mystic nothingness (76–77). The arrival of day, in Rossetti's text, brings light that will serve as a kind of sundial, revealing time's passage, as well as making it possible to perceive perspective. The speaker's almost violent emergence from darkness to the awareness of mortality connects on a fundamental level with myths of death and resurrection, as well as to Rossetti's vision of the erotic. On a metaphorical level, darkness precedes the creation of the temporal world that encompasses both love and mortality. This poem is consistent with Rossetti's statement, in her interview with Sharon Keefe Ugalde, that she seeks through the erotic to reach "los principios de vida en vez de los principios de muerte" (the principles of life instead of the principles of death), though fully understanding the contradiction that "la principal esencia de la vida es que termina"(the principal essence of life is that it ends) (157).

In the next poem, as John Wilcox noted, first-person verbs make their initial appearance within *Punto umbrío*, as the ego asserts itself against the philosophy of renunciation:

> Pero qué debo hacer
> Dónde estará el sosiego
> cuando en mi corazón duran las sensaciones
> inquietantes del mundo y no puedo ordenar
> en un caleidoscopio
> la fragmentada imagen del recuerdo.
> Ni entre los atropellos de voces y rumores
> ni en el retroceder hasta un tiempo anterior
> de todos los reflejos que voy acumulando
> encuentro algún lugar para la ciudadela
> inmóvil del silencio.
> Un desbrozado espacio
> Para asentar la nada.
>
> (23)

> [But what should I do.
> Where can calm be
> when within my heart disturbing impressions
> of the world persist and I can't arrange
> in a kaleidoscope
> the fragmented image of memory.
> Not even among the intrusion of sounds and voices
> nor in retreating to a time before all the reflections
> that I'm gradually accumulating
> do I find any place for the immobile citadel
> of silence.
> A cleared-off space
> to situate nothingness.]

The speaker is perturbed because s/he can't find a fortress against the anguish of memories and the world around him or her—"algún lugar para la ciudadela inmóvil del silencio" (any place for the immobile citadel of silence). His/her enmeshment in temporality is also an enmeshment in language ("voces" [voices] versus "silencio" [silence]). The broken images that s/he can neither contain nor order (as a kaleidoscope might) suggest the weight of his/her own history and (in the writing process) the previous texts that s/he weaves into her own. In telling his/her story, s/he draws on this verbal/experiential past, but the result—a collage of clichés—highlights the impossibility of escaping mediation. In *Punto umbrío*, in fact, s/he expresses his/her own experience in terms of fictional types or of specific literary characters: the tyrant, Alice in Wonderland, the fugitive figure in an action movie, Ramón del Valle-Inclán's Don Juan (the Marqués de Bradomín, who like Rossetti objectifies his heart and discusses its death and regeneration[12]), but these representations are more abstract and fragmented than in those of Rossetti's novel *Mentiras de papel*, where the protagonist shifts roles from fashion model to filmmaker, at the same time acting out a new version of the Cinderella story.

Until this point in the collection, the speaker's self has been longing for peace beyond temporality. But the poem that begins "Se traiciona a la desesperación" (One proves false to one's desperation) brings a shift:

> Se traiciona a la desesperación si se pide auxilio:
> *Porque el que pide, espera.*
> Se reniega de la soledad, manifestándola:
> *Porque lo que es expresado, se comparte.*
> Se contradice el silencio, si se explica.
> Y aun si no se explica:
> *Porque, el silencio, si se le atiende, habla.*
>
> (25)

> [One proves false to one's desperation if help is requested:
> *Because whoever asks for something, hopes.*
> Loneliness is renounced when displayed.
> *Because what is expressed is shared.*
> Silence is contradicted, if it's explained.
> And even if not explained.
> *Because silence, if attended to, speaks.*]

Rossetti's irony and humor surface in this portrait of human resilience. The sleepless agony of existential aloneness has led the speaker to cry for help—which means, ironically, that s/he is beginning to communicate. Existential aloneness turns out to be as unattainable as perfect union: where there's life there's communication. Silence itself speaks, paradoxically destroying itself. This poem takes the reader beyond the anecdotal situation of the protagonist to a consideration of all communication as treasonous. The text suggests, however, that although writing inevitably fails to capture reality, the act of writing itself creates a new reality as it comes into being. *Punto umbrío*, then, chronicles not only an affair of the heart but a writer's crisis as well. Like his/her erotic entanglement, the speaker's love affair with the word has failed, but renunciation and the realization of the inevitability of failure are followed by new attempts. As an allegory of the writer facing the mystery of the creative process, the book then is about itself, an event as well as a referential work. Within this story of the writing process, which parallels the chronicle of the speaker's love experiences, this particular text is a fulcrum, speaking of silence, but also foreshadowing communication to come.

The relationship between writing and Eros develops further in the next poem, beginning "Aun la escritura deja atrás sus renglones" (Writing still leaves behind its lines). Instead of conquering time by giving fixity to events, writing is merely the detritus left behind in the self-consuming writing process. Ironically, our very impulse to live carries us toward death, even as the pencil with which words struggle to "organizar su pervivencia" (organize their survival) grows shorter. The writing journey leaves in its wake a fast-fading string of words:

> Aun la escritura deja atrás sus renglones
> desatando su incontenible estela:
> impronta que reseca su lacada herida; sentimientos que
> se alejan hasta desvanecerse, hasta abismarse, veloces,
> en las ráfagas nubladas del principio.
>
> (27)

> [Writing still leaves behind its lines
> Loosing its uncontainable wake:
> An imprint that parches its lacquered wound;
> Feelings that retreat until vanishing, until plunging, swift,
> Into the clouded gusts of the beginning.]

The rest of the poem continues to describe the writing process as a kind of journey. Material words, with their fragile meanings, are like goods on "vagones de carga perecedera" (freight cars full of perishable cargo). In the end, the speaker says, "seguir no es sino ... ahondar la saeta en el último tramo, / fingiendo desdeñar, o desmentir, el pacto que liga la / fragilidad a la existencia" (continuing is only to sink the arrow into the last stretch, / pretending to disdain, or to disprove, the pact that links fragility to existence). The image of shooting an arrow (evoking both the phallus and the pen) into the last leg of a journey captures the illusory nature of coincidence between words and experience, of communication and union. Even if one hits the bull's eye, the target itself is continually fading away into the past.

The five poems that I have examined so far take the protagonist from almost total retreat to a clear-eyed contemplation of the human condition. At this point, he/she is able to leave numbness and existential loneliness behind and to embark upon a new sexual/amorous entanglement. The eighteen poems that follow describe the affair's tortuous path: communication, temptation, union, and passion, then disappointment and the recognition of the union's impossibility—and finally resurging vitality despite all. In one of the most arresting images of the book, the speaker addresses his/her broken heart that has miraculously repaired itself: "tus fragmentos estallados se han ido / buscando, encontrando, cohesionándose como gotas de / mercurio, sin cicatriz ni señal" (your exploded fragments have kept / looking for each other, finding each other, and uniting like drops of mercury, without any scar or sign) (59). In the last two poems of the collection, which form a kind of coda, the speaker revisits his/her existential aloneness, but then surrenders to his/her own mortality—to love or to the life force, which also implies death.

In the penultimate poem (63), which opens with the words "Navío desvelado, corazón mío" (Sleepless ship, my heart) the speaker chooses the word "desvelado" to combine a suggestion of sleeplessness with an allusion to a ship without a sail. The desolate heart, surrounded by emptiness, responds pathetically and tragicomically to the mechanical sweep of a lighthouse beacon by smiling and donning ceremonial flags "para saludar a un quimérico puerto" (to salute a chimerical port). The ship's horns beep and the compass goes crazy, but in the end, the speaker addresses his/her heart with these words: "Pero el horizonte, imperturbable, sólo muestra tu íntimo precipicio, tu inabarcable desierto interior" (But the horizon, imperturbable, only reveals your intimate precipice, your uncontainable inner desert).

In a significant shift, the final poem expresses acceptance of life on its own terms. This text continues Rossetti's attempt to transcend gender, not only by masking the sex of the protagonist but also by employing a masculine-dominated form of discourse —the adventure movie. The speaker, a fugitive caught in the flashlight's glare, realizes there is no escape and thus surrenders to his/her fate:

> Como si una linterna me arrancara
> de en medio de la noche,
> así me descubriste, así me señalaste.
> Así horadaste mis silencios escarpados y troquelaste
> las fronteras de mi isla.
> Nombrándome me expones, me sitúas en el ojo de la
> diana.
> No hay lugar para el ardid, no hay escondite.
> Soy blanco paralizado, centro de tu voluntad, destino
> de tu atención y tu advertencia.
> ¿A qué esperas?
> No rehúyo la luz.
> Hágase en mí lo que tu dardo indica.
>
> (65)

> As if a flashlight grabbed me
> From the midst of night
> That's how you uncovered me, that's how you marked me,
> That's how you perforated my steep silences and cut around
> the edges of my island.
> By naming me you expose me, you place me in the center of the
> Target.
> There's no place for cunning, there's no hiding place.
> I'm a paralyzed target, the center of your will, the destination
> Of your attention and your warning.
> What are you waiting for?
> I'm not avoiding the light.
> Do with me what your arrow suggests.

Rossetti alludes to cinematic discourse in this poem, but in postmodern fashion she combines the contemporary with the traditional, employing also imagery borrowed from Spanish

Catholicism. The text suggests a speaker chosen by a divine agent, and in a sense the imagery of penetration evokes a metaphorical recasting of the Annunciation. Yet even stronger perhaps is the resonance of Christ's final days. The poem's final line echoes Christ in the darkness of Gethsemane: "Padre, si quieres, aparta de mi este cáliz; pero no se haga mi voluntad, sino la tuya" (Father, if thou be willing, remove this cup from me: nevertheless not my will, but thine, be done) (Luke 22:42). The light as the force that singles out the protagonist recalls the characterization of Jesus as "la luz verdadera que alumbra a todo hombre" (the true Light, which lighteth every man) (John 1:9), of Christ as the word made flesh. The Rossettian paradox of life as death also recalls the biblical account of the spikenard ointment used by a woman to anoint Christ, an act criticized by those present as wasteful. Christ responds by associating her breaking of the vessel, a symbolic act of love, with anointing his body for burying: "Esta hizo lo que pudo; se ha anticipado a ungir mi cuerpo para la sepultura" (She hath done what she could: she is come aforehand to anoint my body to the burying) (Mark 14:3-9). The poem thus endows human existence with an unmistakable holiness. Not only does the text construe the life of those made in God's image as a martyrdom similar to Christ's, but it also advocates embracing the miraculous privilege of living, even on life's own uncertain terms. Hints of mysticism, as well as an intense eroticism, appear in the immanence of consummation.[13] Thus Rossetti, whose iconoclastic poetry could at times be called irreverent, nevertheless interprets human life in *Punto umbrío* as infused with images of the divine.

In recycling her passion for martyrdom (accounts of which fascinated her as a child as a forbidden fruit [Ugalde 152]), Rossetti demonstrates the continuity of her vision of the cosmos. At the same time, she has progressed from a spectator to the role of protagonist (as writer) and creator of a protagonist (as speaker). Rossetti's poetry suggests the complexity of human consciousness and the arduous task of negotiating the vast field of words, symbols, and roles that we acquire along with our culture. The union of the male and female principles (seen in the annunciation/crucifixion duality of the last poem) represent Rossetti's attempt to challenge the rigidity of cultural roles and to suggest a broader range of possibilities for each individual.

Punto umbrío reveals itself to be consistent with Rossetti's other works. Rossetti continues to insist upon the paradox of the life force that inevitably leads to death and to view human beings as conditioned and constructed by the language and roles they inherit. While insisting upon the importance of giving oneself up to life, of accepting life, at the same time she recognizes the individual's role in rebelling against oppressive tradition. Thus Rossetti inscribes herself and her work as an active political force, attacking in various ways the conventional limitations of gender in the area of human creativity.[14]

It is important to consider *Punto umbrío* in relation to the literary politics of gender. In the volume, Rossetti rewrites the role of "poetisa" (poetess) first by purposefully creating a speaker of indeterminate gender and then by using martial imagery and intertextual allusions.[15] Continuing her fascination with the master narratives of the fall from Eden and redemption by Christ's crucifixion, she confronts issues of twentieth-century Spain—gender, sexuality, and religion, tradition and transgression. Through the mixture of intertextual citations ranging from the Bible to Luis Cernuda to Ramón del Valle-Inclán to Lewis Carroll to movie clichés (in which Spain becomes the colonized, not the colonizer) she responds to the polemic of Spanishness. Like Valle-Inclán, whose Marqués, surveying the "viejas cicatrices" (old scars) that mark his heart after many wounds, finds consolation in comparing his past to Spain's history ("En una Historia de España, donde leía siendo niño, aprendí que lo mismo da triunfar que hacer gloriosa la derrota" (In a History of Spain, where I used to read as a child, I learned that a glorious defeat is just as good as winning) (Valle-Inclán, 114–15), she puts sentimental battles into the context of heroic struggles. She ends up, finally, doing what she said she couldn't do—imposing order on cultural fragments, as if in a kaleidoscope, to make a beautiful picture.

The opening up of Spanish culture in the post-Franco era sometimes obscures the fact that even in the 1990s Spanish writers have had to continue to address long-standing cultural issues: the quarrel between Spanish tradition and cosmopolitanism, the rigidity of gender roles, and the weight of religious history. As Aurora Morcillo Gómez has pointed out, the Franco regime concerned itself with roles of men and women, and to do so, "manipulated traditional sacred images," particularly "Saint James, the

Virgen del Pilar, and the Sacred Heart," as well as Santa Teresa de Jesús (56). Francoist rhetoric defined women principally through the role of motherhood, a subject that Rossetti, although she is a mother, tends to avoid (unlike many of Spain's twentieth-century women poets, some of whom are particularly devoted to the theme).[16] Rossetti was in her late twenties when controversy erupted over the rigid gender roles associated with the epitome of Spanishness, the festival of San Fermín in Pamplona. This masculine ritual, immediately after the Civil War, was cast as a demonstration of the Navarrese youths' bravery as in war (Puértolas, 100). In *Punto umbrío* Rossetti transgresses through her military imagery the rigidity that places women "outside the arena." Rossetti indeed refers in *Punto umbrio* to the texts and words of the past, but she combines her Catholic upbringing with her imagination and creative openness in order to reinterpret Christianity in a humane and humanistic way. She refashions Christ's message of giving oneself up to death, which is at the same time life, and through the mending of her protagonist's heart portrays the resurrection that occurs *within* the life span. In continuing to develop her vision of death as part of life, Rossetti does not address life after physical death but explores such metaphorical aspects of religion as the courage of martyrdom in the face of sacrifice and the yearning for union that transcends temporality. Without a doubt, *Punto umbrío*'s verbal richness, complexity, and philosophical depth add a new dimension to Rossetti's art.

Notes

I would like to thank the Foundation of the University of North Carolina at Charlotte for providing funding that helped make possible the preparation of this essay. All translations of poems, titles, and excerpts from critical works are my own.

1. A multitude of literary theorists from Northrop Frye to Roland Barthes have challenged the view of language that postulated a simple connection between words and objective reality. Focusing on the way that components of the linguistic system relate to each other, instead of on how words capture a reality outside the web of words, they emphasized the interconnectedness between texts of various kinds. "Poetry can only be made out of other poems," stated Frye in 1957 (97), focusing on literature as a system at the same time that his European contemporaries were developing "classical" structuralism (Eagleton, 94). With the advent of poststructuralism, new ways of conceptualizing the rift

between words and meaning emerged, including the view of the text not as a "closed entity, equipped with definite meaning which it is the critic's task to decipher" but rather "as irreducibly plural, an endless play of signifiers which can never be finally nailed down to a single centre, essence or meaning" (Eagleton, 138). Categories that had previously been taken for granted as natural givens, such as those of gender, and experiences which seemed to emerge viscerally from the prelinguistic core of the self, such as erotic desire, have become problematized, cast as part of the vast web of social meaning-making activity that traps and conditions human beings.

2. Víctor García de la Concha termed this work a significant advance over Rossetti's earlier books of poetry. In 1998, in a conversation with me, Rossetti expressed her desire that this work receive the attention she thought it deserved. The following words, written in 1995 about her books *Los devaneos de Erato* (Erato's Idle Pursuits) (1980), *Dióscuros* (1982), and *Devocionario* (Book of Prayers) (1985), could apply to *Punto umbrío* as well: "One tradition that the poet uses almost as a central organizing principle is the story of humanity's fall from Eden. She often relates sexuality to temptation. She also portrays the crucial moments when carnal knowledge replaces innocence and when, as a result, wholeness gives way to a sense of differentiation, and stasis to a temporal flow of desire. The erotic impulse she depicts signifies vitality but also leads to death. And instead of portraying sexual union as a path to self-transcendence and a fusion with the cosmos in which time and death are momentarily abolished (à la Jorge Guillén), she sometimes depicts desire as triangular and self-consuming, inflamed by what proscribes or limits it and constitutionally destructive of its very source and object. Rossetti's elaborate explorations of sexual curiosity, loss of innocence, and the complexities of erotic attraction thus acquire at times a dark and even tragic sense" (Miller 1995).

3. This title is an invented word and I have therefore not provided a translation.

4. Salvador Fajardo also explores Rossetti's treatment of the relationship between the world and the word in his article "Ana Rossetti: The Word Made Flesh." His perspective is that Rossetti's female speaker through bodily experience rewrites the male tradition (145).

5. Zaldívar suggests that Rossetti uses ekphrasis to question and subvert women's status as "other," by using a double lens—that of the way women are viewed by society and that of their own view (24–25).

6. This combination is part of her genealogy: her father, she states, liked tradition, while her mother broke with established norms to become an expert plumber (Ugalde, 149–50).

7. Rossetti counts among her works the libretto for a one-act opera, *El secreto enamorado* (The Secret Lover), which premiered in 1993. This is just one of many examples of her interest in theater.

8. See Servodidio for an explanation of Rossetti's attempt to overcome the limitations of the perspective of just one gender (320).

9. For specific examples, see my article "Continuidad y ruptura" (Continuity and Rupture).

10. In keeping with the text's demands, I will refer to the speaker as s/he and use the possessive his/her. Although these constructions may lack grace,

they are made necessary by Rossetti's attempt to transcend linguistic and social categories in her work.

11. Rossetti's use of the terms "conjunciones," "conjugaciones," "conjuraciones," and "abjuraciones," suggesting verbal expression but connoting also the drama of union and separation, emphasizes the connections between the verbal and the erotic.

12. In *Sonata de estío*, the Marqués refers to his heart as follows: "Mi corazón estaba muerto, y desde que la coitada diera las boqueadas, yo parecía otro hombre" (My heart was dead, and ever since the poor thing had kicked the bucket, I seemed like a different man) (96).

13. The connection between sexuality and mortality is made in Christian myth in the story of Adam and Eve.

14. Other recent works likewise have a political agenda: the "novela rosa" (romance novel) *Mentiras de papel* rewrites the Cinderella story. Although she maintains the fairy tale convention of the happy ending after a struggle, she suggests a change in gender roles allowing women agency instead of passivity.

15. In a conversation with me in May 1999, Rossetti indicated she had avoided gender references on purpose.

16. In the novel *Mentiras de papel*, motherhood enters the picture, though not as the traditional version. The protagonist is a single mother with a successful career. At the end of the novel, the suggestion of her reuniting with the child's father is present but in a relationship of equality.

Works Cited

Cirlot, J. E. 1971. *A dictionary of symbols*. 2nd ed. Trans. Jack Sage. New York: Philosophical Library.

Eagleton, Terry. 1982. *Literary theory: an introduction*. Minneapolis: University of Minnesota Press.

Fajardo, Salvador. 1999. Ana Rossetti: The word made flesh. *Letras femeninas* 25, (1–2): 137–54.

Frye, Northrop. 1957. *Anatomy of criticism: four essays*. Princeton: Princeton University Press.

García de la Concha, Victor. 1995. Review of *Punto umbrío*. *ABC Cultural* 185 (19 May): 22.

Miller, Martha LaFollette. 1995. The fall from Eden: Desire and death in the poetry of Ana Rossetti. *Revista de estudios Hispánicos* 29: 260–77.

———. 2000. Continuidad y ruptura: *Punto umbrío* de Ana Rossetti. *Alaluz* 32, (1–2): 31–41.

Morcillo Gómez, Aurora. 1999. Shaping true Catholic womanhood: Francoist educational discourse on women. In *Constructing Spanish womanhood: Female identity in modern Spain*. Edited by Victoria Lorée Enders and Pamela Beth Radcliff. Albany: State University of New York Press.

Persin, Margaret H. 1997. *Getting the picture: The ekphrastic principle in twentieth-century Spanish poetry*. Lewisburg: Bucknell University Press.

Puértolas, Clotilde. 1999. Masculinity versus femininity: The Sanfermines: 1938–1978. In *Constructing Spanish womanhood: Female identity in modern Spain*. Edited by Victoria Lorée Enders and Pamela Beth Radcliff. Albany: State University of New York Press.

Rossetti, Ana. 1987. *Indicios vehementes: poesía 1979–1984*. 3rd ed. Madrid: Hiperión.

———. 1994. *Mentiras de papel*. Madrid: Ediciones Temas de Hoy.

———. 1995. *Punto umbrío*. Madrid: Hiperión.

Servodidio, Mirella. 1992. Ana Rossetti's double-voiced discourse of desire. *Revista hispánica moderna* 45:318-26.

Ugalde, Sharon Keefe. 1991. *Conversaciones y poemas: La nueva poesía femenina española en castellano*. Madrid: Siglo Veintiuno.

Valle-Inclán, Ramón del. 1988. *Sonata de primavera: Sonata de estío*. Madrid: Espasa-Calpe.

Wilcox, John. 1996. *Punto umbrío*: Ana Rossetti's introspective gaze. Talk presented MLA conference, December, Washington DC.

Wilde, Oscar. 1965. The priority of art. From *The decay of lying*. 1889. Reprint in *The modern tradition: Backgrounds of modern literature*, edited by Richard Ellmann and Charles Feidelson, Jr. New York: Oxford University Press.

Zaldívar, María Inés. 1998. *La mirada erótica en algunos poemas de Ana Rossetti y Gonzalo Millán*. Santiago de Chile: Red Internacional del Libro.

Staging Immanence: Of Space, Time, and Luminous Reality in Dionisia García's *Lugares de paso*

Michael Mudrovic

In a brief overview published in 1995, Biruté Ciplijauskaité asserts that with the publication of each of her works, Dionisia García's writing "gana en andadura más individual, en concisión, es decir, en firmeza" (gains in individual style, in concision, that is to say, in certainty) (353). Ciplijauskaité further defines the fundamental characteristics of García's poetry when she states:

> Desde los primeros libros, la evocación ocupa un lugar importante en su poesía. El pasado suele estar intrínsicamente unido al presente.... Al llegar a *Diario abierto,* el énfasis se traslada de lo perdido a lo recogido... La atención se centra en los pequeños detalles de la vida cotidiana de la mujer, instantes sueltos que se eternizan en cuadros de estructura casi totalmente nominal. (353)[1]

> [From her first books, evocation occupies an important place in her poetry. The past is wont to be intrinsically linked with the present.... On reaching *Open Diary*, the emphasis shifts from what has been lost to what has been garnered.... The focus centers on the small details of the daily life of a woman, random moments that become eternal in scenes structured almost entirely of nouns.][2]

The poems of García's most recent work to date, *Lugares de paso* (Points of Passage) (1999), may be less static in their presentation of precise scenes, but they, too, reflect the joyful serenity with which the poet accepts the events of everyday reality, "una aceptación gozosa resultante de largas reflexiones" (a joyful acceptance resulting from long meditations) (Ciplijauskaité, 354). Grounding these poems in a concrete anecdotal reality that often specifies historical monuments as the setting, García explores how these "immutable" spaces evoke a sense of the passing of time, making them stages of immanence; that is, timeless platforms on which the drama of life's changes is played out.[3] In addition to the contrast between the personal events that take place in a public setting, these poems emphasize the relationship between the fleeting and the lasting, between the time and space that the poet will fuse in and through the act of writing.

W. J. T. Mitchell provides useful insight into this interaction in his essay "Spatial Form in Literature: Toward a General Theory" in which he maintains that "we never apprehend space apart from time and movement.... Instead of viewing space and time as antithetical modalities, we ought to treat their relationship as one of complex interaction, interdependence, and interpenetration" (275). Adopting a taxonomic approach to space in literature, Mitchell delineates a "four-level system" of space in literature (282–84).[4] The first of these levels, which he designates as "the literal level," consists of the physical existence of the text itself, the poem situated on the page. The "descriptive level," according to Mitchell, then involves the reader in the mental activity of reading and of converting the signifier into the signified. The words on the page represent "a spatial realm that has to be constructed mentally during or after the temporal experience of reading the text" (283). The third level of spatiality involves perception of the "structure" or "form" of the text, which entails our perception of the sequential presentation governing the text and our temporal movement through it. Mitchell asserts that the fourth level is the most difficult to discuss as it entails the movement from experience to interpretation and often creates a sense of simultaneity of perception. He labels this level "*dianoia*," the simultaneous apprehension of multiple levels of insight. As we shall see when we discuss García's poems, these levels are often imbricated and interrelated, and not necessarily hierarchical in their exposition.

Keeping these levels in mind, this essay explores the intersection of space and time that leads to epiphanic illuminations of everyday reality in three poems from García's *Lugares de paso*. These poems are similar in that an arch presides over each public setting in which the poem takes place. Symbolically, an arch represents a passageway or threshold leading from one world to another. Moreover, the circular or pointed apex of the arch signals an aspiration or elevation toward perfection. (The semicircle synecdochically evokes the circle as symbol of eternity and perfection.) The arch is often associated with triumph or achievement, and it can even represent a connection of opposites (as the arch of a bridge or a passageway between buildings).[5] Indeed, in each of the poems studied here the arch leads the speaker-poet to a different discovery.

Of the three poems I will discuss here, "Arco de Santo Domingo" (The Arch of Santo Domingo) stages the action in the most colloquial setting. The literal "Arco de Santo Domingo" is an archway extending over one end of a narrow street that connects two plazas in Murcia (the poet's home town) and serves as a local landmark frequently used for arranging rendezvous between friends.[6] As frequently happens, the area has become so familiar to local residents that it has lost its charm:

> He visto el arco sucio,
> pasadizo que comunica calles,
> sobre él la ventana,
> que ya no aloja.
> Pero es bello el rincón
> con su mugrienta edad,
> y el trecho transitado.
> Años sin elevar los ojos
> hacia los muros,
> viejos de tanto soportar
> decenios de indigencia.
>
> (1999, 22)

> [I have seen the dirty arch,
> a passageway that joins two streets,
> above it the window,
> that no longer houses anyone.
> But this corner is beautiful
> with its dingy age, and the crowded passageway.
> Years without raising my eyes
> toward the walls,
> aged by so much tolerance
> of decades of indigence.]

The description of the archway as "sucio" (dirty) and as a "rincón / con su mugrienta edad" (corner / with its dingy age) emphasizes its lack of attractiveness. Likewise, the focus on "los muros, / viejos de tanto soportar / decenios de indigencia" (walls / aged by so much tolerance of / decades of indigence) calls attention to a long period of neglect and a narrow perspective on reality. It is almost as if the speaker had been wearing blinders. The verb "soportar" is ambivalent, meaning physically "to hold up" but also "to tolerate." This ambivalence not only subtly personifies the arch but also highlights civic and personal indifference and neglect. Even the alliteration and rhythm of the phrases "su mugrienta edad" "el trecho transitado" (crowded passageway) and "decenios de indigencia" suggest repetition and monotony. Moreover, the detail of the window where no one lives any longer points to emptiness and a lack of vitality.

Nonetheless, the speaker has undergone an epiphany. On the day in question she has lifted her eyes and rediscovered a certain beauty beneath the quotidian landmark. Her act of raising her eyes adopts symbolic proportions that indicate she has gone beyond the familiar surface of reality, as she states in the opening phrase "He visto" (I have seen) (which has biblical overtones) and in the simple declaration "es bello" (it is beautiful). Therefore, when she comes to a stop beneath the arch, "en ese punto fijo de las citas" (on the spot designed for meetings), the scene before her becomes enlivened with movement and color:

> Me detengo en la arcada,
> en ese punto fijo de las citas,
> y observo el movimiento de la calle,
> el río de colores.
>
> (1999, 22)

> [I stop in the archway,
> on the spot designated for meetings,
> and I observe the movement of the street,
> the river of colors.]

Ironically, the poet chooses the ambivalent image of the river to describe the scene. As a symbol of transient passage and of permanent presence, the river enfolds the static and the dynamic in both spatial and temporal dimensions. Although the arch functions as a threshold defining the speaker's epiphany, she has stopped precisely in this liminal space used for reunions, where she has discovered new meaning and life. It is no mere detail, then, that the arch is named "Santo Domingo" (Saint Dominic), a reference to resurrection and revitalization, a specific moment in time that leads to eternal life.[7]

The second poem under consideration, "Instantánea" (Polaroid), is set in a more recognizable, historical, and public space, the Puerta de Alcalá in the heart of Madrid. One of the original entrances to the formerly walled city, this series of arches is located in the center of a circular plaza into and from which several main arteries of the capital flow. As the title indicates, this monumental space provides a flash of memory that recalls a trip the speaker and her father made to the city nearly thirty years before. At that time a street photographer took a snapshot of her and her father with the Puerta de Alcalá as backdrop.[8] Thus the photograph that she recalls as having captured and frozen this one moment in time contrasts with the passage of thirty years, with the same setting as the backdrop. Hence the space of the plaza imbricates past and present and foregrounds the speaker's perception of time.

The poem begins with the memory of that day long ago when the speaker as a young girl was holding onto her father's arm. In fact, the first sentence is a fragment of perceptions that not only explains the purpose of the visit but also equates the mood of the young speaker with the exciting atmosphere of the capital in the ambivalent adjective "airosa" (breezy):

> Del brazo de mi padre por la avenida airosa,
> en busca del amigo, que al fin vimos.
> Era marzo con sol, y se acercó un fotógrafo
> dispuesto a detener aquella escena.
> Nuestros abrigos largos, la sonrisa;
> el gozo elemental de la existencia,
> marcado para siempre en blanco y negro.
> Presidía la puerta de Alcalá,
> con sus rosas y grises en la piedra,
> rodeada de atmósfera inocente.
>
> (1999, 11)

> [On my father's arm along the breezy avenue,
> in search of a friend, whom we finally saw.
> It was a sunny March day, and a photographer approached

eager to capture that scene.
Our long overcoats,
the smile;
the elemental joy of existence,
patent forever in black and white.
The gate of Alcalá presided over the scene
with its pink and gray stone,
surrounded by an innocent atmosphere.]

The act of holding her father's arm implies the young speaker's insecurity as well as her graceful, even jaunty entry into a new world, the vital capital. Like the March weather, she combines the instability of the windy weather with the confidence of warmth in the sun, "el gozo elemental de la existencia" (the elemental joy of existence).

The same errand that brought the speaker and her father to Madrid thirty years earlier has brought her back in the present. While on her way to visit her father's old friend, she passes by the Puerta in a taxi. Although it is the same time of year, the change in the speaker's attitude is reflected in her description of the scene:

> Han transcurrido más de treinta años,
> y atravieso el lugar en automóvil,
> al paso, las arcadas de piedra ennegrecidas,
> su insolente esplendor ajeno a la premura.
> Voy a ver al amigo, anciano y solo.
> Es primavera inquieta, sin fotógrafo,
> y mi padre no está.
>
> (1999, 11)

[More than thirty years have passed since then,
and I cross the same place in a car,
just passing through, the stone arches grown blacker,
their insolent splendor foreign to the rush.
I am going to see our friend,
aged and alone.
It is a restless spring, without the photographer,
and my father is not here.]

Now, instead of the rose and gray colors she recalls from the photo (even though it is in black and white), the arches of the city gate have become "ennegrecidas" (grown blacker) suggesting pollution, disillusionment, and the loss of innocence. The perception of this change again represents a projection of the speaker's view of the world because of her growth and greater maturity and worldliness. The monument even seems to be insolent, holding itself proudly and disdainfully above the traffic and bustle of the city, "ajeno a la premura" (foreign to the rush). Time is so precious that people must rush from one place to another in cars, buses, and motorcycles unaware of the tranquility and dignity in their midst, unaware of the value tarnished by neglect.

The circular repetition of space, time, and memory has a quite different effect on the speaker. As before, she has returned to Madrid in the spring to visit her father's friend, "anciano y solo" (aged and alone) like the Puerta de Alcalá. But on this trip the speaker is acutely aware of the differences in herself and her world because her father has died. She herself is the same person she remembers in the photograph, but of course she has changed. The brief, "instantaneous" glimpse of the Puerta de Alcalá opens the door to a memory so complex and saturated with time, heritage, and change that it evokes the sensation of simultaneity (the past coinciding with the present). Mitchell identifies this phenomenon as the concept of *dianoia*. As Mitchell explains, what he calls "the fourth level of spatiality in literature is difficult to discuss because it approaches that point where the interpretation of literature (presumably a rational, sequential activity) converges with the experience of it" (375). Quoting Northrop Frye, Mitchell notes that "*dianoia* conveys, or at least preserves, the sense of simultaneity caught by the eye. We *listen to* the poem as it moves from beginning to end, but as soon as the whole of it is in our minds at once we 'see' what it means. More exactly, ... we have a vision of meaning or *dianoia* whenever any simultaneous apprehension is possible" (275). In keeping with this definition, the speaker's description of the Puerta de Alcalá represents "a 'vision' of the whole ... one of those valuable but ephemeral flashes of insight" (376) evoked by the spatial setting. Hence the title "Instantánea" is superbly apposite.

In keeping with the motif of the arch, the third poem in this discussion, "Tino en la caída" (Hitting the mark) takes place in the shadow of the Arc de Triomphe in Paris. This unforgettable poem turns on a meeting between the speaker and a friend. The grandiose setting takes in the "explanada" (esplanade), dwarfing and diminishing the human figures of the speaker and her friend:

> Esperabas puntual, mi vieja amiga,
> y crucé con premura
> la grandiosa explanada.
> Aparecías quieta
> bajo el Arco del Triunfo.
> Lágrimas de emoción,
> y tu lengua tudesca
> se hacía más difícil.
>
> (1999, 38)

> [You were waiting punctually, my old friend,
> and I crossed quickly the grandiose esplanade.
> You appeared quiet
> beneath the Arc de Triomphe.
> Tears of emotion,
> and your Germanic tongue
> became more difficult.]

It seems that we look at this scene from the temporal distance of the speaker's retrospective reflection. But as she approaches the arch and recognizes her friend, the perspectives elide past and present, and we enter the scene more intimately. This meeting stirs the emotions of the other woman, making her cry and interfering with her ability to speak. Her contradictory tears of joy add to the harsh, gutteral sounds of her "lengua tudesca" (German tongue). Moreover, the confluence of different nationalities points to the difficulty of communication.

An absolutely absurd occurrence interrupts this poignant reunion and effectively puts an end to the speaker's recounting of it. As they are just walking away, a pigeon falls from the sky, hits the friend on the head, and comes to rest on her backpack.

> Entre risas, dejamos el ensanche.
> Inesperadamente,
> queda un palomo azul en tu cabeza,
> sin poder ascender, por muerte súbita.
> Temblaron nuestras manos
> al percibir lo inerte,
> y no saber qué hacer con aquel cuerpo,
> alojado después en tu mochila.
> Te marchaste y no supe su terminal destino.
>
> (1999, 38)

[Amid laughter, we left the wide space.
Unexpectedly,
a blue dove rests on your head,
unable to ascend,
because of sudden death.
Our hands trembled
on perceiving its stillness,
and not knowing what to do with that body,
then ensconced on your backpack.
You marched away and I never knew its final destiny.]

All we know of this pigeon is that it is blue and that it is no longer capable of flight because it has died. Although these details seem trivial, the color blue softens and even idealizes the tone, and the inability to ascend to greater heights (those of the arch and its symbolic triumph) connotes a certain resignation and humility. We should also note that the pigeon is gendered as male ("palomo" rather than "paloma") so that it does not refer to either of the two women specifically. However, that it ultimately lands on the friend's backpack suggests a burden this friend carries with her. (That is, there is no premonition of the death of the other woman, but possibly an oblique reference to the death of someone in the friend's family—husband, son or father—since the "palomo" is gendered as male.) The speaker never knows how her friend disposes of the dead bird, cryptically dropping the scene at that point. This incident does provoke her nevertheless to question how such an event can come about, can "fall from the blue" and indelibly mark the connection between the two women.

Confundida pregunto,
qué fuerza natural
pudo impulsar al ave,
en el último instante,
para exhalar su aliento en tu persona.
                                              (1999, 38–39)

[Confused, I ask
what natural force
could impel the bird,
in its last instant,
to exhale its breath on your person.]

In this poem the arch represents the threshold to a contemplation of the towering presence of fate and death in our lives. The pure coincidence of this bird expiring at that exact moment depends upon an inexplicable "fuerza natural." Yet there is irony beneath the speaker's confusion. Her recognition of this force in the word "impulsar" includes the pulse of life, while the exhalation infuses the lives of the women with its "aliento," a symbol of inspiration and life with religious overtones of the descent of the Holy Spirit. By changing from the more specific "palomo" to the more categorical "ave," the speaker evokes various contradictions centering around the intersection of space and time.[9] As Mitchell says, "space is the body of time, the form or image that gives us an intuition of something that is not directly perceivable but which permeates all that we apprehend. Time is the soul of space, the invisible entity which animates the field of our experience" (276). Likewise, in this poem the trivial and miniscule are privileged over the grandiose and monumental; the massive arch is secondary to an insignificant and absurd event of a meeting marked by a dead pigeon. The bird itself adopts symbolic proportions of all the experiences we carry with us, and especially of the omnipresence of death in our lives, which causes us to appreciate life all the more (cf. Heidegger).[10] Here, the vivid emotions of friendship become perceptible through a face-to-face meeting in which the physical presence of the other allows the emotions to surface and acquire meaning, even though they are inexpressible.

In contrast with but in no way disconnected from the other poems in *Lugares de paso*, the final poem is titled "Del poeta y el poema" (Of the Poet and the Poem). A disjunction in the language at the beginning of this poem creates (con)fusion between the poet and the reader within the space of the poem:

> Quien sus palabras sigue
> no se instala en lugar definitivo.
> Afirma las historias,
> cuantos temas propuso en la escritura,
> pero él es diferente con el paso del tiempo,
> y cambia la mirada al presenciar la vida.
> Su paisaje más íntimo
> se muestra en ocasiones lleno de soledades:
> otras es el fulgor inesperado

que no sabe de sí, y tiene que dar cuenta.

(1999, 50)

[One who follows his words
does not settle in a definitive place.
He affirms the stories,
as many themes as he proposed in the writing,
but he is different with the passage of time,
and changes his view on witnessing life.
His most intimate landscape
is revealed on occasions full of solitude:
other times it is an unexpected glow
that knows nothing of itself, and has to bear witness.]

It is unclear in the first verse whether the "Quien sus palabras sigue" refers to the poet who follows words to discover new experiences or to the reader who attends to the words written by the poet. In either case, both find themselves in an indefinite space, that of poetic experience. This disjunction belies the definitive presence of the words on the page and the identifiable public spaces evoked, and alludes to the shifting floor of the spatial map formed by the text. "El paso del tiempo" that encourages writer and reader to affirm "las historias, / cuantos temas propuso en la escritura" changes our perception of that reality. As Mitchell again asserts:

> "Temporal form" . . . is not the antithesis of spatial form but the term we apply to a temporal experience whose spatial pattern or configuration has been discerned. Any time we feel that we have discovered the principle which governs the order or sequence of presentation in a text, whether it is based on blocks of imagery, plot and story, the development of character or consciousness, historical or thematic concerns—any time we sense a "map" or outline of our temporal movement through the text, we are encountering . . . spatiality. (284)

The perception of textual space can shift and change in the course of reading and as we discern different levels of meaning. And as the poem concludes, this space can paradoxically be "lleno de soledades," or it can present a flash of insight, "un fulgor inesperado," a vision that we must both attempt and fail to capture in words (the poet's or the critic's). The poems of Dionisia García's *Lugares de paso* illustrate the problematics of representation and signification by means of language and attest to "the tendency of spatial form to unite (while preserving the relative distinction between) analytical and experiential aspects of reading" and writing (Mitchell 289).

It is obvious from the reading of these three poems that Dionisia García is highly cognizant of the metapoetic implications of her work. The *Lugares de paso* portrayed on the "descriptive" level in these poems represent the space of poetry itself, its literal existence on the page (see Mitchell). Hence the overly familiar passageway in "Arco de Santo Domingo" defines the worn-out, everyday language with which the poet has to work. The arch allows us to cross a threshold and behold a "río de colores," the varied nuances and shadings of all-too-familiar words. Likewise, in "Instantánea" we recognize growth and change, difference and similarity when we revisit a text. Past and present are imbricated in an experience of *dianoia* while we simultaneously perceive the gap between them. The complexity of this insight precludes an easy paraphrase because of the multiple levels of space and time on which the text functions to illuminate reality. The arch in "Tino de la caída" points to the luck and the skill ("tino" means both) involved in participation in the writing and reading process. The falling bird thus represents the unexpected arrival of insight and illumination (the color blue) that evokes experiences we carry with us. The sharing of a common experience calls attention to separation and union between the poet and the reader in the spatial context of the poem, its literal words and its symbolic magnificence, a relationship "of complex interaction, interdependence, and interpenetration."

Likewise, these poems raise the issue of the relationship between art and life precisely because they are situated in empirical reality. All of these settings exist in the real world as well as in their representation in the words of the poem. As such, these poems epitomize the theme of this collection of essays: "poetry's impulse to create a self-contained reality and the competing impulse to remain vitally connected to the world."[11] Through the intersection of time and space in these poems the "permanent" becomes transient (an empty signifier) while the "transient" becomes lasting though intangible (the ever-vital signified). By concentrating on the representation of space in these poems, we can observe how spatial form moves through and submerges in "the texture of the work and . . . the texture of life" (Mitchell 298). These poems become monuments to the passing of time, staging and perpetuating transient events.

Notes

1. *Diario abierto* (Madrid: Trieste, 1989) is included in a collection of the poet's work, *Tiempos del Cantar (Poesía 1976–1993)* (Barcelona: El Bardo, 1995).

2. All translations are my own.

3. Here I use the term "immanence" as the opposite of "permanence." Specific human events are immanent and therefore transient, elusive, fleeting, ephemeral, evanescent as opposed to that which is permanent, i.e., lasting or "transcendent." I am basing this distinction in part on Gérard Genette's discussion in *The Work of Art: Immanence and Transcendence*. However, the etymology of "immanence" defines an inherent trace that "dwells within" fleeting reality. The ambivalence in my usage is intentional.

4. Mitchell's discussion is based on but goes significantly beyond Joseph Frank's seminal essay, "Spatial Form in Modern Literature," in that Frank concentrates primarily on modern literature. His essay can be found in *The Widening Gyre*.

5. According to Jean Chevalier and Alain Gheerbrandt, the archway "like the niche combines the spatial elements of the cube and the chalice. The archway is a triumph over the banalities of the material world." Quoting Chanpeaux and Dom Stercks they continue, "The archway soaring up its keystone proclaims the lasting triumph of the upward striving of the unconscious over the clogging flesh" (Chevalier and Gheerbrandt 40).

6. I am grateful to the poet for supplying me with this information and a photograph as I was preparing this article for a conference on "Space in Literature" held at SUNY-Binghamton in March 2000, and then for her hospitality and generosity during my visit to Murcia. The Calle Arco de Santo Domingo connects the Plaza Julián Romea and the Plaza de Santo Domingo. The arch is located at the end of this short, narrow street, next to the entrance to the church of Santo Domingo.

7. Literally, the phrase "Santo Domingo" refers to the saint, whereas "Domingo Santo" would refer more specifically to Easter Sunday. One cannot deny, however, that St. Dominic's name in Spanish is "Sunday." Moreover, St. Dominic is pertinent in this context. Domingo de Guzmán (1170–1221), born in Caleruega, Castilla la Vieja, established the Order of Friars Preachers, also known as the Dominicans. The order was founded with the express purposes of preparing preachers to proclaim the Word and of reforming the corrupt or heretical. According to *The Encyclopedia of Religion*, "The influence of Dominic perdures in the shared vision of a religious family of men and women dedicated to preaching the gospel to all people while living in a community that is committed to common prayer and simplicity and whose members are

jointly responsible for their life and mission" (418). As we shall see, the metapoetic dimension of the proclaiming of words (whether gospel or poetry) and the social aspect of language are implicated in this reference to the "Arco de Santo Domingo." I am indebted to my colleague Viviana Rangil for challenging my univocal reading.

8. I am grateful to the poet for showing me this photograph and providing autobiographical information that underlies my reading.

9. At the conference on "Space in Literature" (see note 5 above), Salvador J. Fajardo pointed out that the word "ave" opens a semantic space that is more expansive than the word "palomo." As a result, the poem represents a quiasmus as the "visual," "physical" space narrows and the semantic space widens.

10. Chronologically forming part of the so-called "Generación de los 50" (Generation of the 50's) García would probably have read Heidegger's *Being and Time*. It seems that much of Heidegger's philosophy undergirds these poems. In addition to the concept of "being-toward-death" and "freedom" that we find here, in "Arco de Santo Domingo" the speaker recognizes in a moment of *aletheia* her involvement in "everydayness" while at the same time turning toward "authenticity." Likewise, "Instantánea" deals with the theme of temporality and reliance on the past for self-definition. These themes are also dominant in Claudio Rodríguez's poetry.

11. I quote from the letter sent by the editors, Cecile West-Settle and Sylvia Sherno, inviting participation in this project.

Works Cited

Chevalier, Jean, and Alain Gheerbrant. 1994. *A dictionary of symbols*. Trans. from the French by John Buchanan Brown. Oxford: Blackwell.

Ciplijauskaité, Biruté. 1995. Hacia la afirmación serena: Nuevos rumbos en la poesía de mujer. *Revista de estudios hispánicos* 29: 349–64.

Frank, Joseph. 1963. *The widening gyre: crisis and mastery in modern literature*. New Brunswick, NJ: Rutgers University Press.

García, Dionisia. 1989. *Diario abierto*. Madrid: Trieste.

———. 1999. *Lugares de paso*. Sevilla: Renacimiento.

Genette, Gérard. 1997. *The work of art: immanence and transcendence*. Trans. G. M. Goshgarian. Ithaca: Cornell University Press.

Heidegger, Martin. 1962. *Being and time*. Trans. John Macquarrie and Edward Robinson. New York: Harper.

Mitchell, W. J. T. 1980. "Spatial form in literature: Toward a general theory." In *The language of images*. Chicago: University of Chicago Press.

Giving the Vampire Voice: Monstrous Metaphors in Recent Spanish Poetry by Women

Margaret Persin

The vampire story has been a staple of the cultural forces of subversion from its birth in the dark recesses of the human imagination, having been told and retold as a means of confronting the prohibitions and taboos of structured and hierarchical social constraints. In addition, it also offers a means through which conventional society can lay claim to that which remains outside the norms of acceptability, responsibility, and customary codes of conduct.[1] Recent theory and criticism of the late twentieth century reflect this subversive reading of the vampire's cutting figure, and offer for the discerning reader various and sundry visions and interpretations of contemporary bloodletting, hunger, and violence by suggesting their relation to the vampire's unquenchable thirst. In her *Our Vampires, Ourselves*, for example, Nina Auerbach bases her reading of the vampire mode on the confrontation with unspoken fears and the uses and abuses of power. For this cultural critic, Dracula's offspring lurk in the darkened hallways of Ronald Reagan's Washington, the patriarchy's reaction to the rise of feminism, and the social hysteria occasioned by the gay rights movement and the AIDS epidemic. In the edited volume by Joan Gordon and Veronica Hollinger, *Blood Read: The Vampire as Metaphor in Contemporary Culture*, the vampire figure looms large but is hidden in plain sight in our contemporary setting: the vampire figure may be perceived in the odd neighbor worthy of cinematic rendering, a Hollywood swinger, the homosexual "other" or the anorexic teenage girl who literally consumes herself, all the life blood drained out of her by society's imposition of unrealistic standards for a svelte, supposedly female body that, paradoxically, loses its female curves and ability to produce the monthly menstrual blood flow. This version of feminine beauty is based on lack or absence—the virtual disappearance of the female body—where the young girl's life as well as menstrual blood are sucked away by a spectral image of beauty whose attainment results in death. Thus, within this context vampirism is evoked by the coupling of female beauty, blood, and death.[2]

In this essay, I will explore the uses of the vampire and other monstrous metaphors by several female Spanish poets whose work has appeared in the waning years of the twentieth century. But first, let me consider the vampire from two different perspectives: on the one hand, as a social construction that calls into question conventional modes of conduct and underscores cultural fascination with the outcast or subliminal other. In the case of the vampire, the alien "other" inhabits a territory that consistently remains outside cultural knowing, but paradoxically resides within, just beyond the reach of consciousness. And on the other hand, the patriarchy often has associated this dark territory with the patriarchal fear of the feminine, specifically forbidden feminine desire. Thus, gender underlies and underwrites patriarchy's bloodlust in the vampire mode. The vampire traditionally has been associated with the male imaginary, Dracula and his brood being the most egregious example. Here I will give special consideration to the vampire motif in recent Spanish poetry by women, in order to explore not so much the role of the hapless and helpless female in the conventional vampire narration, but rather the female and even feminist vampire whose function is to contravene the aforementioned patriarchal control of female desire.

As James B. Twitchell comments in the introduction to his study of the vampire in romantic literature, this outcast has been used to "explain human interactions" (4) and to cast a dim and denied light on the subliminal other that is carried within. To wit, this critic traces the vampire's presence in nineteenth-century romantic representations of the attraction/repulsion to the maternal figure, the incestuous relationship, oppressive paternalism, adolescent love, avaricious love, the struggle for power, homosexual attraction, repressed sexuality, female domination, and "the artist himself exchanging energy with aspects of his art" (5). In all of these cases, the protagonist struggles with the dark and alien other who resides within and who attempts to thwart the numbing confines of conventional society. From a more contemporary viewpoint, Gordon and Hollinger point out that "many writers now narrate their horror stories from the inside, as it were, filtering them through the consciousness of the horrors that inhabit them. Not surprisingly, the impact of this shift from human to other perspective works to invite sympathy for the monstrous outsider at the same time as it serves to diminish the terror generated by what remains outside our frame of the familiar and the knowable" (2). Thus, readers are invited to get the inside story on the alien other who is known all too well by the denying self. Second, these two authors point out that in contemporary literature, the manifestations of the vampire often are metaphorical roles that represent the sickness in modern life that contemporary society refuses to recognize or name, and comment that "contrary to the old legends that tell us that vampires have no reflection, we do indeed see many diverse reflections—of ourselves—as the vampire stands before us cloaked in metaphor" (3). Further, from a metaphorical perspective, the vampire may "help us to construct our own humanity, to provide guidelines against which we can define ourselves" (5), the monstrosity of our own cultural values that we are at pains to recognize, much less confront and correct.

The patriarchal fear of the feminine finds creative expression in vampire lore from a variety of perspectives. For example, the vampire's existence on the margins of social acceptability defies the domestic milieu, and thus plays to masculine longings for freedom from the routine and confinement of conventional society. His nocturnal travels mimic or merely reflect, from a patriarchal perspective, the much longed for rejection of domestic existence and the restrictive hierarchy presupposed by that particular way of being within the social context.[3] Thus, the male vampire persona represents a means and model of escape from the strictures of family life, which normally revolve around a maternal figure. Another aspect of the vampire's modus operandi that underscores the masculine desire to escape social strictures is that of the intense bond of friendship that typically serves as a means of initiation into the vampire brotherhood of the "undead."[4] In speaking of the intertextual relationship between Byron's vampire fragment and the 1819 tale, *The Vampyre*, by

John Polidori, Nina Auerbach wryly comments that "In societies where families are inescapable and marriage is enforced, friendship may be a more indelible taboo than incest" (19). Polidori's protagonist impresses on his male travel companion to "Remember your oath," that is, to preserve the protagonist's honor by "concealing his predatory life and apparent death" (14). In this manner, intense friendship—male or female—circumvents prescribed social convention and acceptability, and subverts the laws that not only support familial loyalty but also celebrate the division of the living from the dead.

Fear and loathing of the feminine finds expression in the patriarchal cast of the male vampire's tale not only in the ravishing of the sleeping maiden by means of the erotic bite, but also in the projection of that very fear and loathing onto the vampire who now takes on female characteristics within the modernist context. Erika Bornay, in her *Las hijas de Lilith* (The Daughters of Lilith), notes that "it is not surprising that, around 1900, men would perceive in the vampire the closest rendering of the feared *New Woman*, covetous of sex, power and money. From this period proceeds, equally, the still valid denomination of 'vampire' for the ghastly woman" (285).[5] Similarly, in his *Idols of Perversity*, Bram Dijkstra makes note of the patriarchy's devastating binary opposition of female identity at the end of the nineteenth century which effectively negates for women any possibility for independence, self-determination, or self-expression. Not surprisingly, the vampire casts a shadow over the woman who would dare to attempt escape from this stifling system of classification: "The virgin and the whore, the saint and the vampire—two designations for a single dualistic opposition: that of the woman as man's exclusive and forever pliable private property, on the one hand, and her transformation, upon her denial of man's ownership rights to her, into a polyandrous predator indiscriminately lusting after man's seminal essence, on the other" (334). Dijkstra then cites one William J. Robinson, MD, who, in 1922, published a scathing denunciation of the woman whose sexual needs exceed those of her spouse:

> [T]here is the opposite type of woman, who is a great danger to the health and even the very life of her husband. I refer to the hypersensual woman, to the wife with an excessive sexuality. It is to her that the name vampire can be applied in its literal sense.

> Just as the vampire sucks the blood of its victims in their sleep while they are alive, so does the woman vampire suck the life and exhaust the vitality of her male partner—or victim. And some of them—the pronounced type—are utterly without pity or consideration. (90)

Thus, according to Dijkstra, the good doctor is positing "a direct equation between woman's supposed hunger for seminal substance and her bestial blood lust, (...) thought to be precipitated by her insatiable need to replenish the blood incessantly lost to her system as a result of her degenerative subjection to the reproductive function and its attendant sexual cravings" (334).[6]

A prime example of the misogynist intent in equating female hungers with the figure of the vampire is the rendering by Charles Baudelaire, whose work no doubt is known to contemporary Spanish poets. In two of his poems he offers for consideration a representation of the insatiable woman by means of the image of the vampire; both of the texts, "The Vampire" and "The Metamorphoses of a Vampire," hail from *Les fleurs du mal* (The Flowers of Evil).[7] In the former, the male lyric voice bemoans his fate, having been seduced by the charms and delights of sexual intoxication. But his irresistible female lover becomes the "sharp-edged brand," and the speaker in a keening voice creates a series of similes to construct an image of the loss of the masculine self in the abyss of fickle sexual attraction, attachment, and addiction: "As is the convict to his chain, / as reckless gambler to his play, / Or as the drunkard to his wine, / Or vermin to their putrid prey." The poem ends with the speaker imploring either poison or the sword to free him from his folly; but they refuse, noting that the speaker willingly gave himself over to the woman's seduction. Their shared kisses have sealed his monstrous fate. In the second text, "The Metamorphoses of a Vampire," the speaker lends more attention to the various permutations of the female figure in the telling of the story of seduction, pleasure, and final horror. In this version, the speaker initiates a sexual relationship with a woman, most probably a prostitute, who, after lusty lovemaking, metamorphoses first into a "leathery wineskin filled with pus," then to an indiscriminate scattering of bones, more akin to "a weathervane, / Or like a signboard on an iron pole." As has been noted in the opening comments in regard to the vampire motif, this mythical figure has been imbued by the patriarchy with its own fear of the feminine, whether the female's creative potential, her sexuality, or her ability to ensnare and enslave her unknowing partner in the chains of her presumably insatiable hungers, whether for sex, power, or simply the ancient bloodlust of energy and life itself. Thus, Baudelaire projects the vampire's destructive powers onto the female figure and allows the vampire to embody the patriarchy's fin de siècle anxieties concerning changing social and cultural mores, customs, demands and expectations for women, no matter their social class.[8]

At this point, it would be well to review briefly the vampire's ability to express the danger zones of cultural anxiety: to narrate the horror story from within, to explore cultural attitudes toward the alien other, to embody an ideal metaphor for generalized sickness in society, to posit a means of subverting traditional family structure via an intense perhaps homosocial and homoerotic friendship, and to give voice to heretofore ignored hungers and desires, previously deemed too dangerous to be named. Moreover, the vampire is commonly associated with the moon and being buried alive. In contemplating this list, it becomes obvious why several contemporary Spanish women poets opt to utilize the figure of the vampire—whether in the male or female form—in order to defamiliarize and thus underscore the position of woman as alien other in a society whose values consistently marginalize, trivialize, brutalize, or totally erase female experience. Thus, the horror of being buried alive may pertain to Dracula's offspring as well as to a contemporary woman facing her everyday woes. In giving voice to the vampire in any of its various permutations, women poets point to the "horror story" of female existence and the monstrosity of contemporary life, whether within the domestic, the psychosocial, or purely libidinal context. The vampire imagery or metaphorical manifestations of violence that emerge from the female imaginary do not so much repeat the blood and gore of the *machista* undertaking of possession and domination by force, but rather may call attention to the violence of existence in contemporary life as well as to the passionate female desires that await an acknowledgment and, more importantly, a naming.[9] To wear the subversive cloak of the vampire may be metaphorically expressed, for example, in telling of the dread of imposed domesticity, of the possibility of illicit and transgressive (pro)creation outside the heterosexual bond, of the need to pursue and nurture aspects of the shadow self, or of the perverse and numbing enjoyment of violence as a means of entertainment.

Now let us consider some specific examples of the vampire legacy in contemporary Spanish poetry by women. The first to be considered here, written in 1976, is taken from María Victoria Atencia's *Marta & María* and carries the title of "El Conde D" (Count D).[10] It is up to the reader to deduce that the name implied with the modest and enigmatic initial is that of Dracula himself:

> Cada noche te espero desde antes de acostarme,
> Y cuando sobrevienes, agregada presencia
> A mi quehacer, pareja de topacios que rompe
> Contra la piedra azul serena de los míos,
> Dócilmente interrumpo mi sueño y, pues prefieres
> Las sombras, me levanto y cierro las cortinas.
> Ya puedes reclinar tu cabeza en mi hombro
> Y aposentar tus dientes con su sed en mi aorta,
> Boá de Transilvania que me cercase el cuello.
> El mosto de la muerte con su empacho te alienta.
> Me voy quedando fría en tanto que amanece
> Y sorbes acremente mi paz a borbotones.
> (Atencia 1990, 59)

> [Each night I wait for you from before I retire,
> And when you come up, collective presence
> To my task, partner of topazes that breaks
> Against the serene blue stone of mine,
> Gently I interrupt my dreams and, since you prefer
> The shadows, I get up and close the curtains.
> You can now put your head on my shoulder
> And nestle your teeth with their thirst in my aorta,
> Transylvanian boa that surrounds my neck.
> The musty smell of death with its blockage inspires you.
> I am getting cold as dawn approaches
> And you sip pungently my peace welling up.]

Similar to the lyric rendering in Delmira Agustini's modernista poem entitled "El vampiro" (The vampire), here Atencia creates an active female poetic voice to stand in counterpoint to the customary passive feminine body who awaits the vampire's bite. In the opening verse, she states "Te espero" (I wait for you), much as a besotted Juliet longs for her Romeo. Rather than a Sleeping Beauty ravished by the night prowler's unbridled thirst, here the female lyric voice is conscious of the rhythm of the vampire's custom "cada noche" (each night). She willingly interrupts her sleep to hand herself over "dócilmente" (gently) to his embrace, and in a fine domestic touch, adjusts the curtains to his liking. Her complicity in the scene is made evident by her implied permission—"Ya puedes reclinar tu cabeza en mi hombro / y aposentar tus dientes con su sed en mi aorta" (You can now put your head on my shoulder / And nestle your teeth with their thirst in my aorta)—and in her acknowledgment without recrimination that "sorbes acremente mi paz a borbotones" (you sip pungently my peace welling up). The openly erotic charge of this scene, including the unembarrassed description of the exchange of bodily fluids, permits a reading of this poem other than the straightforward one of spectral coupling: namely, it suggests a metapoetic perspective, in that Dracula may be viewed as the male poetic muse whose nocturnal visits allow the female lyric persona to (pro)create herself, in this instance in her self-representation in the poetic text.[11] This metapoetic reading is suggested by the parallel but asymmetric leitmotif of the male poet's visitation by the female muse in the dead of night. The female muse interrupts his sleep, but remains passive and distant, always just out of reach. The poet, in striving to possess her, creates the text that reflects his longing and captures only imperfectly the object and inspiration of his desire. Gustavo Adolfo Bécquer's poem that begins with "Yo soy ardiente, yo soy morena" (I am aflame, I am dark-haired) is an ideal example of this model. Atencia's poem is a parallel yet asymmetric rendering of this emblematic lyric mode, because the subject of the text is female, a female poet, and her muse is male. Moreover, Atencia subverts the cliché of the passive, distant female figure both by inverting the roles and by having the female of the text express and enact volition in regard to sexual coupling. In admitting Dracula to her bed rather than a conventional, human, heterosexual lover, this female speaker implicitly calls into question the validity of that relation, if a woman is to be in possession of her full creative capacity. The question that it implicitly poses is whether a woman can express her full artistic potential if her creative energies are consumed by the patriarchy, especially within the context of matrimony, or at least the prescribed passive role for women in heterosexual coupling. By permitting her unconventional lover to drink aggressively—"sorbes acremente mi paz a borbotones" (you sip pungently my peace welling up)—she in turn invests herself and her Self in the process of (self-)discovery by her muse. Her offspring from the well of the self-same is the poem itself, "El Conde D" (Count D). Atencia thus subverts the traditional submissive role of women, their silence and passivity within the patriarchy, and suggests an alternate route of (pro)creation, one based upon the word. It is a well-worn cliché that vampires customarily bypass the male/female coupling, by means of a bite and the exchange of blood. This woman poet uses the sign of the vampire to 'skirt' the conventional form of (re)production and (pro)creation. From this self-referential perspective, poetry itself is the 'bite' as well as the offspring of the female poet and her muse that, in turn, seduces the reader—and the literary critic—into participating in this subversive way of life/death, reading, knowing, and being outside the patriarchy.[12]

Aurora Luque, a Spanish poet born in 1962, also makes veiled reference to the process described in the Atencia text, wherein the female lyric persona is 'bitten by the poetry bug' in a text entitled "Del descifrar" (On deciphering):

>   Fluir en la corriente sagrada de los versos
>   De una noche a otra noche
>   Y ser atropellada, ser mordida
>   Por la negra belleza que estalla en las palabras.
>   Y qué saturación sentir el aire
>   . . . .
>   O un placer sumergido
>   En las aguas más hondas de la vida:
>   Carne que se entreviese
>   —erótico fulgor rosado y denso—
>   Bajo el encaje oscuro del poema.
>   (Benegas and Munárriz, 415–16)

[To flow in the sacred current of verse
From one night to the next
And to be run over, to be bitten
By the black beauty that erupts in words.
And what saturation to feel the air

> . . . .
> Or a submerged pleasure
> In the deepest waters of life:
> Flesh that is barely glimpsed
> —erotic glow rosy and dense—
> Underneath the dark lace of the poem.]

The vampire's cloak (dis)covers "la negra belleza" (the black beauty), the erotics of (pro)creation beyond penetration, and the female poetic speaker's pleasure in handing herself over to the lover's bite of her dark muse that will produce the body of the text,—"carne que se entreviese" (flesh that is barely glimpsed)—beneath the darkened lace of the poem itself. Thus, the poem appears at the end—the last word—thanks to the coupling of the female poet with the nocturnal visitor inclined to carnal nibbling.

The vampire's representation of the "undead," a category outside the conventional binary opposition of life/death or alive/dead whose gendered options are of course male/female, opens up the option to women poets to explore the patriarchy's equivalencing of women with death, and to suggest alternate and subversive possibilities for rereading this mythic tradition from a female and feminist position. For example, in Guadalupe Grande's "Oficio de crisálida" (Craft of the Chrysalis) the first-person speaker declares at the opening of the poem,

> Durante un tiempo estuve muerta:
> hubo hambre y cansancio,
> y el sonido del mar y el aroma de los alimentos
> y la luz de la vida poblándose, reuniéndose;
> pero algo estuvo muerto.
> (Benegas and Munárriz, 589)

> [For a while I was dead:
> There was hunger and weariness,
> And the sound of the sea and the aroma of food
> And the light of life filling, reuniting,
> but something was dead.]

In this particular poem, the speaker explores the absences that result from death, whether the disappearance of possibilities, such as to "rastrear los pies en el tapiz" (dragging one's feet on the carpet), or more significantly, the disappearance of memory.

But given the opening line of verse cited above, it is obvious that this female speaker is referring not so much to the loss of a loved one through physical cessation of life, but rather to a death of the self that is a reality in so many women's lives.

The lyric voice lends a note of quiet desperation to this experience by comparing the state of (un)death as represented in the chrysalis to that of her own. The need for recognition is not forthcoming from the distanced "tú" (you) whose "dócil y atónita bondad" (docile and astounded goodness) masks indifference with superficial courtesy:

> Durante un tiempo estuve muerta
> Como una crisálida guardada en una caja de cartón,
> Detenida en el umbral, olvidada del gusano y de la mariposa.
> Instante perpetuo, cómo duele despertar de tu sosegada
> Indiferencia,
> De tu dócil y atónita bondad.
> (Benegas and Munárriz, 590)

> [During a time I was dead
> As a chrysalis kept in a cardboard box,
> Held in check at the threshold, forgotten by the worm and the butterfly.
> Perpetual instant, how it hurts to wake from your peaceful
> Indifference,
> From your docile and astounded goodness.]

Here, the female lyric voice rejects the passivity of the woman-death motif by bestowing voice upon the "undead" female speaker of the poetic text. She does so in order to explore the means to leave behind the threshold's shadow and emerge as the graceful butterfly, symbol of resurrection and transformation, that was alluded to in the text. As in the case of both the Atencia and Luque poems, the text itself is the means by which the poet subverts the patriarchy's commandeering of the figure of the dead woman as a source of poetic inspiration. In this poem, the undead woman utilizes that image subversively in order to awaken her voice, to put into motion the transformation from chrysalis to butterfly, and to counteract the loss of and memory of the female presence.

The enriching and subversive possibility of the shadow self, yet another manifestation of the vampire motif, finds expression in Teresa Agustín's "Me visto para la luna" (I Dress for the Moon). In this poem colored with romantic tones, the female first-person speaker makes reference to the clichéd context of the vampire's nightly prowls, and like the actively motivated co-conspirator of the Atencia text, she participates in the process of seduction and surrender. A gothic ambience is suggested by the moon, the nightly visits, the lovers' tryst among some ruins, and the pathetic fallacy that informs the speaker's anticipation, "y canto mi miedo a los ríos salvajes / que crecen bulliciosos mientras fluye la noche" (And I sing my fear to the wild rivers / that grow restlessly while the night flows) (Benegas and Munárriz, 482). However, the referent of "mi único enamorado" (my only beloved) to whom the female lyric voice makes reference in the opening lines of verse is not an aspiring Dracula in the classical manner. In a subversive twist, the speaker reveals the beloved's identity as residing within, the shadow self whose identity must be both sought after and protected from social norms, if female identity is to be nurtured to its fullest form:

> Es el triunfo de lo invisible sobre lo visible,
> Es el grito el que subyace:
> Yo, siempre yo
> Y la desconocida yo.
> Me visto para la luna
> Que influye sobre mi único enamorado.
> Como Endimión, yo también la espero.
>   (Benegas and Munárriz, 482)
>
> [It is the triumph of the invisible over the visible,
> It is the underlying shout:
> I, always I
> And the unknown I.
> I dress up for the moon
> Who influences my only beloved.
> As Endymion, I also await her.]

The death conventionally feared by woman's public persona that was formed by the patriarchy must be pursued, so that "la desconocida yo" (the unknown I) may emerge. The reference to Endymion in the final line of verse casts a metapoetic shadow over the pursuit of this hidden self, and clearly suggests a female reappropriation of male poetic desire:

> The story of Endymion has a peculiar charm from the human meaning which it so thinly veils. We see in Endymion the young poet, his fancy and his heart seeking in vain for that which can satisfy them, finding his favorite hour in the quiet moonlight, and nursing there beneath the beams of the bright and silent witness the melancholy and the ardor which consumes him. The story suggests aspiring and poetic love, a life spent more in dreams than in reality, and an early and welcome death. (*Bullfinch's Mythology*, 204)

Denial of domesticity, dedication to a life of creativity usually denied to women, and the acknowledgment as well as pursuit of a same-sex intense friendship personified in "la desconocida yo" as the "único enamorado" here contribute to the expression of the vampire motif as well as the feminist questioning of conventional patriarchal strictures for women, their creativity, and their hidden and thus dangerous desires.

A less idealized version of the shadow self than that offered in the previous text appears in Rosa Lentini's rendering, with distinct tonalities of the feminized vampire that lives within:

> Esta mujer que viene a encontrarse conmigo cada noche
> descubre mi sueño de blanco vestido
> Mientras hace sonar cascabeles que se clavan
> Entre los hombros y el cuello.
> (Benegas and Munárriz, 325)
>
> [This woman who comes to meet with me each night
> Discovers my dreams dressed in white
> While she makes little bells ring that are set
> Between my shoulders and my neck.]

After declaring that "La luz excesiva mata tanto como la oscuridad" (Excessive light kills just like the darkness)—a clear allusion to the vampire's aversion to sunlight—and making references to metaphorical bloodletting in daily life such as "el odio nos haga clavar las uñas en otros ojos" (hate makes us bury our nails in others' eyes) or "faltas que nadie enmienda / y ningún lugar para otras heridas" (faults that no one corrects / and no other place for other wounds), the speaker at the end identifies those shadow defects whose presence on the surface of the self commits the wounding and fault finding so divisive in daily exchange, and contributes to the death of intimacy and a healthy social contract:

> Ella es el nombre que he violado,
> La intonación que me niego,
> Una devoción de culpa ajena,
> Y el espíritu que, dormido a mis pies,
> Vuela y vuelve del país sin edad,
> A transgredir toda medida.
> (Benegas and Munárriz, 326)

> [She is the name that I have violated,
> The intonation that I deny,
> A devotion to someone else's guilt,
> And the spirit that, asleep at my feet,
> Flies and returns from the ageless country,
> To transgress all measure.]

This poetic speaker thus acknowledges the bloody, destructive vampire presence that dwells within. The poem serves to "bring to light" the defective shadow and encourage its leave taking, much as the vampire flees the approaching daylight to return to its protective lair.

The elision of love and vampirism finds expression in the six-line poem entitled "El exceso" (Excess) by Josefa Parra, where excess may refer to the absorption of one lover by the other, either in the strict sense of the conventional exchange of blood in the vampire tradition, or to the loss of the self within the context of romantic love. The vampire motif is suggested by the first line of verse, as well as the reference to literary tradition, and the symbolic kisses that seal the newly initiated lover's fate, that separate him/her from the rhythms of daily life and the clear demarcation between the living and the dead:

> He de beberte a sorbos muy pequeños,
> Deletrear las frases, hacer alto
> Después de cada encuentro,
> Cerrar los libros de las confidencias,
> Amarte muy despacio, y distanciando
> Los besos como islas.
> (Benegas and Munárriz, 603)

> [I must drink you in little sips,
> Spell the sentences, halt
> After each encounter,
> Close the books of confidences,

> Love you very slowly, and distancing
> The kisses as islands.]

In contrast to several other poems considered here, in the case of this text, no gender determination is offered for either the lyric voice, the pursuer of the romantic pair, or of the receptive "tú" (you), which thus suggests the possibility of a homoerotic reading, totally consonant with the vampire tradition of the "intense bond of friendship" that was mentioned earlier. It should be noted that the receiver of the amorous yet bloodthirsty advances remains in the passive role reminiscent of the traditional vampire tale. It is up to the reader to determine the gender implications of this enigmatic text and to ponder the negative connotations that are suggested by the possibility of vampirelike absorption of romantic love. This absorption of the "tú" by the speaker is reflected in his/her total passivity within the context of the amorous advances, and the "tú's" representation only through the lyric voice of the first-person speaker.

The final category to which I should like to make reference is to that of the metaphorical vampire whose footprints may be fleetingly perceived in the violence of daily life, and specifically in the monstrous metaphors that make reference to but do not name the sickness of contemporary society. Blanca Andreu's verse is drenched in surrealistic blood that becomes the objective correlative for the horror that permeates human exchange and the loss of a sense of self, connectedness, and the possibility of human intimacy:

> O viene Rilke el poeta
> a contarme que sí, que de veras tú pasas a mi sangre
> pero de qué nos sirve.
> Veneno y sombra extraña, extraño no decirlo, de metales
> Muy fríos
> y faltos de latido:
> amor, es eso, yo bebo violas rotas,
> pienso cosas quebradas,
> En verdad yo me bebo la infancia del coñac,
> Bebo las locas ramas virginales,
> bebo mis venas que se adormecen para querer morir,
> bebo lo que me resta cuando dejo mi cuello
> bajo la luna de guillotina,
> bebo la sábana de los sacrificios y bebo el amor que salpica

sueño
pero de qué nos sirve.

(Andreu, 39)

[Or Rilke the poet comes
to tell me yes, that truly you pass through to my blood
but what good does it do.
Poison and strange shadow, strange not to say it, of metals
That are very cold
and lacking a heartbeat:
love, it is that, I drink broken violas,
I think broken things,
In truth I drink up the infancy of cognac,
I drink the crazy virginal branches,
I drink my veins that nod off in order to want to die,
I drink what remains when I leave my neck
Under the guillotine moon,
I drink the sheet of the sacrifices and I drink the love that
spatters
Dreams
But what good does it do.]

The metaphorical vampire "I" turns upon its ungendered self to absorb the life force run amok but declares at the close of this unsettling text, "But what good does it do," not a question but a disembodied plaint of social anxiety and unease.

In her poem entitled "Anoréxica" (Anorexica), Isla Correyero evokes the spectral image of the anorexic victim of the patriarchy's imposition of an impossible standard of female and supposedly feminine beauty. As was pointed out earlier, the blood images associated with this textual body refer to a lack, a loss, whether of the healthy glow of female adolescence or the menstrual flow. This particular victim is also tellingly compared with the legend of Sleeping Beauty, but in this case, sleep and death are the final solution to the hunger to achieve the loss and lack prescribed by the pursuit of beauty and acceptance:

> La bella es sangre de esqueleto
> Translúcido,
> Es aire y huevo de lo ido,
> De la histeria es aire,
> De lo fugaz,
> De la velocidad agujereada.

. . . .
Es la bella anoréxica lujosa
Que va a morir mañana,
Sin desayuno,
Con la privación de la hermosura.
               (Benegas and Munárriz, 296–97)

[The beautiful young woman is skeletal blood,
Translucent,
She is the air and egg of the departed,
Of hysteria she is the air,
Of the fleeting,
Of perforated velocity.
. . . .
She is the beautiful, luxurious anorexic
Who is going to die tomorrow,
Without breakfast,
With the privation of beauty.]

The speaker points out that a woman's freedom to make choices for herself in this case leads her paradoxically to become enslaved within a system over which she has no control. Her supposed liberty as an emancipated—and emaciated—female is a delusion, given that "es artificio de la crueldad / su libertad / su boca, / el estómago blanco, / el recto loco de sacrificio / y éxtasis" (Her liberty is the artifice of / cruelty, / her mouth, / her white stomach, / her mad rectum [the artifice] of sacrifice / and ecstasy).

The violence that pervades contemporary society in the guise of entertainment also conjures up for the discerning reader traces of the unnatural alien other, whether vampire or some other monstrous manifestation. In Luisa Castro's *Los versos del eunuco* (Verses of the Eunuch), this female poet gives voice to social unease, "En un esperpento aceptado, el teatro de la pasión y la farsa del desamor se combinan y alternan como protagonistas de la impotencia enmascarada y la conquistada falsedad de quienes sobreviven a la mueca diaria del eunuco" (In an accepted absurdity, the theater of passion and the farce of indifference are combined and alternate as protagonists of masked impotence and conquered insincerity of those who survive the daily grimace of the eunuch).[13] The figure of the impotent eunuch pervades even a romantic interlude, and leads to the acceptance of violence as performance and a means of senseless distraction:

Y nos queremos con el hilo
Hermoso
De la tarde hueca,
Y nos queremos, sí, si el eunuco
De pronto
Osa escalar la dura arquitectura de mi sangre.
Estaremos en la sangre,
Beberemos otra vez la tibia sangre,
Compraremos un billete a ver la sangre.
                                    (L. Castro 1990b, 33)

[And we love each other with the beautiful
Thread
Of the empty afternoon,
And we love each other, yes, if the eunuch
Without warning
Dares to scale the hard architecture of my blood.
We will be {awash} in blood,
We will once again drink the lukewarm blood,
We will buy a ticket to see the blood.]

The vampire casts its shadow and inhabits "la mueca diaria del eunuco" (the daily grimace of the eunuch). The deadening effects of violence turned entertainment play out in the speaker's choice for an amorous afternoon's pastime, where blood and gore drench the spectator's conscience and sensibility, leaving the death of humanity's shame in their wake.

Two poems from the pens of Luisa Castro and Juana Castro, whose focus is that of the monstrous nature of domesticity, defamiliarize this common terrain, and present the horror of indoctrination for the young. For the knowing reader, it is easy to spot the blood-drenched shadow of the vampire lurking in the background. The first text, "El cerdo" (The Pig) by Luisa Castro, presents for the reader a text vocalized in the first-person by an adult female speaker who conjures up a bloody, highly wounding memory of the past. The poem begins innocently enough, with the remembrance of village festivities and special clothing donned for the yearly event:

Me habían puesto una falda nueva porque llegaba gente,
El agua de colonia,
Rescatada de la profundidad de los armarios,
Resbalaba por mi frente

Una vez al año, por diciembre,
Tibia.

(L. Castro 1990a, 19)

[They had dressed me in a new skirt because people were coming,
Cologne,
Rescued from the depths of the cupboards,
Slipped across my forehead
One time per year, in December,
Lukewarm.]

The speaker admits that "Tengo una capacidad de olvido propia de la niñez" (I have a capacity to forget, typical of childhood), but what cannot be washed away from consciousness is the slaughter of "el cerdo" (the pig) of the poem's title, not so much the end result, for "las tripas, el riñon, el corazón, el hígado / desaparecen pronto de mis sueños. / Su llanto en mi cabeza reproduce débiles resonancias," (the intestines, the kidney, the heart, the liver / soon disappear from my dreams. / Their crying in my head reproduces weak resonances), given the forgiveness of the passage of time of visual and auditory stimuli. Rather, that which haunts the speaker is the olfactory assault: "Pero el olor a sangre, / adherido para siempre en las bombillas tan tenues, alimentaba todos mis malos pensamientos" (But the smell of blood / sticking forever to the tenuous light bulbs, fed all my dark thoughts) (20). The suggestive nature of this olfactory image taints the present context, with the implication of slaughter, bloodletting, and a living hell for the female sensibility within the domestic milieu. That which is underscored is the questionable validity of the sanitized version of domesticity as well as of the human relationship to the production of food based on animals, and the role of women within the patriarchal, domestic context. Also, the violence inherent in food production of traditional village practices suggests a metonymic relation to the violence visited upon women within that same context. The festive slaughter of animals enacts a lack of sensibility hardened into custom that also finds expression in the treatment of women.

The second poem, by Juana Castro, is number XVIII of her *Fisterra* (Earth's End), and from a third-person perspective, recounts the village tradition of porcine slaughter and the consequent bout of sausage-making, once again in the month of December.

The slaughtered pigs appear only metonymically as "redondos, / están gigantes blancos / desangrados, que entregaron su grito/ a la negra alborada / de diciembre y su frío" (round / they are giant white [masses] / drained of blood, who handed over their shriek / to the black dawn / of December and their cold) (40). Work is accomplished along a gendered divide, with women who "enhebran las tripas, / lavan las cabezas / y ungen con la masa / de carne roja el viento / del comino, la sal y la pimienta" (thread the intestines, / wash the heads / and anoint the wind with the dough / of red meat / of cumin, salt, and pepper), and the men "afilados cuchillos, / de las piezas colgadas / separan los jamones, abren / el vaho denso del vientre, con el machete cuentan / el costillar y el lomo" (sharpened knives, / from the hanging pieces / they separate the hams, they open / the dense vapor of the belly, with the machete they count / the ribs and the loin). The domestic normality of this bloody scene where nurturing and human sustenance are accompanied by the carnage, blood, suffering, and sacrifice of animals play havoc on the sensibilities of a girl-child overcome by the wash of feelings awakened by "(d)el griterío, la sangre, / tanta carne batiendo / untuosas manos, las paredes, / las sillas y las puertas" (the shouting, the blood / so much meat beating against / sticky hands, the walls / the chairs and the doors). Her only means of self-defense when faced with an experience so ambivalent is that of escape:

> Sola niña,
> Sin nadie,
> Huye lejos, al campo
> Verde y limpio de musgos,
> Al aire de las rocas
> Y los cielos abiertos.
> Sola niña, aterida,
> Sin comprender,
> Llorando.
>
> (J. Castro, 41)

> [Solitary girl,
> Without anyone,
> Flee far away, to the countryside
> Green and clean of moss,
> To the air on the rocks
> And the open skies.

> Solitary girl, terrified,
> Without understanding,
> Crying.]

The solitary little girl seeks comfort in her escape to the green hills, where she can find solace in the fresh air and open sky. The reader is left to ponder the enigmatic message the residue of which remains somewhere between a pessimistic contemplation of the child's eventual return, indoctrination, and desensitization to the animals' necessary sacrifice and the woman's submission to patriarchal violence, and a more optimistic possibility of the girl-child's eventual escape to another world outside the confines of village life, patriarchal violence and control, and human sustenance—whether physical, political, or ethical—based upon the monstrosity of domination and the death of body, mind, and spirit.

As has been demonstrated by the creative permutations of the vampire motif in recent Spanish poetry by women, the ancient legend of the nocturnal monster from a distant land who paradoxically resides within continues to hold fascination within the contemporary context. The women poets of contemporary Spain who have given voice to the vampire, as manifested in these unsettling texts, confront the darkness not only of the shadow self, but also that of the modern milieu that exerts the same violent and death-producing force upon women as Dracula and his minions. The metaphorical and metonymic extensions of the vampire legend, rather than inducing the demise of the unsuspecting, passive, and somnolent maiden, here invigorate the female textual body and contribute to the revivification of the vampire legend from a decidedly female and feminist perspective. In the forceful and confident appropriation of the vampire legend, these female poets not only face the monster within, but also those who dwell in society's shadows. In addition, their inversion, revision, and subversion of this ancient motif opens to possibility the female poet's active participation in the questioning of patriarchal interpretation and control of female existence and experience, including that of the creative impulse.

Notes

1. For a review of the figure of the vampire, see especially Auerbach, Dundes, Gelder, Gordon and Hollinger, Heldreth and Pharr, and Rickels.

2. See Sandra Tomc's "Dieting and damnation: Ann Rice's *Interview with the vampire.*"

3. This function is similar to that of the male hero who left domesticity behind to explore the American West.

4. The strong bond of male friendship suggested by the traditional vampire tale also gives rise to the inscription of the homoerotic.

5. Bornay also offers several very telling examples of this interpretation of the *New Woman* as a vampire from the visual arts.

6. And from a more contemporary perspective, taking the metaphorical turn suggested by Gordon and Hollinger, the present-day reader could well extrapolate from Dr. Robinson's "scientific" findings a reading of woman's hunger(s) that subverts patriarchy's condemnation of female identity, to infuse the figure of the female vampire with vitality, will, and an empowering sense of self-determination and nurturance.

7. The English version of "The vampire" and "The metamorphoses of the vampire" used in the preparation of this manuscript were taken from *Baudelaire in English* (Clark and Sykes, 1997).

8. The figure of the female vampire was developed in the romantic literary tradition as a subcategory of the male version. See especially chapter 2, "The female vampire," in Twitchell's *The Living Dead.* In *Our Vampires, Ourselves*, Nina Auerbach examines the nineteenth-century female vampire as well, but also extrapolates this function to the patriarchal interpretation of the rise of feminism in the 1970s. But from a twentieth-century female perspective, the vampire persona holds special attraction: "Feminists in the 1970s were discovering, just as the vampire's lovers do, the multiorgasmic versatility of women's eroticism, which, despite the admonitions of male experts, requires no penis for arousal" (149–50). As we shall see in succeeding examples, this bypassing of heterosexual intercourse for (pro)creation lends itself easily to the possibility of a metatextual reading for the vampire text, whether from the perspective of a male or female writer.

9. Spanish women poets are not the first to take advantage of the obvious subversive possibilities of the vampire motif. Within a Hispanic context, the modernist Uruguayan poet Delmira Agustini formulated an early feminist response to Baudelaire's misogynist vampires in her poem "The vampire," in which she creates a self-actualizing female voice to counteract the silencing enacted by the French poet. See the excellent article by Patricia Varas, "Modernism or *Modernismo*? Delmira Agustini and the gendering of turn-of-the-century Spanish-American poetry" as well as Gabriela Mora's "Decadentismo y vampirismo en el modernismo hispanoamericano: un cuento de Clemente Palma."

10. The version of the text that I used in the preparation of this manuscript appeared in Atencia's *La señal: Poesía 1961–1989*. The translation of this poem and other translations, unless otherwise indicated, are my own.

11. John Wilcox utilizes this text as an example of Atencia's commitment "to the revision of androcentric myths" (255). The feminist rewriting of Dracula from the point of view of the woman, here seen not so much as a victim as a coconspirator, leads to enticing possibilities for (pro)creation without penetration and the penis. In this case, the pen really is mightier than "the sword."

12. For a consideration of Romanticism's equivalencing of the artist and the vampire, see Twitchell's chapter 5, "The Artist as Vampire." He also contends that today's modern literary critic has co-opted the role of the hapless victim of the traditional vampire: "The critic has been made artist once removed, and the unknowing artist now depends upon him [sic] for information and sustenance, as well as the reverse" (143).

13. Taken from the back cover of *Los versos del eunuco*.

Works Cited

Andreu, Blanca. 1994. *El sueño oscuro: poesía reunida 1980–1989*. Madrid: Hiperión.

Atencia, María Victoria. 1990. *La señal: poesía 1961–1989*. Málaga: Excmo. Ayuntamiento de Málaga.

Auerbach, Nina. 1995. *Our vampires, ourselves*. Chicago: University of Chicago Press.

Benegas, Noni and Jesús Munárriz, eds. 1997. *Ellas tienen la palabra: dos décadas de poesía española*. Madrid: Hiperión.

Bornay, Erika. 1990. *Las hijas de Lilith*. Madrid: Cátedra.

Bullfinch's mythology. 1979. New York: Avenel Books.

Castro, Juana. 1992. *Fisterra*. Madrid: Durendal Ediciones Literarias.

Castro, Luisa. 1990a. *Los hábitos del artillero*. Madrid: Visor.

———. 1990b. *Los versos del eunuco*. Madrid: Hiperión.

Clark, Carol and Robert Sykes, eds. 1997. *Baudelaire in English*. New York: Penguin Books.

Dijkstra, Bram. 1986. *Idols of perversity: fantasies of feminine evil in fin-de-siècle culture*. New York: Oxford University Press.

Dundes, Alan, ed. 1998. *The vampire: a casebook*. Madison: University of Wisconsin Press.

Gelder, Ken. 1994. *Reading the vampire*. New York: Routledge.

Gordon, Joan and Veronica Hollinger, eds. 1997. *Blood read: the vampire as metaphor in contemporary culture*. Philadelphia: University of Pennsylvania Press.

Heldreth, Leonard G. and Mary Pharr, eds. 1999. *The blood is the life: vampires in literature*. Bowling Green, OH: Bowling Green State University Popular Press.

Mora, Gabriela. 1997. Decadentismo y vampirismo en el modernismo hispanoamericano: un cuento de Clemente Palma. *Revista de crítica literaria latinoamericana*. 46: 191–98.

Rickels, Laurence A. 1995. *The vampire lectures*. Minneapolis: University of Minnesota Press.

Tomc, Sandra. Dieting and damnation: Ann Rice's *Interview with the vampire*. In *Blood read: the vampire as metaphor in contemporary culture*, edited by Joan Gordon and Veronica Hollinger. Philadelphia: University of Pennsylvania Press.

Twitchell, James B. 1981. *The living dead: a study of the vampire in romantic literature*. Durham, NC: Duke University Press.

Varas, Patricia. 1997. "Modernism or *Modernismo?* Delmira Agustini and the gendering of turn-of-the-century Spanish-American poetry." In *Modernism, gender, and culture: a cultural studies approach*, edited by Lisa Rado, 149–60. New York: Garland Publishing, Inc.

Wilcox, John C. 1997. *Women poets of Spain, 1860-1990: toward a gynocentric vision*. Urbana: University of Illinois Press.

The Queer Poetics of Ana María Moix

JILL ROBBINS

THIS ESSAY WILL EXPLORE HOW A QUEER DISCOURSE ELABORATED by the Catalan woman Ana María Moix rhetorically disrupts the gender stereotypes underlying the Spanish nationalist narratives of Franco's regime and the transnational capitalist strategies of the 1960s and 1970s. Queer theory has made limited inroads into Spanish literary studies, particularly into the study of literature by women, where it is often regarded as one more factor that will keep women writers on the margins of canonicity. It is true that the intellectual and aesthetic equality of women's writing is still questioned in contemporary Spain, and that critics' focus often shifts to the personal life of the writer if she is a woman. Lesbianism invites exactly this sort of gossipy criticism, to the detriment of serious attention to the texts. This article, therefore, walks a fine line between the naming or representation of a particular homosexual subject and the rhetorical devices an author may use to produce a "queer effect," that is, to mark the discontinuities within the dominant discourse or to signal issues that cannot be publicly named.

Although Moix wrote her poetry in the late 1960s and early 1970s, at the time when gay and lesbian militancy was beginning in Spain, and clearly before the articulation of queer theory, her work conforms more to the parameters of the latter than the former. David Halperin explains that queer identity is "a positionality that is not restricted to lesbians and gay men but is in fact available to anyone who feels marginalized because of his or her sexual practices" (62).

Unlike gay identity, which, though deliberately proclaimed in an act of affirmation, is nonetheless rooted in the positive fact of homosexual object-choice, queer identity need not be grounded in any positive truth or in any stable reality. As the very word implies, "queer" does not name some natural kind or refer to some determinate object; it acquires its meaning from its oppositional relation to the norm (62).

Moix's work is a perfect example of the disjunctions between articulations of the lesbian and the queer, as critics of her fiction have noted.[1] In her letters to Rosa Chacel, Moix criticizes the confrontational tactics of the student protest movement, so it should not surprise us that her poetics avoid explicit criticism of oppression, dovetailing with theories that problematize subjectivization, that is, the articulation of power relationships and the construction of national subjects with specific gender and sexual characteristics.[2]

In the case of Spain, those subjects were emphatically heterosexual, based upon models derived from Catholicism and a skewed reading of the Spanish imperial past. Thus, although my title refers to a lesbian poetics, lesbianism did not officially exist in Franco's Spain.[3] Of course, by that I do not mean that women did not have erotic relationships with other women, but rather that their sexual practices were invisible because women—decent women, that is—did not have sex for other than procreative purposes, according to the dominant ideology. Particularly in the early decades following the Civil War, women's sexuality was made invisible by the discursive cloak of maternity, which was confounded with concepts of the Spanish nation, "la Madre Patria" (the Motherland), Catholicism, and empire, as numerous historians, sociologists, and art historians have explained in recent years.[4] According to the "ideology of domesticity," the ideal woman was limited to the private sphere, and the "private woman" was her man's domain. Even the women who escaped the literal enactment of marital possession by becoming nuns reenacted it symbolically in their seclusion and submission to the patriarchal hierarchy of the same church that provided the ideological justification for the domestic gender order. In both cases, the women's names were erased and replaced by others chosen for them. The male, whether husband, priest, or father, had the duty of keeping the private woman inviolate, safe from foreign invasion, and her only possible transgression—either by allowing invasion or abandoning the private sphere for the public—would make her "una mujer pública" (a public woman), signaling and justifying her symbolic or literal death, the stain cleansed with her own blood.[5] This image of the private woman came to embody the Spanish national ideal in the early postwar period: the virginal, Catholic Madre Patria safely guarded within her national and cultural borders. Xenophobia was internally displaced onto the public woman—the worker, the prostitute, the lover—who had been rhetorically identified with the republican, or loyalist, cause during the Civil War, and was thereafter depicted as foreign, inherently without honor (roja [red]), and reduced to her sex, forever at the disposal of the male.

Only "las raras" (the rare ones)—the unmarriageable, the unmarried, the professional women—remained outside the public/private paradigm underlying the symbolic system of Francoism. "Una mujer rara," as Carmen Martín Gaite has explained, would always be considered a social outcast, but she was pitied rather than scorned because the dominant ideology cast her as a woman who had failed to find a husband, rather than as one who did not desire men. The connotation of lesbianism is indeed a shadow behind the term "rara," but it was not made explicit because lesbianism was simply *not conceptually possible* in the symbolic order of Francoist Spain, where female sexuality and desire could only be seen as a reflection of male desire. Even a 1985 study of homosexuality in Spain says the following about lesbianism: "se observa . . . que es en el polo de lo masculino donde aparece la sexualidad y el deseo. Por contra, el lugar de lo femenino será el lugar de 'afectividad' y del no deseo" (one observes . . . that it is on the masculine pole that sexuality and desire appear. On the other hand, the place of the feminine is the place of "affection" and of lack of desire)[6] (García Martín and López Fernández 1985, 50). More than biological difference, this assertion reveals an assumption of sameness, as Luce Irigaray has explained: a normal woman is a kind of man; she is, at the same time, the negative image of man (desire/no desire) and "a man minus the possibility of (re)presenting oneself as a man" (27). What, then, is "una mujer rara"? She is unimaginable, and she thus escapes symbolization, registering only as a stutter or a shadow behind the looking glass. She therefore remains undefined and unexamined, made invisible and silenced. This blind spot, this silence, this conceptual gap, this queerness, provides a vantage point from which to examine and reveal the reversibility and lacunae in the gendered social order; it makes visible the invisibility of all women, save as reflections or negatives of male desire.[7]

The perspective that queers Francoism's isolationist foundations also provides a space from which to critique the economic policies that the state adopted in the 1950s and 1960s in order to rejoin the world order. The transnationalization of capital that began after World War II and accelerated through the Cold War (though especially following it and in the wake of technological advances, leading eventually to present-day globalization) brought with it a promise of increased liberalism, that is, the spread of democracy to formerly "oppressed" countries, as national boundaries weakened and traditional class and gender distinctions became less relevant. The development of a Western feminism in Spain in the 1960s can therefore be seen in light of the economic, political, and cultural transformation of the country that ensued from the Economic Stabilization Plan of 1959, which brought traditional, nationalistic concepts of Spanish purity into an uncomfortable marriage with the very foreign fashions, mores, pedagogies, and intellectual movements that Franco had earlier demonized. This union revealed the internal inconsistencies in both systems, invalidating the hegemonic discourses of the right and the left that had dominated Spanish aesthetics in the early decades of Francoism. This rupture, as Guillermo Carnero has called it, appears in the cultural production of the 1960s, which exhibited a mixture of high and low forms and allusions to foreign and domestic texts, while also critiquing the new materialistic international economic order. In these complex circumstances, a Spanish woman speaking as a man and using Spanish, Catalan, and international models to discuss questions of agency and disillusionment produced a stutter in the discourses of both the national and the world orders. Her questions belie both the particular homogeneity of "Spanishness"—"España es diferente" (Spain is different)—and the universality of Western discourse and capital.

It is exactly as a stutter and a shadow that such queerness emerges in Ana María Moix's poetry, originally published between 1969 and 1972 and later collected in the volume *A imagen y semejanza* (In the image and likeness) in 1983. Moix, one of the original *Nueve novísimos poetas españoles* (Nine new Spanish poets) anthologized by José María Castellet in 1970, that is, a founding member of arguably the most important group of Spanish poets since the Generation of 1927, is perhaps best known now as a novelist, short-story writer, and an editor of the prestigious publishing house, Editorial Lumen. Her books of poetry—*Baladas del Dulce Jim* (Ballads of Sweet Jim) (1969), *No Time for Flowers* (1971), *Call Me Stone* (1972)—tell and retell stories of love, disillusionment, death, and despair, using a variety of characters, locales, and poetic and narrative forms. The stories themselves may seem traditional: a love triangle, a broken heart, unrequited love, strictly heterosexual. The foregrounding and parody of romantic conventions, however—including phrases, emotions, poetic structures, and plots—expose the gendered nature of love stories and hint at a hidden homoeroticism behind the compulsory heterosexuality of those models.[8] This queerness is highlighted by the comments of the speaker, gendered as female, who plays her identity off the romantic male figures of the poems. The other female figures in these books are passive, archetypal, nearly nonexistent; they seem to be merely anonymous voices that perpetuate male legends, or else pretexts for or victims of men's actions.[9] The books thus also play out the problem of identity within a gendered social order for a female who does not wish to become a "normal woman"—meaning "a lesser man"—yet lacks the ground for "exceptional womanhood," except as what Rosa Chacel calls "una feminidad varonil" (virile femininity) in a 1966 letter to Moix (Rodríguez Fisher, 121).[10] At the same time, the references to and intertextualities with foreign texts and contexts reproduce a cultural exchange and suggest that the disillusionment and gender stereotypes are not confined to Spain.

Rachel Blau DuPlessis reminds us that lyric poetry is always gendered:

> To talk about lyric, one must say something about beauty, something about love and sex, something about Woman and Man and their positionings, something about active agency versus malleability. This is a cluster of foundational materials with a gender cast built into the heart of lyric. The foundational cluster concerns voice (and silencing), power (appropriation and tran-

scendence), nature (as opposed to formation and culture), gaze (framing, specularity, fragmentation), and the sources of poetic matter–narratives of romance, of the sublime, scenes of inspiration, the muse as conduit. (71)

Any writer of lyric poetry is immediately confronted with these foundational materials, and the gender/power inversion clearly makes such a confrontation more complicated and disturbing for the female writer than for the male. Moix's response is to foreground the conventions and their hidden gender implications, making them appear and sound strange and unnatural.

Let us examine this process in the first text of *Baladas del Dulce Jim*. The poem begins with images characteristic of romantic verse—"Un hombre triste, su barco" (A sad man, his ship)—reminiscent of José de Espronceda's Romantic poem, "Canción del pirata" (The pirate's song). The following words, however, undermine the romantic image by separating the man from his boat, from the Spanish context, and from the speaker: "Un hombre triste, su barco, Alegre, ese fue Jim. Dulce conmigo, mas no risueño: qué corazón" (A sad man, his ship, Happy, that was Jim. Sweet with me, but not cheerful: what [a] heart). The names in this line—Alegre and Jim—create a dissonance, marking a rupture with the romantic image of the unfettered outlaw/hero. The name of the boat conflicts with Jim's character rather than symbolizing it, creating a schism that cannot be resolved in the statement, "ese fue Jim." The hero's unheroic English name also clashes with the image of Espronceda's pirate, reminding us perhaps of the role that English pirates played in the decline of the Spanish empire, yet also of the "Dulce Jim," Jim Hawkins of *Treasure Island*.[11] What is more, the Spanish pronunciation of Jim—"him"—makes this figure representative of his gender, as "El" (Him), "Ella" (Her), and "Aquella chica" (That girl) will be in *No Time for Flowers*. The punctuation of the sentence also marks separations and undercuts the passion of romantic sentiment, as does the prosaic form of the lines, which will conflict with the internal assonant rhyme in the following stanzas. The stanza form is, in effect, more reminiscent of Allen Ginsburg's *Howl* than it is of poems in the Spanish literary tradition, an intertextuality that will be reiterated in the references to Lorca, Cernuda, Vallejo, "the best minds of [a] generation destroyed by madness" (the Generation of 1927, destroyed by the

Civil War), and in the criticism both of Spanish cultural myths and of the effects of capitalism.

The speaker inserted herself into the above lines as a nameless character in the story, one of many witnesses who "knew Jim" and had a relationship with him. She continues speaking of Jim in the following stanzas, but she does so by mimicking prototypical female choral voices—one who fears him, one who admires him—who comment upon Jim's comings and goings:

> Jim en el parque, y sin sombrero.
> Ay Dios, qué miedo si es un matón.
> Ay Dios, qué pena si un día parte como llegó.
> (15)

> [Jim in the park, and without a hat.
> Oh God, what a fright if he's a killer.
> Oh God, what a pity if one day he departs just as he came.]

The stock expressions and characterizations of Jim highlight the power differential of gender inherent in the lyric: Jim appears as an image, walking alone, whereas the women are invisible, reduced to the kind of anonymous voices that predominate in popular verse, praying to God to save them from Jim's violent passions and wanderlust. Still, the use of periods rather than exclamation marks downplays and/or renders ironic Jim's grandeur and the women's sentiments of fear and longing.

The high drama and passion of romanticism, and the exaltation of Jim's figure, are further undercut in the following lines by the girl's observation that Jim is a clown, followed by Jim's own subsequent clownish behavior:

> Tiene los ojos rojos y on the sea mira como un traidor.
> ¿Serás payaso?, dije, y sobre el césped se revolcó.
> Y eso que no soy niña que con desconocidos antes hablara yo.
> (15)

> [He has red eyes and on the sea he looks like a traitor.
> Could you be a clown?, I said, and on the lawn he rolled around.
> And I'm not a girl who had ever talked to strangers before.]

The girl emphasizes her conformity to the image of the good girl who does not talk to strangers in a rhythmic line that completes the assonant rhyme. The preceding sentences, however, break the rhythm, interrupt the linguistic uniformity with an English phrase, and disrupt the traditional lyric imagery with the words "payaso" (clown) and "césped" (lawn). The speaker's discourse therefore reveals that she is "rara," seeing Jim not as a romantic hero but as a clown even though she knows his story as well as the other women:

> Cortaste lirios en las praderas y a Johnny mataste en Nueva York.
> Fue por amor: bailaba en Broadway Nancy Flor.
> (15)

> [You cut lilies in the meadow and killed Johnny in New York.
> It was for love: on Broadway danced Nancy Flor.]

The switch to consonant rhyme here signals that this is a story of high culture, but the rhyme is only consonant in its oral, or popular, form. What is more, the prosaic form and the reference to Broadway musicals undermine the concept of "high art." These dissonances highlight the conventions they rupture, and the voice of the girl particularly disrupts the seriousness of romantic sentiment, a role that will continue in the poem as she comments upon Jim's desperate but selfish search for the "quimera de su roto corazón" (the chimera of his broken heart).[12]

Jim searches for his heart in the women who hear his story; that is, he depends upon the sentiments of female readers to enact his history, which is a fairy tale like any other:

> Una ilusión es la quimera de su roto corazón: que, con la primavera, a puerto arribará, y, en los parques de las ciudades, historias a las muchachas contará: la del príncipe y la chica fea, la flor de Nancy, la habanera y Johnny el Prometedor.
>
> Un amor tiene cualquiera
> mas Dulce Jim, jamás.
> Si muere Jim, ¿llorarás tú? Va preguntando a las mujeres, arrabaleras, niñeras, quinceañeras.
> Parte su barco, rojo por dentro, antes de oír el sí o el no. Ya las respuestas no le interesan. Ya nunca baila en Broadway Nancy Flor.
> (15–16)

> [An illusion is the chimera of his broken heart: that, in the Spring, he'll come to port, and, in the city parks, tell the girls

tales: the one about the prince and the ugly girl, Nancy's flower, the Cuban girl[13] and Johnny the Promiser.

Everyone has a love
But Sweet Jim, will not.
If Jim dies, will you cry? He goes around asking the women, slum dwellers, nannies, sweet sixteens.
His ship departs, red within, before he hears the yes or no. The answers matter to him no more. On Broadway no longer dances Nancy Flor.]

When he leaves, Jim becomes a legend—the sad man in the red boat—but his fame and his identity depend upon the ears, mouths, and hearts of the working class women who tell and listen to such tales. They spin them into the "feminine" verse of ballads, oral poems with octosyllabic lines and assonant rhyme, such as the one we see here, others ("habaneras," Broadway tunes) that are mentioned, and still others that we hear. The speaker provides one of those voices—after all, she knows the story by heart and tells it to us here—but she does so from a queer perspective, maintaining her distance, observing and commenting upon the spectacle, disrupting the form, and turning Jim into a clown desperate for the pity of his female public.

The final lines of the poem hint at the ambiguity of this love story, the stutter of the love triangle, and the role of the flower—Nancy Flor—that will mediate between the soul brothers, Johnny and Jim: "Y tiene un perro que ladra fuerte cuando regresa de madrugada al barco que fue de Johnny y de su amor" (And he has a dog that barks loudly when at dawn returns the boat that belonged to Johnny and his paramour). But who is that love? The answer may come in the third poem of the book, the only poem written entirely in verse form and an approximate consonant rhyme, in which Nancy Flor exists solely as the object of desire that links the two men. She dances again, it is true, but only in Jim's dreams. In the middle of the poem, the stanza form is broken by a single, long line that links the two men to each other even more than to Nancy: "Eran hermanos los dos adoradores de Nancy Flor" (They were brothers the two adorers of Nancy Flor) (20). The final stanza suggests that Nancy Flor does not really exist autonomously, but has been created by Johnny, who "pintaba flores de azahar" (painted orange blossoms) (19). The real affair is between the two men who compete for possession of her through art, be it dance or painting:

> Una flor era Nancy para Jim,
> mas una flor pintada antaño
> por un solo enamorado
> que no fue Jim, sino John.
>
> (20)
>
> [A flower was Nancy for Jim
> but a flower painted before
> by a single lover
> that wasn't Jim but John.]

By foregrounding the traditional love triangle, including its poetic and artistic representation, Moix reveals the queerness of the convention and its foundation in female invisibility.

Throughout *Baladas del Dulce Jim*, the women are either the cause of heartbreak (Nancy) or the victims of it (Charo, Rossy), but the female speaker of the poems is not. She is not the object of the poems, but the subject of them, and she therefore has to project herself, not into these female heroine/victims, but into the male heroic poets, dreamers, rebels, who, nonetheless, die as well in a world in which "las palabras se vendían" (words were for sale) (22). This projection takes the form of mimicry or indirect citation of well-known artists, political figures, or characters. In the latter case, the point of view from which the speaker narrates the stories is particularly relevant. Compare, for example, the fifth text of *Baladas del Dulce Jim* with the eighth poem, both cited below. In the former, the female speaker mimics the first-person narration of the typical male protagonist of a hard-boiled detective novel or film noir. In the latter, she narrates in third person the strange—because "normal"—experience of a young girl who dies of a broken heart. Her identification is clearly with the active male figure.

> Yo hubiera deseado verme entrar enfurecida en la pequeña sala del Café Boscán y pistola en mano buscar entre las mesas su rostro ladeado hacia otro rostro. Hablaba palabras húmedas, enmohecidas. Hubiera pegado a su frente el cañón de la pistola y, tan sublime como siempre fue, aún me daría las gracias por haberle proporcionado el frescor del hierro en los últimos momentos de

su vida. Los gavilanes de medianoche se levantaron, sobrecogidos, de las mesas. En mitad del fox se oyó un disparo y al encenderse las luces me vieron a mí, besando la sangre que cruzaba el rostro de la sombra. (22)

[I would have liked to see myself enter, furious, into the small lobby of the Boscan Café and pistol in hand look among the tables for his face turned toward another face. He was speaking humid, moldy words. I would have placed the barrel against his forehead, and, sublime as ever, he would still thank me for having bestowed the coolness of metal upon him in the last moments of his life. The midnight hawks stood up, fearful, from the table. In the middle of the foxtrot a shot was heard and when the lights came on they saw me, kissing the blood across the shadow's face.]

El corazón de Charo flota sobre las aguas del Delta como una flor endamascada. Fue asesinada al amanecer. En los raíles del tren se han encontrado fragmentos del dietario de su amor. Relatos de luna llena, caligrafía imposible, Cristo crucificado, ¿qué pasó? Adamo guarda silencio en el Olimpia y las monjas del Sagrado Corazón cubren el cuerpo mutilado con flores de azahar. Qué historia más extraña la de algunas colegialas. (25)

[Charo's heart floats on the waters of the Delta like a damasked flower. She was murdered at dawn. On the train tracks they found fragments of her love diary. Stories of full moons, impossible handwriting, Christ on the Cross, what happened? Adam keeps quiet on Olympus and the nuns of the Sacred Heart cover the mutilated body with orange blossoms. What a strange story some schoolgirls have.]

In other poems, the mimicry of poetic texts and styles allows the speaker to bring the dead or foreign visionaries to life and to identify with them, as in the following poems, where she evokes Federico García Lorca and César Vallejo:

Charo se volvió al Delta en un barquito de papel y se secó el océano. Recuerdo que llevaron la noticia los periódicos. Qué extraño es a la una de la madrugada saber la ciudad, calle a calle oscura y sosegada, y hacer ver que uno ha olvidado que las casas permanecerán hasta siempre más deshabitadas. A pesar de todo, aún se oye la sirena de los transatlánticos. Es entonces, Federico, cuando mi corazón tiembla arrinconado como un caballito de mar. (31)

[Charo returned to the Delta in a paper boat and the ocean dried up. I remember they carried the story in the papers. How strange it is, at one in the morning, to know the city, street by dark and still street, and to be made to see that one has forgotten that the houses will remain always more uninhabited. Despite everything, you can still hear the siren of the trans-Atlantic cruisers. It is then, Federico, that my heart trembles cornered like a seahorse.]

Moriré en París, como César, una tarde de frío y aguacero. Se lo dije a la sombra antes de que se fuera: Habrá un muerto que no saldrá en los periódicos. Y sonrió con labios de fantasma y risa hueca. (39)[14]

[I will die in Paris, like César, some cold and rainy day. I said it to the shadow before it left: There will be a death that won't appear in the papers. And it smiled with phantom lips and an empty laugh.]

This identification with revolutionary male figures and the adoption of their symbolist visions and surrealist images makes the speaker "una rara," given the paucity of women artists in the Spanish avant-garde and the Falangist demonization of female republicans as "mujeres públicas y/o raras" (public and/or queer women). The identification is doubly queer, however, for several reasons. First, Francoist discourse construed the avant-garde as satanic, republican, and queer, as José María Pemán specifies in the prologue to his epic poem, *Poema de la Bestia y el Angel* (Poem of the Beast and the Angel) (1938):

> toda una generación, arrojada de cabeza al mar de una pura incoherencia intuicionista, ha vivido en pleno pecado de "angelismo", en plena ambición de lograr un conocimiento intuitivo y directo, sin intermedio alguno reflexivo, empresa que excede las posibilidades del mecanismo intelectual del hombre.... El ángel quiso ser superángel, y acabó en diablo. El hombre quiso ser superhombre, y acabó en pobre diablo de cuello escotado y pelo con ondas. (919)

> [an entire generation, thrown headlong into the sea of pure intuitionist incoherence, has lived in the clear sin of "angel-ism," in full ambition of achieving an intuitive and direct knowledge, without any reflective intervention, an enterprise that exceeds the possibilities of man's intellectual mechanism.... The Angel

wanted to be an archangel, and ended up as a devil. Man wanted to be a superman, and ended up as a poor devil, with a plunging neckline and curled hair.]

In effect, many of the authors Moix cites—Lorca, Cernuda, Ginsburg—are homosexual, though discussion of their sexuality, and often the texts themselves, were suppressed in Francoist Spain. Some of them are also indeed identified with republicanism—this is the case for Lorca, Cernuda, and Vallejo—or they may be identified as Marxists fighting against cultural and economic imperialism, like Allen Ginsburg and Che Guevara. What is more, their texts were largely unknown within Spain during the Franco dictatorship, due to their foreignness or their sexual or political content, so the citation of them is queer in the Spanish context, recognizable and coherent to readers that "entienden."[15]

The last poems I will mention here foreground the cultural and sexual issues I have discussed, implying that Spain is already queer under Franco, that is, homosocial and ambiguous. The following poem, for example, portrays the relationship of two men, Bécquer and Che Guevara, from different countries and historical eras, as a shadow behind the everyday reality of Francoist Spain:

Pasaban de las doce de la noche cuando regresaba a casa, y juro que no bebí, pero allí estaban los dos, jugando a cartas a la vuelta de la esquina. Eran dos sombras para siempre enamoradas: Bécquer y Ché Guevara. (48)

[It was after midnight, when I was returning home, and I swear I hadn't been drinking, but there were the two of them, playing cards just around the corner. They were two shadows forever in love: Bécquer and Ché Guevara.]

It is possible to discuss this homosexual love explicitly in the text only because the temporal and geographical separations make such a relationship appear wholly symbolic and materially impossible, yet the speaker sees it and portrays it as a love between men, making visible the hidden specter of homosexuality in the homosocial relationships of romanticism and revolution.

Another poem clearly links the female speaker/subject with the Spanish nation, implying the queerness of both: "Ay madre, ya soy como la España; ni chicha ni limoná, loquita del corazón y dura como la caña" (32) (Ay mother, I am already like Spain, neither one nor the other, crazy of heart and hard like cane). Again, a reader "que entiende" (who "gets it") will recognize the connotations of "ni chicha ni limoná," of "loquita," and of a female who is "dura como la caña." This queer subtext undermines the conventions of the poetic form of this text, generally reserved in traditional verse for female speakers lamenting lost loves to their mothers. In those poems, there is an implied understanding and identification between mother and daughter in the face of male heartlessness. We may infer from the intertextuality, then, that the mother of this poem also understands—that is, "entiende"— the gender ambiguity of the daughter as well as its relation to the Spanish nation, "la Madre Patria," which is presumably also "rara."

The final examples are taken from "Una novela" (A novel). Ricardo Krauel has studied in depth the generic queerness of this text, which appears at the end of *Baladas del Dulce Jim* and which Moix calls a novel, despite the poetic concision of each "chapter."[16] The entire content of chapter six is the following: "el galle de la periu ara plora, ara riu" (the cock now cries, now laughs) (57). The use of Catalan here is not incidental, given the prohibition of its public use in Francoist Spain. Indeed, Andrew Bush has explained that the "predominance of Castilian in (Moix's) work and the subversive interference of Catalan reflects, on the one hand, a political reality beyond the linguistic sphere, and on the other, constitutes at the most fundamental level of language a case of doubling or split identity" (139).

Chapter eight is also succinct, telling us only that "Manitas de Plata sale del pueblo en busca de Cara Cortada" (Manitas de Plata leaves town looking for Scarface) (60). Like the initial texts of *Baladas del Dulce Jim*, this "chapter" reveals the homosexual shadow behind the love triangle, as Manitas de Plata and Cara Cortada pursue one another outside the reference of any heterosexual love, since no woman appears in any chapter of "Una novela" with either man. This pursuit also implies a queer relationship between Spanish nationalist stereotypes—such as the flamenco guitarist, Manitas de Plata—and the stereotype of the excesses of Anglo-American capitalism, the gangster Al Capone, known as Scarface. The marriage of these two images in the Spain of the 1960s subverts both Francoist nationalist discourse, based upon compulsory heterosexuality, and the supposed liberal bases of capitalism, which ironically financed the oppressive Francoist regime after 1959.

The queerness of *Baladas del Dulce Jim* is not anecdotal or tangential but central to the cultural critique that the book performs, because gender and sexuality lie at the foundations of ideology and genre. We run the risk of missing the point altogether if we ignore this aspect of an author's poetics for fear of marginalizing her. In the Francoist period, the woman intellectual is already marginalized, whether she is lesbian or not, and her relationship to the conventions of "género" (gender or genre) is always already queer. Spain's own national identity in those years is also ambiguous, despite the rhetoric of unity, and those fissures become clearly visible in the cultural production of the 1960s, as evidenced by this text. Finally, international capitalism also contains internal inconsistencies that are brought to light by the image of a homosexual relationship between cultures. An exploration of queer poetics allows us to see and examine these fragmentations because it provides a perspective simultaneously within and without the borders of conventional Spanish paradigms and international identities of genre, gender, and sex.

Notes

1. Linda Gould Levine, for example, tries "to decipher Moix's motive for de-emphasizing the theme of female and lesbian love" (99) in "Las virtudes peligrosas" (Dangerous virtues), and concludes that the silencing of the lesbian subtext reflects "the subordination and silencing of women in the timeless Spanish reality she seems to portray." Rosalía Cornejo-Parriego observes that "En 'Virtudes,' la apropiación y adaptación de una historia de amor heterosexual al deseo de dos mujeres apunta, por una parte, a la carencia de paradigmas literarios para las relaciones amorosas entre personas del mismo sexo. Constituye, así, un acto transgresor que, sin duda alguna, introduce fisuras en el espacio narrativo heterosexual" (616) (In "Virtudes," the appropriation and adaptation of a story of heterosexual love for the desire between two women points to, on the one hand, the lack of literary paradigms for relationships between persons of the same sex. Hence, it constitutes an act of transgression that, doubtlessly, introduces fissures in the heterosexual narrative space). Catherine Bellver does not mention lesbianism at all, but she hints at the queerness of the characters' doubling in *Julia* (1968) and *Walter ¿por qué te fuiste?* (Walter, Where Did You Go?) (1973). "The complexity of doubling," she asserts, "arises from the fact that it signifies a paradox of simultaneous outwardness and inwardness, of difference and identity, and of duality as well as

unity" (30) which marks the characters' identification with and alienation from models of bourgeois identity and relationality. She marks this doubling/identification with the figure of Narcissus, who symbolizes homosexual desire.

2. Ricardo Llamasa and Fefa Vila explain it thus:

La política "queer" incide en el debate "histórico" sobre la cuestión de la identidad para oponerse a los postulados tradicionales de la disolución de las categorías fundamentadas en los referentes freudianos del polimorfismo sexual y la bisexualidad universal. . . . Lo que subyace a la importación del término "queer" y a la renovación terminológica que ha hecho de "bollera" o "marica" terminos de reivindicación es la necesidad de establecer un distancimiento con respecto a las figuras políticas "lesbiana" o "gay.". . . Al mismo tiempo, en este proceso se busca aglutinar aspectos relacionados con la clase social, la identidad nacional, la pertenencia étnica o la "sidentidad." No es ésta la revuelta de las lesbianas y los gays que capitalizan un discurso cada vez menos problemático para el orden socio-sexual. Es, al contrario, una revuelta de bolleras, maricas, locazas, camioneras, sidosos y sadomasoquistas, frente a un conjunto social que ignora y excluye posibles sujetos de transformación. El orden social pasa entonces a ser considerado intolerable porque limita los movimientos y posibilidades de actuación y de articulación de diferencias" (223–24).

[Queer politics enters the "historical" debate on the identity question to oppose traditional postulations of the dissolution of categories founded on Freudian referents of sexual polymorphousness and universal bisexuality. Underlying the term "queer" and the terminological renovation that it has made of "dyke" or "fag" terms of vindication, is the need to establish a distance from the political figures "lesbian" or "gay." . . . At the same time, there is an attempt in this process to agglutinate aspects related to social class, national identity, ethnicity, or AIDS-related identity. This is not the mixture of lesbians and gays who capitalize on a discourse that is increasingly less problematic for the social order. It is, on the contrary, the mixture of dykes, fags, fairies, butches, people with AIDS, and sadomasochists faced with a social order that ignores and excludes possible subjects of transformation. The social order then becomes considered intolerable because it limits the movements and possibilities for the performance and articulation of differences.]

3. This is still true. Lesbianism is largely omitted from studies of homosexuality in Spain, and writings by Spanish women occupy an infinitesimal space in Berkana, the largest gay bookstore in Madrid. A history of lesbianism and a lesbian poetics are included in *conCiencia de un singular deseo* (Conscience of a Singular Desire), edited by Xosé M. Buxán, but Julia Cela's recent study of important homosexual cultural figures in the West, *Galería de retratos: Personajes homosexuales de la cultura contemporánea* [Gallery of Portraits: Homosexual Personages of Contemporary Culture], does not contain a single chapter on a Spanish woman, although Esther Tusquets receives a brief mention. Cela has explained that the omission reflects the reluctance of Span-

ish writers to be identified publicly as homosexual (personal interview, July 1999). Lesbians are likewise omitted from *Identidad y diferencia: Sobre la cultura gay en España* [Identity and Difference: About Gay Culture in Spain], published in 1997.

4. See, for example, the studies by Boyd, Cirici Pellicer, Graham and Labanyi, Martín Gaite, and Nash cited at the end of the essay.

5. Pilar Primo de Rivera, the founder of the Women's Section of the Falange party, stated in 1938 that "El verdadero deber de las mujeres con la Patria consiste en formar familias con una base exacta de austeridad y alegría donde se fomente todo lo tradicional. . . . Lo que no haremos es ponerlas en competencia con ellos,—los hombres—porque jamás llegarán a igualarlos y, en cambio, pierden toda la elegancia y toda la gracia indispensables para la convivencia" (Sánchez López 21–22) (The true duty of women in the Motherland consists of forming families upon a precise basis of austerity and good cheer where everything traditional may be fomented. . . . What we shall not do is put the women into competition with them—the men—because they will never reach their level and, on the contrary, will lose all the elegance and all the grace that are indispensable for living together).

6. All translations are my own.

7. One could argue that this is true for lesbianism even more than for gayness because male homosexuality has a long tradition and recognition in the arts, even if its practice remained illegal in Franco's time. In many senses, it did not disrupt the symbolic order to the same extent because it reaffirmed male hegemony, even as it destabilized the social construction of "masculinity." Jean Baudrillard will claim that transvestism also reverts representation by mimicking the feminine. The result is not the same for lesbians, however, not even for dykes, who mimic male behavior, because of the symbolic capital of masculinity, as opposed to femininity.

8. Eve Kosofsky Sedgwick describes the homosocial drive behind the love triangle in her study, *Between Men: English Literature and Male Homosocial Desire*.

9. They thereby comply with: "Freudian interpretive modalities of the female function rigorously postulated by the pursuit of a certain game for which she will always find herself signed up without having begun to play. Set between—at least—two, or two half, men. A hinge bending according to their exchanges. A reserve supply of *negativity* sustaining the articulation of their moves, or refusals to move, in a partly fictional progress toward the mastery of power" (Irigaray 22).

10. The advice that Rosa Chacel gives Moix in that letter, dated May 8, 1966, highlights this problem: "Ser mujer es muy fácil. Tú tienes un temperamento varonil, que es absolutamente necesario para ser una mujer superior. Pero *para ser una mujer*. Si por el mero hecho de tener un temple masculino se debilita o se falsea la propia naturaleza, todo lo que se consigue es un más o menos mala imitación. De modo que, si mis opiniones te sirven de algo . . . dispónte a vivir difícilmente y valientemente una feminidad varonil" (It is very easy to be a woman. You have a virile temperament, which is absolutely necessary in order to be a superior woman. But, *to be a woman*. If, for the mere reason that one has a masculine temper, one weakens or falsifies one's own

nature, all one achieves is a more or less bad imitation. So, if my opinions mean anything to you, set yourself to live, with difficulty and valor, a virile femininity) (Rodríguez Fisher, 120–21).

11. Andrew Bush argues that the use of English in Moix's poetry "must be read as displacement: the more critical issue involves the relation of her Castilian texts to Catalan, the subterranean language that breaks through to the surface now and again . . . but that haunts her every page as a mark of alienation" (139).

12. Bush comments upon the disruptions in Moix's verse: "The form of Moix's poetry is deceiving on a second count as well, for the continuous prose lines . . . mask the jarring discontinuity of their content. Images, frequently related to dreams, are juxtaposed in a technique that recalls the surrealists. And in those poems which are primarily narrative rather than lyric (which is to say the majority of her poetic production), the changing narrative perspective disrupts the linear development" (140).

13. "La habanera" is also a popular Cuban song and dance.

14. This poem has a clear intertextuality with Vallejo's "Piedra negra sobre una piedra blanca."

15. The verb "entender" means "to understand," but in slang it also means "to be queer."

16. "'Una novela' no prescinde de los elementos constitutivos básicos de una estructura narrativa; antes al contrario, y como hemos visto, los acoge a todos ellos. Lo que ocurre es que, al ponerlos en relación, no los integra en circuitos o bucles cerrados y completos, no les otorga una definición estructural. Eso implica plantear una reorientación del género desde dentro del mismo género, sirviéndose de sus propios instrumentos de juego, y no introductir un patrón de referencia extraño que nada tenga que ver con las bases anteriores del género. En definitiva, 'Una novela' presenta una estructura, pero una estructura que exhibe un grado de apertura que bordea los límites de lo concebible" (Krauel, 646–47). ("A novel" does not overlook the basic constitutive elements of the narrative; on the contrary, and as we have seen, it incorporates them all. What occurs is that, upon incorporating them it does not integrate them in circuits or closed and complete loops, it does not give them a structural definition. This implies presenting a reorientation of the genre from inside the genre itself, making use of its own instruments of play, and not introducing a foreign model that has nothing to do with the established bases of the genre. "A novel" presents a structure, but a structure that exhibits a degree of openness that approaches the limits of the conceivable.)

WORKS CITED

Aliaga, Juan Vicente. 1997. *Identidad y diferencia: Sobre la cultura gay en España*. Barcelona: Egales.

Baudrillard, Jean. 1990. *Seduction*. Trans. Brian Singer. New York: St. Martin's Press.

Bellver, Catherine G. 1987. Division, duplication, and doubling in the novels of Ana María Moix. In *Nuevos y novísimos: algunas perspectivas críticas sobre la narrativa española desde la década de los 60*, edited by Ricardo Landeira and Luis T. Gonzalez-del-Valle. Boulder, CO: Society of Spanish and Spanish-American Studies.

Boyd, Carolyn. 1997. *Historia patria: Politics, history, and national identity in Spain 1875–1975*. Princeton: Princeton University Press.

Bush, Andrew. 1991. Ana Maria Moix's silent calling. In *Women writers of contemporary Spain: exiles in the homeland*, edited by Joan L. Brown. Newark: University of Delaware Press.

Buxán, Xosé, ed. 1997. *conCiencia de un singular deseo: Estudios lesbianos y gays en el estado español*. Barcelona: Laertes.

Cela, Julia. 1998. *Galería de retratos: Personajes homosexuales de la cultura contémporánea*. Barcelona: Egales.

Cirici Pellicer, Alexandre. 1977. *La estética del franquismo*. Barcelona: Gustavo Gili.

Cornejo-Parriego, Rosalía. 1998. Desde el innominado deseo: Transgresión y marginalidad de la mirada en "Las virtudes peligrosas" de Ana María Moix. *Anales de la literatura española contemporánea* 23 (1–2): 607–21.

DuPlessis, Rachel Blau. 1994. "Corpses of Poesy": Some modern poets and some gender ideologies of lyric. In *Feminist measures: Soundings in poetry and theory*, edited by Lynn Keller and Cristanne Miller. Ann Arbor: University of Michigan Press.

García Martín, Antonio and Andrés López Fernández. 1985. *Imagen social de la homosexualidad en España*. Madrid: Asociación Pro Derechos Humanos.

Graham, Helen, and Jo Labanyi. 1995. *Spanish cultural studies: An Introduction*. Oxford: Oxford University Press.

Halperin, David. 1995. *Saint Foucault: Towards a gay hagiography*. New York: Oxford University Press.

Irigaray, Luce. 1985. *Speculum of the other woman*. Trans. Gillian C. Gill. Ithaca, NY: Cornell University Press.

Krauel, Ricardo. 1998. Funambulismo sobre una frontera de un género: "Una novela" de Ana María Moix. *Anales de la literatura española contemporánea* 23 (1–2): 641–53.

Levine, Linda Gould. 1987. Behind the "enemy lines": Strategies for interpreting *Las virtudes peligrosas* of Ana María Moix. In *Nuevos y novísimos: Algunas perspectives críticas sobre la narrativa española desde la década de los 60*, edited by Ricardo Landeira and Luis T. Gonzalez-del-Valle. Boulder: Society of Spanish and Spanish American Studies.

Llamasa, Ricardo, and Fefa Vila. 1997. Spain: Passion for life. Una historia del movimiento de lesbianas y gays en el estado español. In *conCiencia de un singular deseo: estudios lesbianos y gays en el estado español*, edited by Xosé M. Buxán. Barcelona: Laertes.

Martín Gaite, Carmen. 1987. *Usos amorosos de la postguerra española*. Barcelona: Anagrama.

Moix, Ana María. 1983. *A imagen y semejanza*. Barcelona: Lumen.

———. 1985. Las virtudes peligrosas. In *Las virtudes peligrosas*. Madrid: Alfaguara.

Nash, Mary. 1995. *Defying male civilization: Women in the Spanish Civil War.* Denver: Arden.

Pemán, José María. 1947. *Obras completas.* Madrid: Escelicer.

Rodríguez Fisher, Ana, ed. 1998. *De mar a mar. Epistolario Rosa Chacel-Ana María Moix.* Barcelona: Península.

Sánchez López, Rosario. 1990. *Mujer española, una sombra de destino en lo universal: trayectoria histórica de Sección Femenina de Falange (1934–1977).* Murcia: Universidad de Murcia.

Sedgwick, Eve Kosofsky. 1985. *Between men: English literature and male homosocial desire.* New York: Columbia University Press.

Three Apologies For Poetry: Discourses of Literary Value in Contemporary Spain

Jonathan Mayhew

The place of poetry within the cultural context in which it is produced and consumed is a particularly vexing question for contemporary poets and critics in Spain. How and why does poetry matter? What is its standing among the myriad discourses of postmodernity? The most readily available answer to this question, of course, is that the genre has lost whatever larger significance it once possessed: aside from the poets themselves and a few academic specialists, the familiar argument runs, poetry has scant resonance with the public. The emerging field of Hispanic cultural studies grants only minimal importance to poetry, a genre still heavily identified with the values that have shaped the *literary* canon: no contemporary poets are mentioned in Helen Graham and Jo Labanyi's *Spanish Cultural Studies*, except in Chris Perriam's survey of gay and lesbian culture. Within literary criticism, however, poetry is often regarded as a minor genre that began to wane in significance after the glory days of the Generation of 1927. Even truly exceptional Spanish poets often appear to be minor figures when compared to moderately successful novelists.

Even if we accept this pessimistic view, however, the specific claims made on behalf of poetry in contemporary Spain are highly revealing, providing clues about the status of literature as a whole. In the pages that follow I propose to examine the three principal arguments that have guided discussions of poetry in the past fifteen years, with an eye to answering the fundamental question of how poetry can still make a viable claim on the cultural imagination. The division of recent Spanish poetry into three main currents is well established: there is an "essentialist" or "metaphysical" poetry, a poetry of "experience," and a neo-avant-garde poetry of "difference."[1] What I propose to examine here are the issues underlying this three-way split. Each of the main tendencies speaks to a different readership and envisions a markedly different cultural role for poetry. All, however, can be understood as reactions to the "marginal" status of the genre in the closing years of the millennium.

For the first group of poets, poetry does not require external justification; its value does not depend on the number of readers it attracts.[2] This attitude, most clearly exemplified by José Angel Valente, is rooted in the assumptions of literary modernism. While the school of poetry inspired by Valente is usually termed "essentialist" or "metaphysical," I prefer the more inclusive term "late modernist." Valente's recent collection of aphorisms, *Notas de un simulador* (Notes of a Simulator), makes constant reference to the icons of the modern literary tradition, from Friedrich Hölderlin to Juan Ramón Jiménez, Franz Kafka, James Joyce, José Lezama Lima, and Edmond Jabès. He quotes Joyce's definition of the "epiphany" with unqualified approval, as well as the trilogy of aesthetic principles from St. Thomas Aquinas, which Joyce's Stephen Dedalus cites in *A Portrait of the Artist as a Young Man*: "Las tres cualidades de la obra literaria según Sto. Tomás: *integritas* (unidad, totalidad), *consonantia* (coherencia, 'decorum'), *claritas* (capacidad de iluminación de la palabra)" (The three qualities of the literary work according to St. Thomas: *integritas* [unity, totality], *consonantia* [coherence, "decorum"], *claritas* [the capacity for illumination in the word]) (27).

For a poet working within this modernist paradigm, the relationship between literature and history is necessarily oblique:

> En el diario de Kafka las líneas dedicadas a la primera guerra mundial no pasan de cincuenta. Pocas semanas después del comienzo de la guerra sus preocupaciones son la escritura de "La colonia penitenciaria" y el comienzo de *El proceso*. Durante la guerra, Joyce está entregado a la escritura de la primera parte de *Ulises*. El tiempo del escritor no es el tiempo de la historia. Aunque el escritor, como toda persona, pueda ser triturado por ella. (Valente 1997, 34)

[In Kafka's diary the lines about the First World War number less then fifty. A few weeks after the start of the war his preoccupations are the writing of "The Penal Colony" and the beginning of *The Trial*. During the war, Joyce dedicates himself to writing of the first part of *Ulysses*. The time of the writer is not the time of history. Although the writer, like anyone else, can be mangled by it.]

Valente participated in the debates surrounding the social utility of poetry in the 1950s and 1960s, and his own poetry continues to make occasional references to historical events. His argument is not for "art-for-art's-sake," but for an even more exalted conception of the poet's cultural role, one based, implicitly, on his confidence in the superiority of the artist's vision of reality. He consciously models himself after the late-modernist poet Paul Celan, whose holocaust poems are notoriously hermetic. The model of cultural significance implicit in his poetic theory and practice remains an elite one. Valente makes no concessions to the literary marketplace. If he ultimately makes an impact on the larger culture, it will be in the same uncompromising way that Kafka or Beckett have.

The idea of the autonomy of literary value is *residual* in contemporary culture.[3] Respected poets like Valente continue to enjoy a high level of prestige; the idea of the "great poet" still resonates with the public that reads the culture section of *El país* or *ABC* and is curious about which contemporary writer will be elected to the Real Academia. The size of this audience is relatively small. Valente often published new collections of poetry in small, expensive editions, although editions of his collected poems and poetic anthologies still come out with some frequency. According to the modernist paradigm, of course, contemporary readership is not the real issue: a significant work, while read by a miniscule group of initiates at the time of its first publication, will eventually reach a substantial audience. This paradigm continues to show signs of life even at the end of the century: cheap, mass-market editions of Rimbaud, Kafka, Beckett, Pessoa, Lorca, Alberti, and even Gimferrer are available in bookstores and newsstands in Spanish cities. Valente's own poetry remains available in a wide variety of formats, ranging from critical editions to pocket anthologies. Along with his contemporaries Claudio Rodríguez and Francisco Brines, he is likely to remain a part of the literary canon for at least the immediate future. The question, however, is whether this canon itself has lost its centrality in an age in which the educational system is becoming increasingly reluctant to assert the value of "great literature."

If the high-modernist model is *residual*, as prestigious as it is outmoded, there is another school of poetry in contemporary Spain that has defined itself, rather self-consciously, as *dominant*. Since the early 1980s, proponents of "la poesía de la experiencia" have exercised a sort of literary hegemony, often characterizing other aesthetic options as outdated, misguided, and lacking in literary quality. Anthologies of recent Spanish poetry, especially those edited by Villena and José Luis García Martín, give pride of place to this tendency, often to the exclusion of other modes.[4] Luis García Montero, a prolific and persuasive essayist and poet, is the de facto leader of this dominant group, which is composed primarily of male poets born after 1955 or so.[5] Other prominent poets in this category are Felipe Benítez Reyes and Carlos Marzal.

The poets of "experience" reject modernist or avant-garde principles; instead, they propose a "normalization" of poetry that would make it more palatable to the ordinary reader (García Montero 1992). The immediate model for this renewal of contact with the reader is the poetry of the 1950s, including Angel González, Jaime Gil de Biedma, and early Valente. The phrase that has given this school its name derives from Robert Langbaum's study of the dramatic monologue in English poetry, *The Poetry of Experience*, which Gil de Biedma read in the 1950s. Generally speaking, the values to which the dominant poets of the 1980s and 1990s appeal are those of literary realism. García Montero has revived the concept of verisimilitude, while García Martín has coined the phrase "poesía figurativa," making an analogy to figurative (i.e., nonabstract) painting. These poets also like to appeal to the use-value of poetry for the ordinary person; their poetry aims to be engaging, accessible, finely crafted, and relevant to everyday life.

This poetry, then, aims to reach the relatively well-educated public that nevertheless feels relatively alienated from the late-modernist aesthetic championed by José Angel Valente. Unlike the social poetry of the 1950s, however, "the poetry of experience" is not populist; there is no talk here of Blas de Otero's immense majority. The appeal, rather, is to a cultivated, but not excessively high-brow, middle class. There is often a conservative tone in García Montero's rejection of the avant-garde, although he might bristle at this characterization. He proposes a "normalization" of poetry, on the analogy of the normalization of Spanish society in the transition to democracy after the death of Franco (García Montero 1992).[6] Hence, the role he envisions for the poet is that of a well-adjusted citizen speaking to similarly situated subjects.

García Montero's solution to the problem of audience has been successful on its own terms. A prolific poet, he has many books in print and his numerous imitators dominate the anthologies, fostering a small but far from negligible audience for this sort of poetry. The fatal flaw with the poetry of experience, however, is a certain ideological and aesthetic restrictiveness masked by an appeal to the common sense of the "ordinary reader." García Montero's ridicule of avant-garde poetics and of alternative subject-positions has the effect of limiting the sphere in which poetry can operate. We might wonder about a literary climate in which a poem like José Luis Rendueles's "Vindicación del desencanto" (A Vindication of Disenchantment) is considered worthy of anthologizing. The speaker of this poem recounts the course of a love affair in fairly banal language. Here is a representative verse-paragraph:

> A la etapa de la charla interminable,
> de los besos por cualquier excusa tonta,
> siguió la de la camaradería silenciosa.
> Sin habernos dado cuenta
> habíamos cambiado el romanticismo
> por el hábito, pero no era algo tan malo
> después de todo
> ¿no crees?
>
> (Villena 1997, 206)

> [After the stage of interminable talk,
> of kisses for any silly excuse,
> there followed that of silent camaraderie.
> Without having realized it
> we had exchanged Romanticism
> for habit, but it wasn't anything that bad
> in the end,
> don't you think?][7]

Ironically, this poem appears in an anthology that purports to demonstrate how younger poets (ten poets under the age of thirty) go *beyond* the precepts of the poetry of experience, which, by the mid 1990s, had exhausted its limited resources. This poem, obviously, does not mount a serious challenge to the realist aesthetic: its title, in fact, implies a half-hearted acceptance of the world-weary cultural mood commonly labeled "el desencanto." Luis Antonio de Villena, who selected "Vindicación del desencanto" for this anthology, asserts that younger poets have grown restless with the narrow restrictions of the dominant school. This observation may be accurate, but it still falsely assumes that this deliberately subdued poetic realism is the only game in town. In any case, a large number of the poems selected in *10 menos 30* (10 less than 30) fail to signal any clear advance over the "dominant tendency" of the 1980s, despite the subtitle of the anthology: "la ruptura interior en la 'poesía de la experiencia" (the interior rupture in "the poetry of experience").

The most obvious problem with the revival of realist or "figurative" poetry is that it offers very little to the hard-core reader of poetry, who typically demands some combination of highly charged language, expressive intensity, and intellectual stimulation. It might appeal more to readers of prose fiction, who are sometimes content with a fairly ordinary plot recounted in an unexceptional prose style. García Montero's poetry fills a precise niche: it is a poetry that can be consumed without undue exertion by an audience accustomed to the finely crafted novels of Antonio Muñoz Molina and Javier Marías. Since poetry remains a residually prestigious genre, there is a need for an upper-middle-brow poet who reflects the cultural aspirations of a certain sector of society. It is in this context that Raquel Medina has spoken of "la conversión de la poesía en un artículo de consumo para la clase política y la burguesía" (603) (the conversion of poetry into an article of consumption for the political and the bourgeois classes). This astute sociological observation accounts nicely for García Montero's centrist appeal, which is difficult to explain in either late modernist or populist terms.[8]

Another problem with the poetry of experience is its desire to position itself as the central current of contemporary Spanish poetry. Proponents of this sort of writing use words like *dominant* and *hegemonic*, often without a trace of irony (Villena 1997, 12; García Martín 1995, 10). Proponents of the concept of a "dominant tendency," it is true, are quick to disavow the negative implications of this formulation, characterizing this dominance as a natural development of the genre rather than as a pernicious conspiracy to exclude other poetic options.[9] Villena, for example, is relatively nuanced in his assessment of recent Spanish poetry, giving at least minimal credit to alternative tendencies. Still, he is far too invested in the notion of *success*:

> Lo que para mí quedaba claro, en el verano de 1992—cuando realicé la antología [*Fin de siglo*]—era que entre todos los tonos de la generación del 80, la llamada *poesía de la experiencia* se había convertido en el más transitado, el más seguido, el más denostado—clara señal de éxito—y en el que estaban algunos, bastantes, de los poetas clave del momento. (*10 menos 30*, 15)

> [What was clear to me in the summer of 1992, when I did the anthology [*Fin de Siglo*], was that among all the tones of the generation of 1980, the so-called *poetry of experience* had become the most well traveled, the most applauded, the most followed, the most attacked (a clear sign of success), and within it were working some, quite a few, of the key poets of the moment.]

By the same logic, poets who depart from this dominant tendency, are inexorably associated with *failure*:

> Este heteroclítico grupo final—autodenominado de la *diferencia* —está compuesto por poetas de varia edad y condición, cuyo único nexo unitivo es el fracaso, la conciencia de falta de éxito. Explicable en unos por una clara ausencia de calidad y en otros—de mucho mejor página—por un nítido desfase histórico. (*10 menos 30*, 11)[10]

> [This final, heterogeneous group, self-denominated as the poetry of *difference*, is composed of poets of varying age and condition, whose only unifying link is failure, the consciousness of a lack of success. Explainable in some by a clear lack of quality and in others—much better writers—by a clear-cut historical anachronism.]

The reasoning here is circular: poets fail because they don't write well or are out of step with the times. The failure of any poet working outside the "dominant" tendency is virtually tautological: nothing fails like failure.

This poetry of "difference" is the third main current in recent Spanish poetry. If high modernism is *residual* and the "poetry of experience" is culturally *dominant*, this final tendency is perhaps *emergent*. It consists of an amorphous group of poets whose common denominator is not their lack of success, as Villena would have it, but their explicit rejection of the all-too-successful experiential mode. It is the hegemony of the dominant school, in fact, that lends this poetry much of its oppositional force. Without such a well-defined and self-confident orthodoxy, in other words, the *difference* of this group might be more difficult to discern.

No single figure stands out as the most representative poet of this heterogeneous category. Most of the women writing today belong to it almost by default, since they are largely absent from the "dominant" anthologies edited by the two most prolific anthologists of the moment: Villena and García Martín. (None of these anthologies includes more than two women; Villena's *10 menos 30* is exclusively male.) By the same token, anthologies of women poets, like Ramón de Buenaventura's *Las diosas blancas* and Noni Benegas and Jesús Munárriz's *Ellas tienen la palabra*, tend to promote a self-consciously avant-garde or alternative agenda, even though some of the women poets included in them are closer to either residual high modernism or to the mainstream poetry of experience. Beginning in the early 1980s, a whole generation of younger women were inspired by the examples of Ana Rossetti and Blanca Andreu. Isla Correyero, herself one of the strongest of these poets, has recently edited a compilation entitled *Feroces: radicales, marginales y heterodoxos en la última poesía española*. "Difference," as I am using the term here, is not a unitary school of poetry but a blanket label covering explicitly political poets, like Jorge Riechmann; poets who represent extreme or marginal subjectivities, like Leopoldo María Panero and Violeta Rangel; and poets who consider themselves to be linguistically innovative or avant-garde.

The division between "difference" and "experience" is not an absolute one. Many poets are justifiably wary of such labels and categories; some could be included in either grouping, depending on how and where the line is drawn. Esperanza López Parada is included in both the orthodox *Fin de siglo* (the only woman in this anthology!) and in Antonio Ortega's heterodox *La prueba del nueve*. Yet the dividing line is not entirely artificial: at stake, once again, is the crucial matter of poetry's cultural aspirations. In this respect the poetry of difference, *pace* Villena, has also found its core audience. Blanca Andreu's *De una niña de provincias que se vino a vivir en un Chagall* was a publishing success, as were *Las diosas blancas* and *Ellas tienen la palabra*. Correyero's *Feroces* has also made a significant impact. One of the regular book reviewers for the widely circulated monthly *Reseña*, Salustiano Martín, has championed alternatives to the dominant "poetry of experience" regularly throughout the 1990s, often castigating anthologies that limit themselves to this hegemonic school.

The appeal of a self-consciously "marginal" poetry is not difficult to explain. A significant segment of the reading public is not likely to respond well to a poetry that promotes itself as socially normative and hegemonic. This category would include politically active younger people generally, and women readers alienated by a literary establishment that still arrogantly perpetuates male privilege. For members of this group, the marginality of poetry, its status as a minor genre, resonates with their own sense of standing outside the dominant currents of power. Some of the poetry of "difference" continues to draw from modernist and late modernist models, like the poetry of Antonio Gamoneda and José Angel Valente. Other poets speak directly to a generation more attuned to alternative rock than to classic literature. Ironically, "alternative" or "countercultural" movements often have more in common with residual literary modernism than they do with the mainstream culture of the cultivated middle class. The neo-avant-garde poetry of *difference* tends to reject, however, the Olympian viewpoint of high modernism. More engaged in the here and now, it does not seek vindication from posterity.

These, then, are three easily discernible "apologies for poetry" in contemporary Spain. Each addresses and, indeed, *defines* a particular segment of the reading public. The total size of the audience for poetry remains small relative to the population as a whole; hence the surprise when a book of poetry begins to resonate with more than a thousand readers or so. Still, the divisions within this already small group are telling, mirroring larger societal attitudes toward literary culture. In general, readers of literature tend to fall into the three categories outlined above. Members of the literary elite, the smallest group, justify their preferences in terms of literary autonomy, with deliberate disregard for the marketplace. "Middle-brow" readers prefer lighter, less demanding fare, but still seek some degree of intellectual stimulation and cultural prestige. Because this group is more numerous than the first, it has the power to determine which books will be bestsellers and which literary tendencies will be perceived as "dominant" at any given moment. Finally, young, marginal, or progressive readers favor literature that reflects their own "alternative" sensibility.[11]

These categories of readers are somewhat speculative. I have based my categories on anecdotal evidence and on the virtual reading-subjects interpolated in each of the three "apologies for poetry." It is possible that a closer look at actual readership would modify my conclusions.[12] All the same, my categories are not only plausible but virtually tautological: readers will inevitably prefer works that interpolate them as the sort of readers they aspire to be. Thus the rhetorical mode of the text itself is a fairly good predictor of both its intended and its real audience. On the other hand, it could be that the *entire* audience for poetry is a relatively elite one, and that the debate over literary value takes place largely among warring factions of a small literary tribe. That poets belonging to the three major tendencies often publish their books in the same collections (especially those published by Visor and Hiperión) might indicate that the audience for poetry is less divided than I have indicated. In this scenario, elite readers identify with the particular "apology for poetry" that they find most congenial. A professor of literature might read García Montero's poetry and identify with its interpolation of the "ordinary citizen" even though he or she possesses a great deal more cultural capital than the implicit reader. This process is analogous to Blas de Otero's simultaneous address to a virtual "inmensa mayoría" and to a real readership largely comprising leftist intellectuals.

Even if the entire audience for poetry is an elite one—a debatable proposition—the divisions within this audience will still reflect differences of age, gender, status, and ideology. The poetry world would thus be a microcosm of the culture as a whole, a relatively self-contained *mundillo literario* that exemplifies larger cultural currents on a smaller scale. Pierre Bourdieu's theory of the literary field provides a useful model for analyzing this situation:

> The literary field (one may also speak of the artistic field, the philosophical field, etc.) is an independent social universe with its own laws of functioning, its specific relations of force, its dominants and its dominated, and so forth. Put another way, to speak of a "field" is to recall that literary works are produced in a particular social universe endowed with particular institutions and obeying specific laws. And yet this observation runs counter both to the tradition of internal reading, which considers works in themselves independently from historical conditions in which they were produced, and the tradition of external explication, which one normally associates with sociology and which relates the works directly to the economic and social conditions of the moment. (1993, 163)

The independence of the literary field does not mean that it functions without reference to other spheres. Rather, this field acts "somewhat like a prism which *refracts* every external determination: demographic, economic, or political events are always retranslated according to the specific logic of the field, and it is by this intermediary that they act on the logic of the development of works" (italics in original) (Ibid. 164).[13]

The seemingly intractable question of literary "quality" often emerges in discussions of contemporary literature. One common way of conceptualizing this problem is to appeal to the private "taste" of individuals. If taste were a *personal* matter, however, it would be impossible to explain how *any* cultural product could appeal to more than a handful of people whose preferences happened to coincide. Much of the disparity in the assessment of *quality* in recent Spanish poetry is attributable, not to individual differences among readers, but to the social and cultural divisions outlined above. The modernist criterion of literary value is perhaps the easiest to define, since it has dominated the process of canon-formation for quite some time: Valente and Gimferrer have been successful according to the same criteria that have made Juan Ramón Jiménez or Jorge Guillén canonical poets. The poets of "experience" deploy the notion of literary quality in a discernibly different way. Although they still invoke canonical literary values to some extent, in order to claim for themselves the prestige traditionally associated with poetry, they also explicitly link quality to success with a particular segment of the literary marketplace. This poetry often appears well written, when judged by conventional standards, though it may seem *merely* conventional to readers who prefer either high modernist or alternative options. From a perspective outside the dominant one, then, the poetry that has the most invested in conventional ideas of quality can easily appear to be the least stimulating.

The poetry of "difference" is least likely to wrap itself up in the mantle of "quality," since it owes the least to conventional standards of literary value. This very independence, however, lends it a vitality that is sometimes absent from the ostensibly "well-written" poetry of the other two tendencies. Too narrow a definition of quality, evidently, is a hindrance to poetic innovation, since quality is usually defined with reference to already established literary models. Judged by conventional standards, many of the poems collected in Correyero's *Feroces* may seem deficient. Yet it is precisely these standards that this vibrant anthology calls into question. Once again, the poetry of difference has more in common with the late-modernist model than it does with the centrist poetry of "experience." Modernism, though now often perceived as the repository of conservative literary values, is rooted in vanguard movements of past decades. It thus shares more with the contemporary avant-garde than it does with the self-consciously mainstream sensibility of the dominant school. The "elitism" of the residual poetry of modernism is structurally similar to the "marginality" of the contemporary avant-garde: in both cases, value is attributed to poetic practices that diverge from middle-of-the-road taste.

It should be obvious at this point that the author of this article is not a neutral observer of the debate surrounding literary value in contemporary Spanish poetry. It is difficult even to find an objective vocabulary in which to describe this debate, since words like "elite" and "middle-brow" are fraught with negative connotations. As a reader accustomed to difficult modern poetry, in any case, I prefer both residual modernism and the emergent neo-avant-garde to the dominant "poetry of experience." While sympathetic to Valente's intransigent opposition to the marketplace, I welcome the diversity of voices presented in *Ellas tienen la palabra* and *Feroces*. (I also admire Benítez Reyes, despite my antipathy to his professed poetics.) This "exclusion of the middle" is actually quite widespread among academic readers, who disdain middle-brow culture much more than they do the products of mass entertainment.[14] This logic perhaps accounts for the gap between proponents and critics of the poetry of experience. It is not surprising that traditional humanists loyal to the modernist canon join hands with young avant-garde poets to reject the revival of a normative literary realism:

> La esfera de lo que llamamos *real* o *realidad* suele quedar acotada por lo que somos capaces de imaginar en un momento dado. La realidad y sus realismos suelen ser el fruto de una imaginación impotente, no capaz de imaginar otra cosa. (Valente 1997, 27)
>
> [The sphere of what we called *real* or *reality* is usually limited by what we are capable of imagining in a given moment. Reality and its realisms are usually the result of an impotent imagination, incapable of imagining anything else.]

Many scholarly articles on contemporary Spanish poetry consist of a series of textual analyses framed by background information on the poet(s) studied and by a theoretical approach. My description of the cultural field of Spanish poetry obviously departs from this model; yet some concrete examples are necessary to demonstrate the ways in which contemporary poetry dramatizes the issue of poetry's cultural viability. In order to maintain some degree of even-handedness, I have chosen texts from three poets who might be judged among the "best" in each category. An untitled prose-poem by Valente is the first exhibit:

> EJERCEMOS UN ARTE mínima, pobre, no vendible, salvo en contadas ocasiones, nunca públicas, igual que ésta, aquí, en la tarde, en la hora incierta de la absoluta desaparición. (Valente 1992, 99)
>
> [THE ART WE PRACTICE is minimal, poor, unmarketable, save on limited occasions, never public, like this one, here, this afternoon, at the indefinable hour of absolute disappearance.]

Valente emphasizes poetry's residual status: poetry is a threatened art, on the verge of extinction because of its lack of market value and public utility. Presumably, however, this precarious status is a mark of distinction, since it lends poetry its exceptional status. Valente's minimalism conceals his confidence in the privileged status of poetic language.

Benítez Reyes's "Apunte" (Note) is a skillful poem written in the dominant style:

Esos barcos que llegan sigilosos al muelle
tienen algo de símbolo y de fácil metáfora.
El símbolo quizá de lo que muere.
La metáfora, en fin, de una vida ignorada.
De niño los miraba inventando unas rutas
por olvidados mares y por tierras de magos.
Perdiéndose en la niebla, helados por la luna,
los barcos de mi infancia iban siempre de paso.
Perseguían un mundo que no existe. Un mundo
que ha muerto en mí, que está borrándose
al evocarlo ahora desde este mar oscuro
que sólo surcan ya los barcos fantasmales.

(1992, 30)

[Those ships that silently slip into the docks
have something of the symbol or the facile metaphor.
The symbol, perhaps, of all that dies,
The metaphor, finally, of an unknown life.
As a child I looked at them inventing routes
through forgotten seas and lands of wizards.
Fading in the mist, frozen by the moon,
the ships of my childhood were always just passing by.
They were searching for a world that doesn't exist. A world
that has died in me, that is wiped away
as I evoke it now from this dark sea
that is crossed now only by phantasmal ships.]

This poem can be paraphrased thus: "I had stereotypically 'literary' aspirations in my youth, but I have put aside childish things. Nevertheless, my reputation as a poet rests on my skill at manipulating easily recognizable metaphors." (As if distrusting his readers' literary competence, however, he explains the significance of these metaphors.) In keeping with this message, Benítez Reyes's sing-song *alejandrinos* contrast with Valente's spare prose rhythms.

Finally, a dated entry from Isla Correyero, 1996, *Diario de una enfermera*, can represent the poetry of "difference":

29 de septiembre de 1994
Hemos actuado precipitadamente.
No hemos esperado el tiempo necesario para comprobar si
    verdaderamente estaba
muerto.

Le hemos amortajado entre algodón y bromas y hemos sellado
    sus ojos con el
"Nobecutane".
Creímos ver un músculo facial que se movía . . .
Nada.
Trabajamos nerviosos, alegres.
Falta muy poco para irnos a casa.

(Benegas, 309)

[September 29, 1994
We've acted hastily.
We didn't wait the time necessary to confirm that he was
    really dead.
We shrouded him in cotton and jokes and sealed his eyes
    with "Nobecutane."
We thought we saw his face move.
Naah.
We work nervously, gaily.
There's very little time left before we go home.]

Correyero's *enfermera* (nurse) speaks with a different tone: the cadaver (the literary tradition itself?) may or may not be completely dead, but who cares? The speaker's concerns are elsewhere. While this metapoetic reading finds no direct justification in the text (there is nothing to link the supposedly dead man with poetry or literature), the rejection of elegy reveals a decidedly less respectful attitude toward the past.[15] In contrast both to Valente's solemn elegiac mode and Benítez Reyes's self-deprecating but still self-absorbed nostalgia, Correyero's speaker is *desenfadada*.

These three tones of voice reveal three distinct attitudes toward poetry itself. All three poets employ irony, but in each case the irony arises from a different contradiction and results in a markedly different tone. In Valente, the underlying contradiction is between the splendor of the modern poetic tradition and its residual status in contemporary society. In Benítez Reyes, the narcissistic speaker seems to be aware that his images are trite, but is unable to step outside of his stereotypically "literary" patterns of thought: the resulting irony is self-parodic. Finally, Correyero's poem achieves its comic effect through a contrast between the potentially grave error (mistaking a live body for a dead one) and the speaker's flippant tone. In this last case, of course, the irony has nothing directly to do with the status of poetry per se, in part because the speaker of the poem is not defined implicitly as a "poet," as in the other two texts. Correyero is much less encumbered by the weight of literary tradition and by readerly expectations about what poetry should sound like. The *desenfado* that characterizes many of the younger women poets of the past twenty years is a sign of an absence of anxiety about the survival of any particular version of the literary tradition.

If poetry is merely residual in contemporary society, then its future is precarious despite its prestige among a group of elite readers. The poetry of experience, on the other hand, attempts to salvage poetry by appealing to a mainstream audience that cares less intensely about the survival of poetry. As is evident in Benítez Reyes's "Apunte," this dominant school often simply reinscribes the cultural problem in a parodic but ultimately conservative mode. Despite its constant appeal to realism and verisimilitude, the poetry of experience is often surprisingly "literary" or "poetic," in the conventional sense of these terms. The appeal to the real is always a transparently ideological gesture. Realism itself, however, is not inherently reactionary: many of the poets in Correyero's *Feroces* write in a direct, autobiographical mode that approximates the ideal of "experience," though without García Montero's and Benítez Reyes's finely nuanced appeals to the ordinary-yet-cultivated reader.

Both residual late modernism and the poetry of experience have quite a bit invested in particular versions of the literary past; thus they stake their claims to future viability on the survival of specific definitions of poetry. In both cases, the traditions invoked are versions of what was once understood as poetic "modernity." Valente's modernity, on the one hand, derives from a tradition of difficult, linguistically dense poetry (Mallarmé, Celan). García Montero is "modern," on the other hand, in the urbane, conversational mode of Auden and Gil de Biedma. Both traditions are potentially rich sources of poetic innovation; in the current field of literary values, however, both are stuck in a sort of holding pattern. The future of Spanish poetry lies elsewhere: in the alternative poetic practices, some as yet undefined, that were beginning to emerge in the final years of the twentieth century.

One danger in this confident prediction is that it is too respectful of the lines drawn by Spanish poets, anthologists, and critics. Studies of these ideological divisions (including this article) inevitably give inordinate emphasis to anthologies, since these provide prima facie evidence of how the poetry world conceives of itself. The problem is that the same poet, included in anthologies of opposing tendencies, might be read differently. Is the Jorge Riechmann of *Postnovísimos* the same as that of *La prueba del nueve*? Is he the "Jorge Riechman" (sic) of *Feroces*? Is his poetry a left-wing version of the often conservative poetry of experience, or does his commitment to radicalism automatically place him in the category of "difference"? By the same token, the persistent discrimination against women poets in mainstream anthologies tends to obscure the differences among them. Esperanza López Parada is the token woman in *Fin de siglo*. Is she a neoclassicist, as Villena would have it? Or does she fit more comfortably in Antonio Ortega's *La prueba del nueve*, where she is one of three women poets, or in the gynocentric *Ellas tienen la palabra*?

While I am not arguing for a liberation from ideological preconceptions, the tendentious divisions of the poetic field enacted in these anthologies do indeed erect artificial barriers and distort perceptions. What is more, this territorial imperative is not an accidental byproduct, but the main cultural function that anthologies serve. This divisiveness can clarify the ideological and aesthetic issues at stake in the debate, but it also conceals potential points of convergence between seemingly irreconcilable positions. Only one poet—Alberto Tesán—is included in both *10 menos 30* and *Feroces*. These two anthologies, then, offer essentially separate visions of contemporary Spanish poetry. This lack of convergence almost certainly reflects the explicit division between poetic mainstream and poetic margin: Villena and Correyero are equally self-conscious about their advocacy of "orthodox" and "heterodox" poetics, respectively. Yet both of these anthologies, published only a year apart, feature poets of the same age group and promote a revival of poetic "realism" inspired by writers like Raymond Carver and Charles Bukowski. The dominant tone in each anthology reflects the anthologist's overt agenda: Villena's selections tend to be more low-keyed and lyrical, in contrast with the stridency of Correyero's *Radicales*.

Yet this blatant difference obscures a significant commonality between these two groups of poets; poets of "experience," in their attempt to break free from the restrictions of this school, are moving in more or less the same direction as "marginal" poets, to the extent that at least one of these poets finds himself in the strange position of being both a representative of the dominant school and a poetic rebel.

The vigorous debate surrounding the issue of poetic value in contemporary Spain is itself a sign of the continued vitality of the genre. The perceived marginality of poetry in relation to other forms of cultural expression is not necessarily cause for pessimism. An art form with a relatively small but impassioned audience can achieve a concentrated energy that is sometimes lacking in genres that are more directly subject to market forces. Contemporary Spanish fiction, for example, reaches a larger audience but may not enjoy the same degree of creative ferment. In the words of Antonio Gamoneda, a poet ambiguously situated between a late modernist aesthetic and the poetics of difference:

> La poesía, ajena al mercado y escasa en funciones externas, es, por ello precisamente, la única actividad que, dentro de las circunstancias, puede escapar el gregarismo. En el fervor minoritario, en la subjectivación radical, en la amplificación "anormal" del lenguaje, ahí se ha producido la mutación cualitativa que legitima su supervivencia, la que se logra en el carácter de la propia máquina poética y en la intensificación de la vida del emisor y de unos pocos receptores. (21)

> [Poetry, alien to the market and poor in external functions, is, precisely for this reason, the only activity that, in these circumstances, can avoid gregariousness. In the fervor of a minority, in a radical subjectivism, in the "abnormal" amplification of language, there has taken shape the qualitative mutation that legitimates its survival, which is achieved in the character of the poetic mechanism itself and in the intensification of the life of the sender and some few receivers.]

Perhaps, then, a reversal of perspectives is in order: rather than asking how poetry can lay claim to the postmodern cultural imagination, one might ask what hope there is for a culture that neglects the poetic imagination.

Notes

1. See, for example, the opening pages (9–12) of Luis Antonio de Villena's introduction to *10 menos 30*.

2. Responding to my article, "How to be Great," in which I note the persistence of modernist values in the poetic canon, George Yúdice offers "una explicación acaso demasiado simplista. De todos los géneros literarios y artísticos, la poesía es el que está más alejado del mercado, fundamento de evaluación según mucho en tiempos posmodernos. Ese alejamiento del mercado se traduce en escasez de lectores, en especial los que pertenecen al público masivo. El público lector de la poesía hoy en día suele consistir en los poetas mismos" (401) (a perhaps too simple explanation. Of all the literary and artistic genres, poetry is the one most removed from the market, a widely accepted basis of evaluation in these postmodern times. This distance from the market translates into a scarcity of readers, especially those that belong to the masses. The public reader of poetry today tends to be poets [sic] themselves). This observation has very limited validity: it might explain the persistence of a certain late modernism, but it fails to account for the entire field of poetic production and consumption. Hiperión and Visor continue to publish original collections of peninsular and Latin American poetry along with translations of foreign language poets at a brisk rate, suggesting an audience that extends well beyond the producers themselves. The audience for contemporary poetry is actually far larger now than it was in the 1920s, in the heyday of modernism.

3. The terms *residual*, *dominant*, and *emergent* are taken from Raymond Williams's *Marxism and Literature*. My analysis of contemporary Spanish poetry, however, owes more to Pierre Bourdieu's theory of the cultural field. I have analyzed the residual poetry in the high modern tradition in "Nuevos textos sagrados" and "How to be Great."

4. Whereas Villena's *Postnovísimos* is eclectic, *Fin de siglo* is devoted exclusively to the poetry of experience. See the discussion of *10 menos 30* below. García Martín's *La generación de los ochenta* and *Selección nacional* are more restrictive than Villena's anthologies.

5. See the essays collected in García Montero's *Confesiones poéticas*, along with his introduction to Felipe Benítez Reyes's *Poesía* and the book written in collaboration with Antonio Muñoz Molina: *Por qué no es útil la literatura*.

6. For an ideological critique of García Montero's poetics, see my article "The Avant-Garde and Its Discontents."

7. All translations are my own.

8. My negative characterization of García Montero is, of course, open to debate. Indubitably he is a capable writer who has been able to connect with his audience. My point here is that his position as a leading contemporary poet is inexplicable in the hierarchy of values that privileges modernist or late-modernist poets like Rilke, Lezama Lima, or John Ashbery.

9. Felipe Benítez Reyes, writing under the pseudonym Eligio Rabanera, pokes fun at the very idea of a dominant school in his tongue-and-cheek introduction to *El sindicato del crimen*. The real target of his irony, however, are those who view his own faction as too powerful. He proposes a facetious list of goals for poets in this dominant school, including being corrupt, sending Christ-

mas presents to critics, and even "No ser buena persona" (12). The point of this satire, presumably, is to disarm criticism by suggesting that the idea of a corrupt poetic "crime syndicate" dominating Spanish poetry is absurd. Maybe so, but his anthology does include all the "usual suspects." See Medina for a useful account of the debate surrounding the real or perceived dominance of this school.

10. Ironically, the theme of failure occurs frequently in poets of the dominant, ostensibly "successful" school, especially Felipe Benítez Reyes and José Gutiérrez.

11. A fourth segment of the reading public is the mass audience that lacks intellectual or literary pretentions; since these readers are likely to be attracted to popular forms of entertainment rather than to books, many of them are, in fact, nonreaders. In any case, this is not the audience envisioned by contemporary Spanish poets, even by those whose work is written in an accessible style.

12. In October 1999 I interviewed Jesús Munárriz, the director of Hiperión, the largest publisher of poetry in Spain. He envisions the audience for poetry as being predominately young. Affordable pricing is thus a key to reaching this public: most books in the Hiperión collection cost 900 pesetas, slightly more than the price of a movie ticket. There is a core audience who will purchase twenty or thirty books a year. Poetry books are printed in editions of 1,000 to 3,000 copies, and an edition will sell out in a period of time ranging anywhere from a month to ten years. Hiperión's current "bestseller" is José Hierro's *Cuaderno de Nueva York*, which sold 23,000 copies as of October, 1999. Munárriz's eclecticism, in my estimation, is the key to his success: he helped to create the boom in women's poetry in the 1980s, but he has also published numerous books by García Montero and Benítez Reyes.

13. Bourdieu's analysis here is especially pertinent because it describes developments in nineteenth-century French literature that produced the categories still used today to refer to cultural divisions: *avant-garde, academic, bourgeois,* and so on.

14. From this same perspective, the most egregious "elitists" are actually the conservative, "middle-brow" cultural critics. Prestigious intellectuals are presumably sophisticated enough to shun stereotypically "élitist" positions, although they often fail to do so.

Accounts of the high/low split usually avoid dealing with the treacherous middle ground. Among recent theorists, Bourdieu has the most clearly articulated theory of "middle-brow" culture:

> This middle-brow culture (*culture moyenne*) owes some of its charm, in the eyes of the middle classes who are its main consumers, to the references to legitimate culture it contains and which encourage and justify confusion of the two—accessible versions of avant-garde experiments or accessible works which pass for avant-garde experiments, film "adaptations" of classic drama and literature, "popular arrangements" of classical music or "orchestral versions" of popular tunes, vocal interpretations of classics in a style evocative of scout choruses or angelic choirs, in short, everything that goes to make up "quality" weeklies and "quality" shows, which are entirely organized to give the impression of bring-

ing legitimate culture within the reach of all, by combining two normally exclusive characteristics, immediate accessibility and the outward signs of cultural legitimacy. (1984, 232)

While Bourdieu is often read as an antielitist, this description of petit-bourgeois culture is itself written from a decidedly "high-brow" perspective.

15. Although any poem can be read metapoetically, I am hesitant to push this reading of Correyero's poem too far. In fact, it was only through the juxtaposition of this text to the other two poems that this interpretation suggested itself to me. *Diario de una enfermera*, like Valente's "Paisaje con pájaros amarillos," is an elegiac work, dominated by the death of the speaker's father. (Valente's sequence was written for his dead son Antonio.) I would interpret both poems somewhat differently in the context of the books of poetry to which they belong.

Works Cited

Benegas, Noni, and Jesús Munárriz, eds. 1998. *Ellas tienen la palabra: dos décadas de poesía española*. Madrid: Hiperión.

Benítez Reyes, Felipe. 1992. *Sombras particulares (1988-1991)*. Madrid: Visor.

Bourdieu, Pierre. 1984. *Distinction: A social critique of the judgment of taste*. Trans. Richard Nice. Cambridge: Harvard University Press.

———.1993. *The field of cultural production*. Ed. and trans. Randal Johnson. New York: Columbia University Press.

Correyero, Isla, ed. 1998. *Feroces: radicales, marginales y heterodoxos en la última poesía española*. Barcelona: DVD.

Gamoneda, Antonio. 1997. *El cuerpo de los símbolos*. Madrid: Huerga y Fierro.

García Martín, José Luis, ed. 1988. *La generación de los ochenta*. Valencia: Mestral.

———.1995. *Selección nacional: última poesía española*. Gijón: Universos.

García Montero, Luis. 1992. Felipe Benítez Reyes: La poesía después de la poesía. In *Poesía (1979-1987)*, by Felipe Benítez Reyes, 9–25. Madrid: Hiperión.

———. 1993. *Confesiones poéticas*. Granada: Diputación Provincial de Granada.

García Montero, Luis, and Antonio Muñoz Molina. 1993. *¿Por qué no es útil la literatura?* Madrid: Hiperión.

Gutiérrez, José. 1989. *De la renuncia*. Madrid: Trieste.

Mayhew, Jonathan. 1998. How to be great: Canonical strategies in recent Spanish poetry. *Revista de estudios hispánicos* 32 (May): 385–90.

———. 1999a. The avant-garde and its discontents: Aesthetic conservatism in recent Spanish poetry. *Hispanic review* 67 (Summer): 347–63.

———. 1999b. "Nuevos textos sagrados": Contemporary Spanish poetry and the return of the sacred. *Revista de estudios hispánicos* 33 (May): 285–97.

Medina, Raquel. 1998. Poesía española "fin de siglo": la experiencia y otros fantasmas poéticos. *Revista de estudios hispánicos* 32 (October): 597–612.

Ortega, Antonio, ed. 1994. *La prueba del nueve (antología poética)*. Madrid: Cátedra.

Rabanero, Eligio (Felipe Benítez Reyes). 1994. *El sindicato del crimen: antología de la poética dominante*. Sevilla: La Guna.

Valente, José Angel. 1992. *No amanece el cantor*. Barcelona: Tusquets.

———. 1997. *Notas de un simulador*. Madrid: Ediciones La Palma.

Villena, Luis Antonio de, ed. 1986. *Postnovísimos*. Madrid: Visor.

———. 1992. *Fin de siglo: antología (El sesgo clásico en la última poesía española)*. Madrid: Visor.

———.1997. *10 menos 30: la ruptura interior en la "poesía de la experiencia."* Valencia: Editorial Pre-Textos.

Williams, Raymond. 1977. *Marxism and literature*. New York: Oxford University Press.

Yúdice, George. 1998. Posmodernidad y valores. *Revista de estudios hispánicos* 32 (May): 399–414.

Notes on Contributors

DOUG BENSON is Professor of Spanish at Kansas State University, where he has taught Spanish language, culture, and literature since 1980. He is the author of some twenty-five articles on contemporary Spanish and Chicano poetry, as well as essays on pedagogical theory and strategies for teaching language, culture, and literature as an integrated program at all levels of study.

SANTIAGO DAYDI-TOLSON was born and raised in Chile and obtained a doctoral degree in Spanish literature from the University of Kansas. He has taught Spanish and Latin American literature at Universidad Católica de Valparaíso, Fordham University, the University of Virginia, and the University of Wisconsin, Milwaukee. For the last five years he has been teaching at the University of Texas in San Antonio. His academic publications include *Vicente Aleixandre: A Critical Appraisal*, *The Post-Civil War Spanish Social Poets*, *Voces y ecos en la poesía de José Ángel Valente*, a book on Gabriela Mistral, an edition of the correspondence between Thomas Merton and Ernesto Cardenal, and several articles on Spanish and Latin American literature.

SALVADOR J. FAJARDO is Professor of Spanish at Binghamton University (State University of New York). He has written books on Rafael Alberti and Luis Cernuda, edited several collections on contemporary Spanish poetry, and variously addressed the poetry of Moreno Villa, Leon Felipe, Ana Rossetti, and others. He is currently engaged in a study of exile in Spanish poetry. His other interest is Cervantes. His and James A. Parr's annotated edition of "Don Quijote" was published in 1998, and reedited in 2002.

ANITA M. HART is Professor of Spanish and former Chair of the Department of Modern Languages at the University of Nebraska at Kearney. She has published articles on Spanish poets in journals such as *Revista de Estudios Hispánicos, Anales de la Literatura Española Contemporánea, Letras Peninsulares, Explicación de Textos Literarios, Hispanic Journal, Revista Hispánica Moderna,* and *The Journal of Interdisciplinary Literary Studies.*

MARTHA LAFOLLETTE is Professor of Spanish and Chair of the Department of Languages and Culture Studies at the University of North Carolina at Charlotte, where she has taught since 1976. She has published numerous articles and book chapters on twentieth-century Spanish poetry. Her book, *Politics and Verbal Play: The Ludic Poetry of Ángel González* was published in 1995 by Fairleigh Dickinson University Press. She has been the recipient of an National Endowment for the Humanities (NEH) fellowship and has served as an NEH panelist and as president of the Philological Association of the Carolinas. She currently serves as chair of the Advanced Placement Test Development Committee in Spanish.

SARAH A. MARTIN is Associate Dean for Academics and Faculty at Marylhurst University in Oregon.

JONATHAN MAYHEW is Associate Professor of Spanish at the University of Kansas in Lawrence. He received his PhD in Comparative Literature from Stanford University in 1988 and has published two books on contemporary Spanish poetry: *Claudio Rodríguez and the Language of Poetic Vision* (1990) and *The Poetics of Self-Consciousness: Twentieth Century Spanish Poetry* (1994). He is currently completing a third: *Recent Spanish Poetry: The Twilight of Modernity.*

LINDA D. METZLER is Professor of Spanish at Kenyon College in Gambier, Ohio. She has written essays on María Victoria Atencia, Angel Crespo, Carlos Edmundo D'Ory, José Hierro, José Angel Valente, and the Congresos de Poesía held in Spain in the 1950s and re-created in the 1990s. Her current project is a series of essays on musicality in contemporary Spanish poetry.

W. MICHAEL MUDROVIC, Associate Professor of Spanish at Skidmore College in Saratoga Springs, NY, has published several articles on contemporary Spanish poetry as well as a book on Claudio Rodríguez. His next book deals with women's poetry of the post-Franco era.

JUDITH NANTELL is Professor of Spanish in the Department of Spanish and Portuguese and the Vice Dean for Academic and Instructional Affairs in the College of Humanities at the University of Arizona. She is the author of *The Poetry of Francisco Brines: The Deconstructive Effects of Language* (Bucknell University Press, 1994) and a number of published articles on Brines's poetry. Most recently, *Anales de la Literatura Española Contemporánea* published her "Essential Existence in Francisco Brines's *La última Costa*." Nantell has investigated poetry of the famed Generation of 1927 and her *Rafael Alberti's Poetry of the Thirties: The Poet's Public Voice* (1986) won the prestigious 1984 South Atlantic Modern Language Association Studies Award. In following the guidance of one of her most significant mentors, Andy Debicki, she has viewed and endorsed the study of Modern and Contemporary Spanish poetry as a voyage of discovery. Professor Nantell resides in Tucson, Arizona with her husband, professor-philosopher Chris Maloney, and their daughters, Maura and Brigid.

MARGARET PERSIN is the author of *Getting the Picture: The Ekphrastic Principle in Twentieth-Century Spanish Poetry* (1997) and *Recent Spanish Poetry and the Role of the Reader* (1987). Her current projects include a book-length study on the poetry of Concha Mendez, as well as other studies on the emergence of marginalized voices in recent Mexican poetry and the representation of nature in modern Spanish verse. She teaches at Rutgers University, where she also is the Executive Director of the World Languages Institute.

JILL ROBBINS is Associate Professor of Spanish Literature and Culture at the University of California, Irvine. Author of *Frames of Referents: The Postmodern Poetry of Guillermo Carnero* (Bucknell University Press, 1997) and editor of *P/Herversions: Critical Studies of Ana Rossetti* (Bucknell UP, 2004). Her recent work encompasses queer and gender studies in Spain, transatlantic studies, and the effects of globalization upon Spanish literary production.

Index

ABC, 226
Adorno, Theodor, 117 n. 4
Agustín, Teresa: "Me visto para la luna," 191–92
Agustini, Delmira: "El vampiro," 186, 201 n. 9
Alberti, Rafael, 226; *La arboleda perdida*, 40, 55–56 n. 10
Aleixandre, Vicente, 17, 25–29, 34–35, 37; light imagery of, 17, 25, 28–29, 37; loss of sight by, 17, 25, 27; Nobel Prize of, 25; silence of, 25–27; and visionary poetry, 17, 25, 27, 28, 37. Works: *Ambito*, 26; "A mi perro," 34–35; "Conocimiento de Rubén Darío," 26–28; *Diálogos del conocimiento*, 17, 25, 26; "Intermedio," 26; *Poemas de la consumación*, 17, 26; *Retratos con nombre*, 34
Alonso, Dámaso, 26–27, 78, 84
Andreu, Blanca, 194–95, 231; *De una niña de provincias que se vino a vivir en un Chagall*, 232
Andújar Almansa, José, 61–62, 67, 75 n. 7
animals, 33–37, 107–9, 116, 120 n. 16, 173–75, 177
Arancibia, Martín, 117–18 n. 6
Arc de Triomphe, 172–73
archetypal criticism, 16
Arco de Santo Domingo, 168–70, 178 n. 6
Ashbery, John, 242 n. 8
Atencia, María Victoria, 18–19, 123–41, 141 nn. 1, 3, and 4; and connections between self and other/past and present, 123–41, 141 n. 1; interest in painting of, 126; and juxtaposition/dialogue, 141 n. 1; and life and death, 18, 127–29, 140; and photography's interplay with poetry, 19, 124–41; prizes awarded to, 123; use of the vampire by, 186–88; and women's creativity, 186–88, 201 n. 11; and the world of work, 127–32, 133; and young people, 133–40. Works: *A orillas del Ems*, 18–19, 123–41, 141 n. 4; "La casa," 125–26, 140, 141; *Compás binario*, 123; "El Conde D," 186–88, 191, 201 n. 11; "Heinrich und Clärchen," 137–38; "Jefe de estación," 131–32; "Joven con bicicleta," 134–36, 138; "Lavandera," 127–29, 131; *Marta & María*, 123, 186; "La niña," 138–40, 141; *La pared contigua*, 123; "Pareja," 133; *Paulina o el libro de las aguas*, 123; "Posan cuatro ancianas," 132; "El pregonero," 129–32; "Las tres gracias," 136–37, 138
Auden, W. H., 239
Auerbach, Nina, 180, 183, 200 n. 1, 201 n. 8
avant-garde, 215–16, 227, 228, 231, 235, 236, 243 n. 13, 243–44 n. 14
Aviram, Amittai F., 119 n. 10

Bakhtin, Mikhail, 80
Baroja, Pío, 42
Barthes, Roland, 124–25, 127, 129, 130, 135, 140, 162–63 n. 1
Baudelaire, Charles: "Le Chat," 33–34; "The Metamorphoses of a Vampire," 184–85, 201 n. 9; "The Vampire," 184–85, 201 n. 9
Baudrillard, Jean, 220 n. 7
Beckett, Samuel, 226
Bécquer, Gustavo Adolfo, 216; "Los ojos verdes," 31; "Rima LXXI," 31; "Yo soy ardiente, yo soy morena," 187
Beethoven, Ludwig von, 117–18 n. 6
Bellver, Catherine, 218–19 n. 1
Benegas, Noni, 231
Benítez Reyes, Felipe, 227, 235, 242 n. 5, 242–43 n. 9, 243 nn. 10 and 12; "Apunte," 236–39
Benson, Douglas, K., 18
Berg, Alban: *Wozzeck*, 117–18 n. 6
Berkana, 219–20 n. 3
Bhabha, Homi, 119 n. 11
Borges, Jorge Luis, 26
Bornay, Erika, 183, 201 n. 5
Bourdieu, Pierre, 233–34, 242 n. 3, 243–44 nn. 13 and 14
Brines, Francisco, 17–18, 59–75, 226; and affirmation of life, 18, 60–61, 66–75, 75 n. 9; awarding of Premio Nacional de las Letras to, 59–60; and *carpe diem* motif, 69, 75 nn. 4 and 6; critical approaches to, 59–63; and elegy, 18, 59–60, 63–68; and the human condition, 62–63, 69; and journey motif, 67–68, 75 n. 5; and memory, 18, 60–61, 63; and naming, 63; and personal "testimony," 62, 72, 75 n. 7; and poetic traditions, 63; unity in poetic production of, 61–62. Works: "Alocución pagana," 64–65; *Aún no*, 61, 64, 70; *Las brasas*, 63, 68, 70; "La certidumbre de la poesía," 59, 72; "Collige, virgo, rosas," 69, 75 n. 6; "El confín perpetuo," 65–66; "Definición de la nada," 65; "La dimisión del testigo," 69; "Elca y Montgó," 64; "Epitafio del vivo," 71; "Los espacios de la infancia," 70–71, 73; "Está en penumbra el cuarto," 71; "Extinción," 64; "Mi hacedor," 74; "Imágenes en un espejo roto," 74; "Insistencias en el engaño," 65; *Insistencias en Luzbel*, 65, 68, 70; "Interior del paisaje," 71; "Junto a la mesa se ha quedado solo," 63; "El mendigo de lo extinguido," 73–74; "Metáfora de un destino," 74; "El niño perdido y hallado (en Elca)," 74; "Oscureciendo el bosque," 64, 65, 71, 74; *El otoño de las rosas*, 63, 65–66, 68–69, 72, 75 n. 4, 75 n. 6; "El pacto que me queda," 66; *Palabras a la oscuridad*, 59, 64, 65, 70; *Poemas a D. K.*, 60; "Proyecto de la vida eterna," 73; "Reflexión sobre un incidente," 74; "El regreso del mundo," 70, 72–73; "Soliloquio para que lo escuche el otro," 73; "Sombrío ardor," 71; *La última costa*, 17–18, 60–61, 63, 66–75, 75 nn. 7, 8, and 9
Browne, Peter, 78, 86
Bruno, Giordano, 117–18 n. 6
Buenaventura, Ramón de, 231
Bukowski, Charles, 240
Bush, Andrew, 217, 221 nn. 11 and 12
Buxán, Xosé M., 219–20 n. 3
Byron, George Gordon, Lord, 182

Caballero Bonald, José Manuel, 78
Cano, José Luis, 59, 75 n. 2, 95–96
canon, 226–27, 231, 240
capitalism, 204, 207, 210, 217–18
Carnero, Guillermo, 207
Carroll, Lewis: *Adventures of Alice in Wonderland*, 156, 161
Carver, Raymond, 240
Castellet, José María, 208
Castro, Juana, 197; *Fisterra*, 198–200
Castro, Luisa: "El cerdo," 197–98; *Los versos del eunuco*, 196
Catalan writers/writing, 20, 204, 207, 217, 221 n. 11

Catholicism, 20, 160, 161–62, 178–79 n. 7, 206–7
Cavallo, Susana, 67
Cela, Julia, 219–20 n. 3
Celan, Paul, 226, 239
Celaya, Gabriel, 85
Cernuda, Luis, 161, 209, 216; "Historial de un libro," 55–56 n. 10
Chacel, Rosa, 205, 208, 220–21 n. 10
Chevalier, Jean, 178 n. 5
Ciplijauskaité, Biruté, 141 n. 1, 166–67
Cirlot, J. E., 154
Cixous, Hélène, 119 n. 11
Cohen, Ralph, 80
Coleridge, Samuel Taylor, 118–19 n. 7
conceptismo, 81, 91, 93
Cornejo-Parriego, Rosalía, 218–19 n. 1
Correyero, Isla, 231, 232, 235, 239, 240; "Anoréxica," 195–96; *Diario de una enfermera*, 237–39, 244 n. 15
Couperin, François, 117–18 n. 6
Cuesta Abad, José M., 117 n. 2
cultural studies, 224

Dante Alighieri: *Divina Commedia*, 29–31, 152
Darío, Rubén, 26–28, 33, 35–36, 37; "Los motivos del lobo," 35–36
Daydí-Tolson, Santiago, 17, 98–100, 115–16, 117 n. 5
Debicki, Andrew P., 15–18, 20, 25, 63, 75 n. 6, 78–81, 140–41, 141 n. 1
de Beauvoir, Simone, 119 n. 11
de la Cruz, San Juan, 107, 120 n. 16; "Canciones de la esposa," 119 nn. 9 and 14; "Canciones entre el alma y el esposo," 30–31
Dijkstra, Bram, 183–84
domesticity, 192, 197–200, 205–6
Dominic, Saint, 178–79 n. 7
Dundes, Alan, 200 n. 1
DuPlessis, Rachel Blau, 208
Duque Amusco, Alejandro, 62–63

Eagleton, Terry, 143
Echevarría, Juan, 42

Economic Stabilization Plan of 1959, 207
Editorial Lumen, 208
embodiment, 45–48
Engelson Marson, Ellen, 85
Espronceda, José de: "Canción del pirata," 209
Estrada, Genaro, 43, 55 n. 7

Fajardo, Salvador J., 17, 163 n. 4, 179 n. 9
Falange party, 215, 220 n. 5
feminism, 19, 180, 181, 189, 192, 200, 201 nn. 8, 9, and 11, 207
Fernández Quesada, Nuria, 117–18 n. 6
fiction, 229, 241
Fifties Generation, 16, 179 n. 10
formalism, 15
Franco, Francisco, 20, 161–62, 204, 205–7, 215–18, 220 n. 7, 228
Frank, Joseph, 178 n. 4
Frye, Northrop, 145, 162–63 n. 1, 172
Fuertes, Gloria, 18, 78–96; accessibility of poetry by, 79, 80, 95; indeterminacy in poetry of, 18, 78–82, 84–96; and irony, 18, 80–81, 92, 95; and literary convention, 79, 80, 82–84, 92–95; and metapoetry, 79, 92, 94–95; and postmodernism, 79–81, 89–90; and the postwar poets, 78–79. Works: "Accidente," 94–95; "Autobio," 92–94; *Cómo atar los bigotes al tigre*, 82; "Diablito de mi guarda," 82–87, 90; *Mujer de verso en pecho*, 18, 82, 87–96; *Obras incompletas*, 79

Gadamer, Hans Georg, 42
Gamoneda, Antonio, 232, 241
García, Dionisia, 19, 166–79; and *dianoia*, 167, 172, 177; and everyday reality, 166, 169; and historical monuments, 19, 167–73, 175, 177; and the intertwining of space and time, 19, 167, 169–73, 175–78; and writing/reading, 175–77, 178–79 n. 7. Works: "Arco de Santo Domingo," 168–70, 177, 179 n. 10;

"Del poeta y el poema," 175–76;
"Instantánea," 170–72, 177, 179 n.
10; *Lugares de paso*, 19, 166–78,
179 n. 10; "Tino en la caída,"
172–75, 177, 179 n. 9
García de la Concha, Víctor,
163 n. 2
García Lorca, Federico, 42, 94–95,
209, 214, 216, 226; "Reyerta,"
94–95; "Romance de la luna luna,"
95; "Sorpresa," 94
García Martín, José Luis, 227, 231,
242 n. 4
García Montero, Luis, 227–29, 233,
239, 242 nn. 5, 6, and 8, 243 n. 12
García Posada, Miguel, 60
Gelder, Ken, 200 n. 1
gender, 19, 20, 87, 91, 146–48,
159–62, 162–63 n. 1, 163 nn. 4, 5,
6, and 8, 164 nn. 14, 15, and 16,
181–200, 201 nn. 6, 8, 9, and 11,
205–10, 213, 215, 218, 220 nn. 5,
7, and 9, 220–21 n. 10. *See also*
women writers, Spanish
Generation of 1927, 120 n. 22, 208,
209–10, 224
Generation of 1980, 230
Genette, Gérard, 178 n. 3
Gheerbrandt, Alain, 178 n. 5
Gil de Biedma, Jaime, 227, 239
Gimferrer, Père, 26, 117 n. 3, 226,
234
Ginsberg, Allen, 216; *Howl*, 209
Golden Age, 84, 91, 93
Góngora y Argote, Luis de: *Polifemo*,
120 n. 22
González, Angel, 78, 227
Gordon, Joan, 180, 182, 200 n. 1,
201 n. 6
Gorostiza, José, 16
Graham, Helen, 224
Grande, Guadalupe: "Oficio de
crisálida," 189–90
Guevara, Che, 216
Guillén. Jorge, 163 n. 2; "Despertar
español," 57 n. 12; "Sospecha de
foca," 140
Gutiérrez, José, 243 n. 10
Gutiérrez Solana, José, 55 n. 2

Halperin, David, 204
Hart, Anita M., 18–19
Hass, Robert, 99, 101–5, 116
Heidegger, Martin, 54, 175, 179 n. 10
Heldreth, Leonard G., 200 n. 1
Hierro, José, 78; *Cuaderno de Nueva
York*, 243 n. 12
Hiperión, 233, 242 n. 2, 243 n. 12
Hölderlin, Friedrich, 54, 225
Hollinger, Veronica, 180, 182, 200 n.
1, 201 n. 6
Homer, 26
homosexuality, 180, 181, 185, 194,
201 n. 4, 204–6, 208, 216–18,
218–19 n. 1, 219 n. 2, 219–20 n. 3,
220 n. 7, 224
Hora de España, 44, 55 n. 8
Hutcheon, Linda, 79–81

imperialism, Spanish, 20, 205, 209
Irigaray, Luce, 119 n. 11, 206, 220 n. 9

Jabès, Edmond, 225
James, Saint, 161
Jameson, Fredric, 80
Jardine, Murray, 51
Jiménez, José Olivio, 59–60, 62, 63,
75 nn. 2, 5, and 7
Jiménez, Juan Ramón, 225, 234
Jiménez Fraud, Alberto, 55 n. 1
Joyce, James, 225–26

Kafka, Franz, 225–26
Kristeva, Julia, 117 n. 3, 119 nn. 11
and 15
Kruchen, Renate, 124

Labanyi, Jo, 224
Lacan, Jacques, 119 n. 11
LaFollette, Martha, 19, 141 n. 4, 149
Lanchares, Santiago, 117–18 n. 6
Langbaum, Robert, 227
Lentini, Rosa, 192–93
Levine, Linda Gould, 218–19 n. 1
Lezama Lima, José, 225, 242 n. 8
literary theory, 15, 119 n. 11, 143,
162–63 n. 1
Litoral, 124
Llamasa, Ricardo, 219 n. 2

López Parada, Esperanza, 231, 240
Lucio, Francisco, 68, 75 n. 8
Luque, Aurora: "Del descifrar," 188–90
Luque, Francisco, 117–18 n. 6

Machado, Antonio, 39
Madrid, 39, 40, 55 n. 2, 170–72, 219–20 n. 3
Mallarmé, Stephane, 239
Mandlove, Nancy, 78
Manrique, Jorge, 60, 62, 75 n. 6; "Coplas por la muerte de su padre," 129
Marías Javier, 229
Márquez, Miguel A., 120 n. 22
Martín, Francisco José, 62, 75 n. 9
Martín, Salustiano, 232
Martín Gaite, Carmen, 206
Martínez de Mingo, Luis, 68
Marxism, 216
Marzal, Carlos, 227
Mayhew, Jonathan, 20, 63, 117 n. 3, 242 nn. 2, 3, and 6
McIntyre, Alasdair, 46
Medina, Raquel, 229, 242–43 n. 9
metaphysics, 20, 225
Metzler, Linda D., 18
Miller, Martha LaFollette. *See* LaFollette, Martha
Milton, John, 26, 152
Mitchell, W. J. T., 19, 167, 172, 175–77, 178 n. 4
modernism, 27, 28, 37, 225–27, 229, 231, 232, 234–36, 239, 241, 242 nn. 2 and 8
Moi, Toril, 119 nn. 11 and 15
Moix, Ana María, 20, 204–21; career of, 204, 208; and class, 20, 207; and gender, 20, 204, 207–10, 213, 216–18, 220–21 n. 10; and intertextualities, 208, 209, 217, 221 n. 14; and nation, 20, 204, 205, 207, 216–18; poetic style of, 221 n. 12; and queer identity, 20, 204, 207, 208, 212, 213, 215, 216–18, 218–19 n. 1; and romantic conventions, 208–14, 217; use of Catalan by, 217, 221 n. 11. Works: *A imagen y semejanza*, 208; *Baladas del Dulce Jim*, 20, 208, 209–18, 221 n. 14; *Call Me Stone*, 208; *Julia*, 218–19 n. 1; *No Time for Flowers*, 208, 209; "Una novela," 217, 221 n. 16; "Las virtudes peligrosas," 218–19 n. 1; *Walter ¿por qué te fuiste?*, 218–19 n. 1
Mora, Gabriela, 201 n. 9
Morales, Carlos Javier, 60, 62
Morcillo Gómez, Aurora, 161–62
Moreno Villa, José, 17, 39–57; and ballads and romances, 44, 55 n. 8; childhood home of, 39–40; diplomatic career of, 39, 43, 47, 55 n. 6; and exile, 17, 40, 43–45, 47, 49, 51, 53, 54 n. 9; and family, 40–41, 55 n. 7; and Jacinta/Florence, 40, 41, 55 nn. 4 and 5; in Mexico, 39–41, 43, 44, 55 n. 7; and the Residencia de Estudiantes, 39, 44, 55 n. 1; and self-narration, 44–54; and thematics of space and place, 39–42, 45, 49–50, 52–54; and transitoriness (*interinidad*), 40, 41, 43; in the United States, 39–43. Works: "Converso con vosotros," 17, 44–54, 54 n. 9, 56–57 n. 11; *Jacinta la pelirroja*, 40, 42; "Nos trajeron las ondas," 41; *Vida en claro*, 39–45, 55 n. 7
Morris, Brian, 94
Munárriz, Jesús, 231, 243 n. 12
Mundo, El, 79
Muñoz Molina, Antonio, 229, 242 n. 5
Murcia, 168, 178 n. 6

Nantell, Judith, 17–18, 63, 75 nn. 5 and 9
national identity, 20, 161–62, 204, 206, 207, 216–18, 219 n. 2
Navarro Tomás, Tomás, 55 n. 2, 55 n. 6, 118–19 n. 7, 119 n. 12
neo-avante-garde, 20, 225, 232
Neruda, Pablo: "Un perro ha muerto," 36
New Criticism, 15–16
novísimos, 78–79, 95, 208

Ortega, Antonio, 231–32, 240
Ortega y Gasset, José, 42
Otero, Blas de, 78, 227, 233

País, El, 60, 67, 226
Pamplona, 162
Panero, Leopoldo María, 231
Paris, 172
Parra, Josefa: "El exceso," 193–94
Pavese, Cesare, 37
Paz, Octavio, 99, 101–5, 116
Pemán, José María: *Poema de la Bestia y el Angel*, 215–16
Perloff, Marjorie, 79–81
Persin, Margaret, 19, 78, 81, 145
Pessoa, Fernando, 226
Pharr, Mary, 200 n. 1
Pinsky, Robert, 99, 101, 103, 104, 116, 119 n. 13, 120 nn. 18 and 20
"poesía figurativa," 227, 229
poetry: and anthologies, 226–29, 231, 232, 235, 239–40, 242 n. 4, 242–43 n. 9; and audience's cultural expectations, 20, 224–29, 232–35, 243 nn. 11 and 12, 243–44 n. 14; and autobiography, 44, 94; creativity of, 19, 32; of difference, 230–32, 235, 240, 241; of experience, 225, 227–31, 234, 239–41; and gendered lyrics, 208–9; Heidegger on, 54; and history, 15, 226; as knowledge in the making, 123, 133; late modernist (essentialist), 225–26, 229, 231, 232, 234–36, 239, 241, 242 nn. 2 and 8; and participation in reality, 123, 140; and the physical act of reading, 103, 104–9, 111–15, 117 n. 1, 119 nn. 13 and 15; and rhythm, 98–120, 117 n. 3, 118–19 n. 7, 119 nn. 9, 10, and 12; social, 78, 82, 87, 92, 227; status today of, 224–244; visionary, 17, 25, 27–37
"poets of discovery," 17, 18, 25, 78
point-of-view criticism, 16
Polidori, John: *The Vampyre*, 182–83
Porterfield, Richard, 119 n. 8
postcolonialism, 119 n. 11
Postismo, 78

postmodernism, 16, 79–81, 89–90, 159, 224, 241
poststructuralism, 143, 162–63 n. 1
Poteat, William, 45
power, 19, 180, 183, 200, 209, 210
Primo de Rivera, Pilar, 220 n. 5
psychoanalysis, 119 n. 11
Puerta de Acalá, 170–72

queer theory, 204–5, 219 n. 2
"Quinto Regimiento," 55 n. 2

Rangel, Violeta, 231
reader-response criticism, 16
Real Academia, 226
realism, 20, 227, 229, 236, 239, 240
Redon, Odilon: *Eye-Balloon*, 32
religion. *See* Catholicism
Rendueles, José Luis: "Vindicación del desencanto," 228–29
republicanism, 39, 43–44, 47, 49–50, 53, 54, 216
Reseña, 232
Rickels, Laurence A., 200 n. 1
Riechmann, Jorge, 231, 240
Rilke, Rainer Maria, 242 n. 8
Rimbaud, Arthur, 226; *Illuminations*, 33; "Voyelles," 32–33
Robbins, Jill, 20
Robinson, William J., 183–84
Rodríguez, Claudio, 78, 123, 140, 179 n. 10, 226; "Alto jornal," 128–29
Rojo, José Andrés, 118–19 n. 7
Romancero de la guerra civil, 44
Romanticism, 31, 37, 209, 210, 216
Rossetti, Ana, 19, 143–64, 231; appropriation of Western master narratives and literary allusions by, 145, 149, 152, 159–61, 163 nn. 2 and 4, 164 n. 13; and ekphrasis, 145, 163 n. 5; erotic sensibility of, 144, 146–49, 151, 154–55, 157, 158, 163 n. 2, 164 n. 11; and film, 148, 156, 159; and gender, 19, 146–48, 159–62, 163 nn. 4, 5, 6, and 8, 164 nn. 14, 15, and 16; and impossibility of writing/language,

19, 143–47, 149, 151, 157–58, 161, 163–64 n. 10; and the political, 143, 147–48, 161, 164 n. 14; and theater, 145–48, 163 n. 7; varied production of, 148; and Wilde, 143, 145, 146. Works: "Chico Wrangler," 144; *Los devaneos de Erato*, 163 n. 2; *Devocionario*, 163 n. 2; *Dióscuros*, 144, 163 n. 2; "Homenaje a Lindsay Kemp y su tocado de plumas amarillas," 145; "Marinero en tierra," 148; *Mentiras de papel*, 146, 148, 156, 164 nn. 14 and 16; *Plumas de España*, 146; *Punto umbrío*, 19, 143–44, 146–62, 163 n. 2, 163–64 n. 10, 164 n. 15; *El secreto enamorado*, 163 n. 7; "Uno," 144

Salinas, Pedro, 84
San Fermín, festival of, 162
Saussure, Ferdinand de, 143
Schoenberg, Arnold, 117–18 n. 6
Schrag, Calvin S., 46
Sedgwick, Eve Kosofsky, 220 n. 8
self-narrative, 44–54, 72
Servodidio, Mirella, 144, 147, 163 n. 8
Shawcross, Nancy, 125
Sherno, Sylvia, 78, 96, 117 n. 3
Silos, 109–13, 120 n. 19
Sontag, Susan, 141 n. 3
Sotelo, Mauricio, 117–18 n. 6
Spanish Civil War, 17, 43, 44, 47, 49–50, 54, 162, 205–6, 210
Spanishness. *See* national identity
Spanish Republic, 39, 43, 44, 55 n. 2
Stevenson, Robert Louis: *Treasure Island*, 209
Surrealism, 37
Symbolism, 32, 37

Taylor, Charles, 46, 53
Teresa de Jesus, Santa, 162
Teruel Benavente, José, 117 n. 2
Tesán, Alberto, 240
Thomas Aquinas, Saint, 225
Tusquets, Esther, 219–20 n. 3
Twitchell, James B., 181–82, 201 n. 8, 202 n. 12

Ugalde, Sharon Keefe, 141 n. 1, 146, 152, 155
Unamuno, Miguel de, 118–19 n. 7; *San Manuel Bueno, mártir*, 84

Valencia, 39, 55 n. 2
Valente, José Angel, 18, 78, 98–101, 104–20, 123, 133, 225–27, 232, 234, 235–39; awarding of Premio Nacional de Poesía to, 120 n. 21; and the canon, 226–27; and musicality, 18, 98–100, 104–20, 117 nn. 2, 3, and 5; 117–18 n. 6; 118–19 n. 7; and landscape, 109–13; and the lyric subject's search for an "other," 18, 99, 100, 104–9, 111–12, 116; school of poetry inspired by, 225–26. Works: *Breve son*, 117 n. 5; "Las condiciones del pájaro solitario," 120 n. 16; *Fragmentos de un libro futuro*, 113–16, 120 n. 21; *El fugor*, 104, 107; "Graal," 117 n. 3; *Mandorla*, 117 n. 3; *La memoria y los signos*, 109; *Notas de un simulador*, 225; "Paisaje con pájaros amarillos," 244 n. 15; *La piedra y el centro*, 120 n. 16; Poem XXX, 104–7, 119 nn. 14 and 15; Poem XXXV, 107–9, 120 nn. 16 and 17; *Punto cero*, 99; "Silos," 109–13; *Tres lecciones de tinieblas*, 117–18 n. 6; "Verbum absconditum," 119 nn. 9 and 14
Valle-Inclán, Ramón del: *Sonata de primavera: Sonata de estío*, 156, 161, 164 n. 12
Vallejo, César, 209, 214, 216; "Piedra negra sobre una piedra blanca," 221 n. 14
vampires, 19, 180–202; and conventional social/familial roles, 181–83, 185, 188, 191–92, 195–200; and Dracula, 181, 185–87, 191, 200, 201 n. 11; and fear of the feminine, 181–84, 189; general critical approaches to, 180–82, 201 n. 8; and monstrous metaphors, 194–200; and the other, 181–82, 185, 196; and sick-

ness of modern life, 182, 185, 194–97; as used by Spanish women poets, 181, 185–202, 201 nn. 6, 9, and 11
Varas, Patricia, 201 n. 9
Varese, Edgard, 117–18 n. 6
Velázquez, Diego: *La vieja cocinera*, 129
Vendler, Helen, 117 n. 1
verisimilitude, 227, 239
Vila, Fefa, 219 n. 2
Villena, Luis Antonio de, 79, 227, 229–32, 240, 242 n. 4
Virgen del Pilar, 162
Visor, 233, 242 n. 2

Webern, Anton, 117–18 n. 6
Welburn, Andrew J., 32

Wilcox, John, 149, 155, 201 n. 11
Wilde, Oscar, 143, 145, 146
Wilden, Anthony, 119 n. 11
Williams, Raymond, 242 n. 3
Wimsatt, William, 15
women writers, Spanish, 19, 146–47, 162, 181, 183, 185–202, 201 n. 9, 204, 218, 231–32, 240, 243 n. 12
Woolf, Virginia, 96
Wordsworth, William, 118–19 n. 7
World War I, 136

Ynduráin, Francisco, 78
Yúdice, George, 242 n. 2

Zajonc, Arthur, 29
Zaldívar, María Inés, 145–47, 163 n. 5
Zambrano, María, 117 n. 2